Web Design
with HTML and CSS
Digital
Classroom

Web Design with HTML and CSS
Digital Classroom

Jeremy Osborn, Jennifer Smith, and the AGI Training Team

Wiley Publishing, Inc.

Web Design with HTML and CSS Digital Classroom

Published by

Wiley Publishing, Inc.

10475 Crosspoint Boulevard

Indianapolis, IN 46256

Copyright © 2011 by Wiley Publishing, Inc., Indianapolis, Indiana

Published by Wiley Publishing, Inc., Indianapolis, Indiana

Published simultaneously in Canada

ISBN: **978-0-470-58360-9**

Manufactured in the United States of America

10987654321

For general information on our other products and services or to obtain technical support, please contact our Customer Care Department within the U.S. at (800) 762-2974, outside the U.S. at (317) 572-3993 or fax (317) 572-4002.

Please report any errors by sending a message to **errata@agitraining.com**

Library of Congress Control Number: 2009936395

Wiley also publishes its books in a variety of electronic formats. Some content that appears in print may not be available in electronic books.

About the Authors

Jeremy Osborn is the Content Director at American Graphics Institute. He has more than 15 years of experience in web, graphic design, filmmaking, writing, and publication development for both print and digital media. He is the author of the *Dreamweaver CS5 Digital Classroom* and has contributed to many of the titles in the Digital Classroom book series. Jeremy holds a MS in Management from the Marlboro College Graduate Center and a BFA in Film/TV from the Tisch School of the Arts at NYU.

Jennifer Smith is a founding member of American Graphics Institute (AGI) and serves as its Vice President. Prior to founding AGI, she worked in advertising as an art director and served as a principal in a Pennsylvania-based design firm. She is the author of more than 20 books on electronic publishing. Jennifer's 20 years of design experience bridge the gap between technical and creative, and she frequently works with both developers and designers. A renaissance artist with technology, you'll find Jennifer integrating her design skills with web, interactive, and application development projects.

The AGI Creative Team is composed of web design experts and instructors from American Graphics Institute (AGI). They work with many of the world's most prominent companies, helping them use creative software to communicate more effectively and creatively. They work with design, development, creative, and marketing teams around the world, delivering consulting, private customized training programs, and teach regularly scheduled classes at AGI's locations. The Digital Classroom authors are available for professional development sessions at companies, schools and universities. More information is available at *agitraining.com* and *digitalclassroom.com*.

Acknowledgments

Thanks to Kristin Osborn for support and encouragement, and also to Isaiah and the team at AGI for testing smoothies. Thanks to the instructors at AGI for input, assistance and reviews. Thanks to iStockphoto.com for many of the images used in the book.

Credits

Writing
Jeremy Osborn, Jennifer Smith

President, American Graphics Institute and Digital Classroom Series Publisher
Christopher Smith

Executive Editor
Jody Lefevere

Acquisitions Editor
Aaron Black

Technical Editors
Haziel Olivera

Editors
Marylouise Wiack, Karla Melendez

Editorial Director
Robyn Siesky

Business Manager
Amy Knies

Senior Marketing Manager
Sandy Smith

Vice President and Executive Group Publisher
Richard Swadley

Vice President and Executive Publisher
Barry Pruett

Senior Project Coordinator
Lynsey Stanford

Project Manager
Cheri White

Graphics and Production Specialist
Jason Miranda

Media Development Project Supervisor
Chris Leavey

Proofreading
Jay Donahue, Barnowl Publishing

Indexing
Michael Ferreira

Stock Photography
iStockPhoto.com

Starting Up

Lesson 1: Planning Your Website

Lesson 2: Fundamentals of the Web

Lesson 3: Web Design Tools

Lesson 4: Fundamentals of HTML, XHTML, and CSS

Lesson 5: Graphics, Color, and Transparency

Lesson 6: Formatting Text with CSS

Lesson 7: Introduction to CSS Layout

Lesson 8: Advanced CSS Layout

Lesson 9: Browser Compatibility

Lesson 10: Introduction to Interactivity

Lesson 11: Mobile Design

Lesson 12: HTML5 Essentials

About Web Design with HTML and CSS Digital Classroom

Creating effective websites requires an understanding of design principles, as well as the underlying technology that is used to deliver and display content to your audience. The *Web Design with HTML and CSS Digital Classroom* provides the information you need to design, develop, publish, and maintain websites. Whether you are just starting out in the field of web design, or are experienced with design tools like Dreamweaver or Expression Web, you'll find this book helpful at explaining the underlying concepts for organizing, creating, and delivering web content effectively using best practices.

The *Web Design with HTML and CSS Digital Classroom* helps you to get up-and-running quickly. Although you can work through the lessons in this book in any sequence, we recommend that you start in at the first lesson and progress through the book in the sequence in which they are presented. Each lesson includes detailed, step-by-step instructions, background information, companion video tutorials, and lesson files.

The *Web Design with HTML and CSS Digital Classroom* is like having your own expert instructor guiding you through each lesson while you work at your own pace. This book includes 12 self-paced lessons that let you discover essential skills, explore web design, and learn HTML, CSS and image editing techniques that will save you time and allow you to more easily create effective websites. You'll become productive right away with real-world exercises and simple explanations. Each lesson includes step-by-step instructions and lesson files available on the Digital Classroom website at *www.digitalclassroombooks.com/webdesign*. The *Web Design with HTML and CSS Digital Classroom* lessons are developed by the same team of instructors and experts who have created many of the official training titles for companies such as Adobe Systems and Microsoft. Now you can benefit from the expert instructors and clear, detailed instructions provided by the American Graphics Institute team.

Prerequisites

Before you start the *Web Design with HTML and CSS Digital Classroom* lessons, you should have a working knowledge of your computer and its operating system. You should know how to use the directory system of your computer so that you can navigate through folders. You also need to understand how to locate, save, and open files, and you should also know how to use your mouse to access menus and commands. If you are just starting out with using a computer, you should become familiar with its operation first, using resources such as the *Windows 7 Digital Classroom* or *Mac OS X Digital Classroom*.

We recommend that you install a text editor to use when working with the HTML and CSS code. The specific editor is not important, but you should choose and install a text editor so that you can easily open and work with the lesson files presented in this book. If you aren't sure which to use, you can wait until you get to Lesson Three where we discuss working with code and using text editors. However, if you're comfortable installing a text editor, we've listed some options below.

Some Mac OS text editors include BBedit and TextWrangler, both of which are available at *http://www.barebones.com*. Or you can use TextMate which is available for download at *http://macromates.com*. Another Mac OS text editor is Coda which can be found at *http://www.panic.com/coda/*.

If you work on a Windows computer you may wish to use E Text Editor which is available at *http://www.e-texteditor.com* or Microsoft Visual Web Developer Express which can be found at *http://www.microsoft.com/express/Web/*.

If you already have a visual web design tool like Adobe Dreamweaver or Microsoft Expression Web installed on your computer, you can use the coding tools integrated with these software packages instead of installing a dedicated text editor. Although both Adobe and Microsoft offer free trial versions of these software tools, if you don't have either one installed, we recommend skipping them for now and instead using any one of the text editors listed above while working with this book. By using a text editor, you can focus on the design and underlying code rather than learning the user interface and functions of a specific software package.

System requirements

Before starting the lessons in the *Web Design with HTML and CSS Digital Classroom*, make sure that your computer is equipped for creating and managing websites. Because you will be using a variety of software tools, there is no formal minimum requirement for your computer, however we suggest that your computer meet or exceed the following guidelines:

Windows OS

Intel® Pentium® 4, AMD Athlon® 64, or Multicore Intel® processor; Microsoft® Windows® XP with Service Pack 2; Windows Vista® Home Premium, Business, Ultimate, or Enterprise with Service Pack 1; or Windows 7

1GB recommended RAM 1GB of available hard-disk space for working with files

1280 × 800 display with 16-bit video card

Broadband Internet connection

Macintosh OS

Multicore Intel® processor

Mac OS X v10.4 or greater

1 GB of RAM 1 GB of available hard-disk space for working with lesson files.

1280 × 800 display with 16-bit video card

Broadband Internet connection

Understanding menus and commands

Menus and commands within the software tools discussed in this book are identified by using the greater-than symbol (>). For example, the command to print a document might appear as File > Print, representing that you click the File menu, then choose the Print command.

Understanding how to read HTML and CSS code changes

Many of the step-by-step instructions in the book involve typing one line (or more) of HTML or CSS code to a previously existing block of code. In these cases, the new code for you to add is highlighted in red to help you quickly identify the text to be added to your lesson file.

For example, this code represents a line already present in your lesson file:

```
<h1> News </h1>
```

The code highlighted here in red is what you would need to add:

```
<h1 class="frontpage"> News </h1>
```

Loading lesson files

The *Web Design with HTML and CSS Digital Classroom* uses files for the exercises with each of the lessons. These files are available for download at *www.DigitalClassroomBooks.com/webdesign*. You may download all the lessons at one time or you may choose to download and work with specific lessons.

For each lesson in the book, the files are referenced by the file name of each file. The exact location of each file on your computer is not used, as you may have placed the files in a unique location on your hard drive. We suggest placing the lesson files in the My Documents folder or on the Desktop so you can easily access them.

Downloading and copying the lesson files to your hard drive:

1   Using your web browser, navigate to *www.DigitalClassroomBooks.com/webdesign*. Follow the instructions on the web page to download the lesson files to your computer.

2   On your computer, navigate to the location where you downloaded the files and right-click (Windows) the .zip file you downloaded, then choose Extract All or double click on the .zip file (Mac OS).

3   If using a Windows computer, the Extract Compressed (Zipped) Folders window appears. In this window, specify the location where you want to save the files, and click Show Extracted Files When Complete. Mac OS users will find the files extracted to the same location as the original .zip file.

Video tutorials

The *www.DigitalClassroomBooks.com/webdesign* site provides *Web Design with HTML and CSS Digital Classroom* book readers with video tutorials that enhance the content of this book. The videos use the popular Silverlight player for viewing on your desktop or notebook computer, or use iPad-compatible video if you are using an iPad to read an electronic version of this book. Most other ePub devices are not optimized for playing video, and you should use a notebook, desktop, or tablet computer for viewing the video tutorials if you are using a dedicated e-reader such as a nook, Kindle, kobo, or Sony e-reader. An Internet connection is necessary for viewing the supplemental video files.

The videos enhance your learning as key concepts and instructions are discussed by the book's authors. The video tutorials supplement the book's contents, and do not replace the book. They are not intended to cover every item discussed in the book, but will help you gain a better or more clear understanding of topics discussed in many lessons of the book.

Hosting your websites

The websites you will create using this book require only your computer, but eventually you will want to create websites to share with the world. To do this, you will need to put your website on a computer connected to the Internet that is always accessible. This is known as a web server. If you don't want to get involved in creating computers that host a website, you can pay a company to provide space on their web servers for you. A good place to look for a hosting provider is here: *http://www.microsoft.com/web/jumpstart/hosting.aspx*. If you want to set up your own computer for hosting a web server and you are using any Windows computer, you can turn it into a web server at no cost by using the Web Platform Installer available at: *http://www.microsoft.com/web*. If you are a Mac OS user, you can get Mac OS X server from Apple to use a Mac OS computer as a web server.

If you are just getting started, you don't need to worry about web hosting just yet. But you'll find this information useful once you start creating sites.

Additional resources

The Digital Classroom series of books can be read in print or using an e-reader. You can also continue your learning online with the training videos, or at seminars, conferences, and in-person training events led by the authors.

DigitalClassroomBooks.com

You can contact the authors, discover any errors, omissions, or clarifications that have been identified since the time of printing, and read excerpts from the other Digital Classroom books in the Digital Classroom series at *digitalclassroombooks.com*.

Seminars, conferences, and training

The authors of the Digital Classroom seminar series frequently conduct in-person seminars and speak at conferences, including the annual CRE8 Conference. Learn more about their upcoming speaking engagements and training classes at *agitraining.com*.

Resources for educators

If you are an educator, contact your Wiley education representative to access resources for this book designed just for you, including instructors' guides for incorporating Digital Classroom books into your curriculum. If you don't know who your educational representative is, you can contact the Digital Classroom books team using the form at *DigitalClassroomBooks.com*.

What you'll learn in this lesson:

- Defining the goals of web design

- Defining the user experience

- Understanding the difference between wireframes, prototypes, and mockups

Planning Your Website

In this lesson, you'll learn how to improve your website by clearly defining what you want the site to do during the planning process.

Starting up

This lesson does not use any lesson files, so you do not need to load any files before starting this lesson.

See Lesson 1 in action!

Use the accompanying video to gain a better understanding of how to use some of the features shown in this lesson. You can find the video tutorial for this lesson at www.digitalclassroombooks.com *using the URL provided when you registered your book.*

The goals of web design

To understand how to create well designed websites, it is worth understanding the fundamentals of design. Good design creates experiences that makes people's lives easier, and is also aesthetically pleasing. Here are some examples: a well-designed store makes it easy for customers to find products they are looking for, or maybe even products they never knew they wanted. Drivers can see well-designed road signs from a distance and the message of the sign can be immediately understood, even at a high rate of speed while driving. A well-designed chair is comfortable to sit in and also fits in with the style of the room.

A store, a sign, and a chair are all designed with a specific intent.

In all these cases, the designer took time to plan the outcome using their skill and experience, as well as resources such as materials and available budget. Different disciplines require different design tools. The web designer is often required to organize information, give it meaning, and assemble it in a way that is visually attractive using available tools.

When designing for the web, there are some unique challenges compared to other disciplines arising from the fact that web design is still in its infancy and is evolving rapidly. Even the definition of *web design* is evolving and difficult to define. Originally, web design meant designing pages for a web browser. While this is still true, you now need to consider the rapidly evolving nature of mobile devices, tablets, smart phones, and consumer electronics that access the web. Some people make the distinction between mobile design and web design, but this distinction is evaporating as mobile devices are evolving. For many web professionals, this rapid evolution of the medium is part of what makes it such an exciting field.

Although the design of websites is an evolving field, designers do not need to reinvent the wheel. Web design's closest relative is print design, and although the two are distinctly different it is worthwhile to compare and contrast them.

The difference between print design and web design

Print involves seeing; the web involves doing. Books, magazines, posters, newspapers, brochures, and advertisements all contain information, usually text and images, whose intent is to deliver some sort of message or content to a reader. More importantly, designers often try to build a call to action into their work that makes a customer believe there is some action they should be taking as a result of the design.

- A visually exciting movie poster's call to action might be, "Go see this movie!"

- A political campaign displays signs with the call to action, "Vote for me!"

- An advertisement in a magazine offering a free sample might have the call to action, "Contact us to learn more!"

In this 19th century advertisement the call to action implores the customer to see the product before going home.

Compare a print flyer for a shoe sale with its online counterpart. The call to action for the print flyer is, "Show up at the store this Saturday to buy these shoes at a discount." The information regarding the sale might be enough to compel the customer to get in their car and go shoe shopping on Saturday, but the designer helps to present the information in a way that is well organized and gets noticed. Using color, type, and perhaps an illustration or image, the designer helps to convince the potential customer of the value of this sale.

In some sense, you could say that the print designer's job is done when she sends the file off to the printer. If the customer shows up in the store, it becomes the salesperson's job to complete the sale.

Now let's examine the web designer who is largely responsible for leading the prospective customer through the entire process. If an interested customer comes to the shoe store's website, perhaps there is a button that the user clicks to see the shoes that are on sale. The customer then needs some way to gather more data on the shoes; perhaps there is a table listing the available shoe sizes, colors, and brands. If the customer takes the leap and puts a shoe into the site's shopping cart, this shopping process needs to be designed as well.

In both of these examples, the end result is hopefully the same for the shoe store's owner: the customer buys the shoes. In both cases information is transferred from the store to the customer; however, in the case of the website, the designer is involved in all stages of the sale process. This is a crucial concept to understand: the web is an active medium and the term to describe this design process is *user interaction design*.

The web demands user interaction

The experience of a website is defined by the interaction the user has with it. For example, a user *clicks* on navigation or *scrolls* down to read a page.

Even the act of reading a book can be defined as user interaction. In the Western world, people *read* from left to right down a page, they *turn* pages, and *scan* page numbers and tables of contents in order to find a certain chapter or topic.

Coming back to the web, you don't just have readers — you have users. Think of the verbs that describe what you do online: you *search* websites, *watch* the weather report, *transfer* money between accounts, *book* airline flights, and do many other things. The designer needs to think in these terms when designing pages, anticipating the user's motivation for coming to the site.

You not only can read an online newspaper, but search, print, email, tweet, comment and listen.

Defining the user experience

When it comes to user interaction, offering too many options can be just as bad as not offering enough. If there are multiple pathways available to the user, it is the designer's responsibility to make sure the user doesn't get lost. The entire sum of a user's interactions with a website can be called the *user experience*.

The focus on the user experience differentiates websites from printed products more than anything else. This job is so important that there are web professionals called information architects. *Information architecture* is defined as the structure of a website and its pages: how the site and the site navigation are organized. In its strictest form, information architecture is not concerned with issues such as color, type, and graphics. In larger design agencies, it is not uncommon to have an information architect collaborating with the designers, especially at the beginning stages of designing a website.

Designers need to think like information architects to be effective. The designs need to provide the best structure allowing users to get the information they want. For online stores, they should provide the most efficient way to allow a user to put an object in a shopping cart and make a purchase. Designers must fully comprehend the web as a medium and understand its rules and possibilities regarding visual design and text.

User-centered design

It can be difficult to describe how a web designer works because the level of involvement in a project can vary, from developing a project on her own, to being part of a large team in an advertising agency. However, in all cases, the designer's goal is to create sites that serves the needs of the users. The following section outlines the planning process so that you clearly understand what the client wants before you begin.

The stages of the planning process

The stages of the planning process can generally be defined as:

- Defining goals and strategy
- Research
- Information architecture
- Sketching
- Wireframes
- Mockups

You'll learn more about each of these stages in this chapter.

Defining goals and strategy

When designing a website, an important question to ask is, "Why does this website need to exist?" It seems strange but a client might not be able to tell you exactly why they want a website. The answer, "Because everyone else has one," is not a good answer.

Imagine a carpenter who is hired by a homeowner to build a "structure" in their backyard, with little information provided about the final project. The carpenter needs to know the purpose of the structure. Do they want a shed? A bandstand? A garage? Just as structures have different purposes, so do websites. As a designer you should be able to define, or have the client define, the goal of the website in a simple sentence. For example, in this book, you will be designing a site called SmoothieWorld, which has the following goal:

To be the first stop on the web for people looking for Smoothie recipes.

Although the designer may not have defined this objective, she can certainly contribute to the conversation. Here are some of the questions that might arise in discussing the functionality and design of such a site:

- Will the site be free? If yes, will there be advertising and is that something the designer needs to include in the layout?

- Has the client considered how they want to organize the recipes on the site? For example, could a user submit ingredients they have on hand and receive a recipe in return?

- What, if any, user interactions might there be on site. For example, can users submit recipes or simply browse existing ones?

In larger organizations, these conversations might also involve web developers, who would be responsible for any database functionality, along with the marketing department, the sales department, and other interested stakeholders. Even if these discussions take place before you, the designer, are brought into the project, you will want to have a good understanding of the goals of a website before you start any design work.

Research

A designer who is practicing user-centered design needs to have some background on what visitors to a site might be expecting.

Competitive research is one way to find this information. In the SmoothieWorld example, there may not be many competing smoothie sites; however, there are certainly a number of popular recipe and cooking sites. You should understand how these sites are designed and what makes them so attractive to users.

In some cases, research can be objective. Perhaps the SmoothieWorld site has existed for some time and is being redesigned. This is an ideal situation because there should be some data from the history of the site that you can access. You could request the server logs from the client. A *server log* is a record of information that most servers collect by default and is often accessible from the hosting company or Internet service provider (ISP) for the site. The raw data from server logs is not particularly useful until it has been organized. This organization of server log data is done with analytic software. *Analytic software* takes information such as the type of browser the visitor is using, monitor resolution, and which pages are most popular, and then formats this data to provide a useful profile of a site's user base. Often analytical tools are installed on a site and available as the site is running, so you can gather information about the site's effectiveness on a regular basis.

Scenarios and characters

It can be helpful to envision some fictitious users of your site. You can create several characters and think about how they were introduced to your site, what they hope to achieve while using the site, and what are their priorities. By envisioning the experience through others' eyes, you can gain a more user-focused experienced.

Web analytics

You can obtain analytics data in two ways: through the hosting company, and through third-party analytic software such as Google Analytics or Omniture. Although many hosting companies provide free analytics services, the depth of the information might be limited and the data might not be easy to interpret.

Daily Summary

(**Go To:** Top I General Summary I Weekly Report I Daily Report I **Daily Summary** I Hourly Summary I Organiz Report I Browser Summary I Operating System Report I Status Code Report I File Type Report I Directory Rep

Each unit (■) represents 10 requests for pages or part thereof.

day	#reqs	#pages	
Sun	230	165	▬▬▬▬▬
Mon	393	258	▬▬▬▬▬▬▬▬
Tue	474	365	▬▬▬▬▬▬▬▬▬▬
Wed	753	450	▬▬▬▬▬▬▬▬
Thu	654	441	▬▬▬▬▬▬▬▬
Fri	241	159	▬▬▬▬▬
Sat	356	160	▬▬▬▬▬

A simple graph of how many pages were visited over a week.

More companies are using advanced analytic software to maintain and improve their website. Third-party analytic software often requires you to add JavaScript to every page on your website, which allows the software to begin collecting more specific data such as how long, on average, users might be spending on a certain page. In addition to the additional data gathered, another benefit of third-party analytics is the way they present charts and graphs in a more user-friendly way.

(continues)

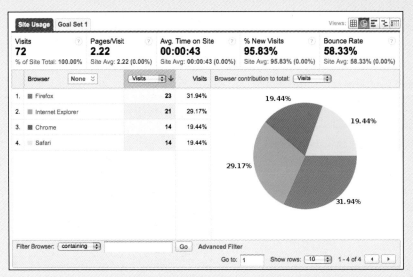

Web analytics (continued)

Third-party analytic software often organizes visitor data in useful ways; this example displays the visitor's browser version.

Although Internet marketers use analytics to improve websites, it can also be useful for design purposes. For example, if analytics data shows that a particular recipe on your SmoothieWorld site has become extremely popular (for whatever reason), a designer might "promote" that page by adding a link or photo to the recipe on the home page. It's a good idea to incorporate analtyics into your site designs so your clients can measure the effectiveness of their sites.

Popular analytics tools

Google Analytics
Google Analytics is a popular choice due to its integration with Google's AdWords campaign, and because it is offered at no cost.

Omniture
Omniture was recently purchased by Adobe, and provides enterprise-level analytics tools for large businesses.

HaveaMint.com
This service has a simple yet powerful interface that makes working with server logs enjoyable and interesting.

Chartbeat.com
Chartbeat combines standard charts and graphs with alert systems to help busy sites stay on top of their server traffic.

For more information on analytics tools and services, see the book *Web Analytics: An Hour a Day* by Avinash Kaushik.

Information architecture

Design is not just about visuals. The word *design* comes from the Latin word *designare*, which means to mark out, devise, or choose. This is a good reminder that you should choose or plan the structure of a website before you consider the visuals. The term used to describe the planning of a website's structure is information architecture. Information architecture is concerned with providing optimal navigation paths for the user and helping them get from point A to point B. For example, the user may need to go from the home page to the best recipe for a mango/banana smoothie.

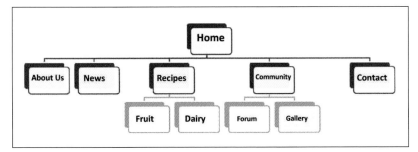

A site map is often used in the discipline of information architecture.

In more formal terms, information architecture is the process of organizing the site's content and defining the hierarchy and navigation of the site. Since most sites have a "client" of some sort, information architecture is also where you discuss the scope of the site. *Scope* relates to the number of pages in a site as well as the features and functionality the site includes. A single-page website with some text and a few images would be a site with a small scope, while a 200-page website that includes a video library, database integration, and sends alerts to a user's mobile phone would be a site with a large scope.

The business of web design

There is an interlocking relationship between the budget of a site and its scope and timeline. A change in one element will affect at least one of the others.

If you are freelance web designer, you may be dealing with a client directly; if you are working in an organization, the "client" might be a manager or a different division or department. In both situations the rules are similar: if the budget, scope, or deadline shifts, it will affect at least one of the other aspects of the project. After you complete the information architecture phase, it is quite likely that the client will ask for new features. As the designer, you need to communicate how this will affect either the budget or the timeline for delivery. In a similar way, if the timeline for delivery changes and the site needs to be delivered sooner than anticipated, then you need to either exclude features or change the budget to reflect this.

Ideally, the client will be able to tell you which of these factors is the most important. For example, if there is a fixed budget for a site and there is absolutely no way the client can exceed it, then you will have to ensure that features can be completed within the budget.

Resources

Issues such as managing projects, legal contracts, and other aspects of web design require attention. Here are some resources to get you started:

AIGA

AIGA is an association dedicated to supporting designers. Although it offers memberships, it also provides non-members access to free resources such as tips on how to create contracts as well as forms you can use.

www.aiga.org/content.cfm/design-and-business

Graphic Artists Guild

The Guild has local chapters in many cities. They publish the *Graphic Artists Guild's Handbook of Pricing & Ethical Guidelines*, which can help you determine the appropriate fees for your services and also provides sample legal forms and tips on how to market yourself.

www.graphicartistsguild.org

A List Apart

An invaluable online resource for all things related to web design, this site has articles about business practices, client management, information architecture, and much more. Each year, the site also conducts and releases a survey of web designers, which provides useful data about salary ranges, job titles, and more. Type **survey** in the search field on their home page to find the most recent one.

www.alistapart.com

Defining the navigation design of the SmoothieWorld site

The nature and content of your layout depend on how you define a site's organizational and navigational structure. One of the benefits of creating wireframes, prototypes, and mockups is to allow you to build your site more rapidly. One popular method for exploring possible navigation in the design phase is to use a pencil, sticky notes, and a blank wall. This lets you rapidly "reorganize" a site, and also allows for collaboration and doesn't require any special skills.

Let's consider two types of site structures that will eventually translate to the navigation menus: wide and deep. First you have a *wide* navigation structure in which the main pages are listed horizontally:

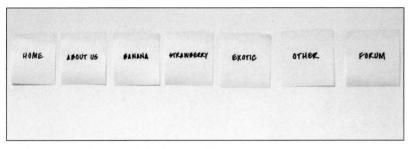

A wide site navigation has primary links always accessible.

In a wide navigation system, the main pages are all visible together and for small sites, this is often a logical choice. With the navigation bar on every page the user can easily jump to any of the main pages with a single click. The disadvantage of a wide navigation structure is that there may be limits to how much information can easily be displayed if there are too many categories. You are limited by the width of the screen and must also remember that if you present too many options, the site may overwhelm or confuse the user.

An alternative method for organizing content is *deep* navigation, which simplifies the main navigation and then groups related pages into categories.

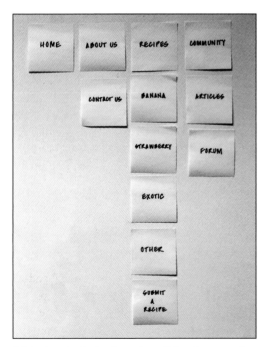

A deep site navigation has fewer primary links and more secondary and tertiary links.

Deep navigation provides simplified entry-points for the user; however, the designer must decide how to organize the pages inside these main links. Common solutions to this problem include drop-down menus and secondary navigation menus.

Rethinking site navigation

The concept of the "home page" may not be as crucial as it once was due to the power of search engines, how their use has influenced users, along with social media such as Twitter and Facebook which make it more likely that a user will enter your site in unique ways. The first time a user experiences your site may not be through the home page, but from a search engine result or a link to an internal page on your site from another website or from a Twitter feed or a Facebook post. Every page on your site now becomes a home, needing to welcome users into your site.

Although this shifts the role of the home page, it also shows the importance of understanding why users are coming to your sites and why you need to provide them clear navigational structure and content that helps them find what they need.

The role of usability testing

Usability testing is related to, but distinct from, the field of design. *Usability testing* is the process of evaluating how users interact with a website. It often involves giving a user a task to complete on a given site and then observing how well they complete the task, whether they can complete it. If a user encounters difficulty or is confused by the process, these problems are noted and solutions are then tested and integrated into the site.

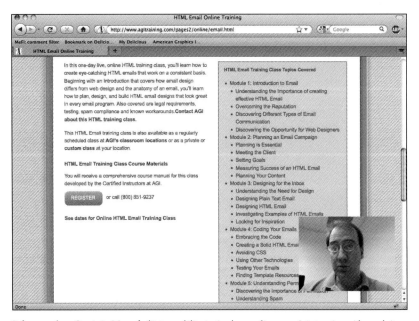

Software such as Camtasia Morae facilitates usability testing by recording a user's interaction with a website, including video of users' reactions.

A common problem with usability testing is that it often occurs too late in the design process. If you have users test the site after you have built it completely, the feedback may be useful but you may need to discard work that you have already completed. For example, if you have completely built a site using a wide navigation, and testing shows you need to revise it to use deep navigation, this will be more difficult if you have already built all your pages and created the graphics.

A usability exercise relating to navigation design

Usability testing must be done correctly or you will receive invalid feedback, or feedback that isn't useful. For example, it's important to conduct testing with subjects who truly represent the target audience, not those who may already be familiar with the site.

To better understand how usability testing works, try the following exercise with another person, putting them in the role of the user and yourself in the role of the tester. Most usability tests ask users to speak their thoughts out loud and they are recorded in order to capture the information. While you won't be recording the user, you will ask them to respond out loud to some questions. First find a suitable website to use as an example, and then ask the other person the following list of questions:

- What are your first impressions of the layout of this page immediately upon viewing it?

- What section of the page does your eye go to first?

- Is that section the most important element on the page?

- What associations do the colors and images evoke? These could be emotions, feelings, memories, places, or anything else the colors bring to your mind.

- Without clicking on anything on the site, describe the navigation choices you see on the home page and indicate what you think they do. Feel free to move around the page by scrolling, but do not click on anything right now.

- Without clicking on anything yet, if you were exploring, what would you click on first and why?

These questions give you a sense of how a usability test works. The next step would be to give the user specific tasks, and pay attention to how they perform them. As you can see, observing users, their reactions, the decisions they make, and any obstacles they encounter is vital to usability testing. We've only scratched the surface in discussing usability testing. For a greater understanding, review the resources below.

Usability Resources

Rocket Surgery Made Easy by Steve Krug
This book provides you with the philosophy and the techniques you can use to integrate simple usability testing into your design process.

User Interface Engineering
Although this is a usability firm that specializes in research, training, and consulting, their website provides free articles that can help you understand the role of usability, as well as useful tips.
www.uie.com/articles

Wireframes, prototypes, and mockups

After you have defined the goals and decided on the information architecture of a website, there are important stages in the design process you should complete before writing a single line of HTML or CSS. If you begin designing visuals or building pages before you are prepared, you may end up discarding your original work. By using wireframes, mockups, and prototypes. you can quickly create to explore different design options and functionality for the site. Making changes before writing code and creating graphics allows you to make changes more quickly and is less costly and more efficient. Whether or not you use all three models generally depends on the size of the project. Larger projects that incorporate complicated elements, such as connection to a database, or use multiple features, will benefit from using all three models.

Wireframes

Wireframes are typically created in black and white or shades of gray, using placeholders for images. Wireframes avoid the visual design of the site and are more concerned with the organization of the content and features. You can create a wireframe in a program like Adobe Illustrator, Adobe Fireworks, Microsoft Visio, or Omnigraffle, or even by using a sketch on paper or a whiteboard. A wireframe does not need to be interactive, and is a fast way to start a conversation between designers, developers, clients, and other members who are involved in a project.

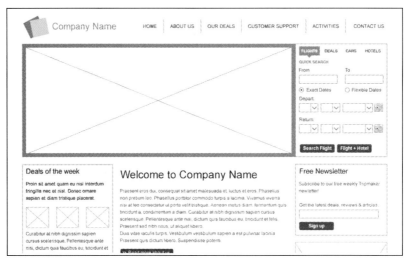

Wireframes use elements such as shapes, lines, and text to begin structuring a web page.

Mockups

Mockups are sometimes the result of wireframes, although it is possible to skip the wireframing step for less-complex sites. You can create them in an image editor such as Photoshop. You create mockups to begin exploring the visual elements of a site, such as the user interface elements such as buttons and navigation bars, typography, layout, and imagery like photographs and illustrations. Some designers prefer to create two or three different styles for clients or collaborators to review. In some cases, the final assets in a mockup might be used directly in the finished application.

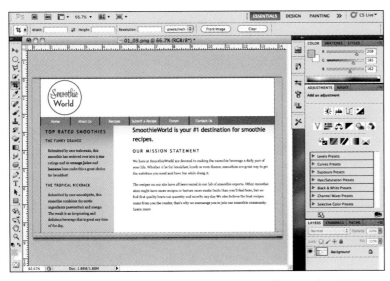

Mockups are often done in a program such as Photoshop and are eventually converted to HTML.

Prototypes

Prototypes are usually built for demonstration purposes. They differ from mockups and wireframes because they show functionality and often demonstrate how the user interacts with elements on a page. For example, if a website will have a shopping cart, a prototype would help define the way the cart will function once it is completed. Aspects of the shopping cart that may be impossible or difficult to display as an image such as animation, response time, or what happens when a user removes an item from the cart are ideal candidates for a prototype. You can build a prototype using HTML, Flash animation, or a program such as Microsoft SketchFlow or Balsamiq Mockups.

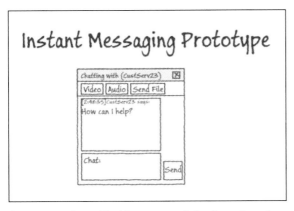

A prototype may have a "sketch" appearance and allow for user interaction such as entering data and clicking buttons. This prototype was created using Microsoft Sketchflow..

The evolving field of interactive prototypes

Traditional wireframes, mockups, and prototypes cannot fully account for the interactive nature of the web. For example, page mockups created in Photoshop are static so they cannot demonstrate how text on the page reflows or how a navigation menu expands and collapses. Wireframes have similar problems because they are not interactive.

Wireframing and prototyping software has evolved over the years, and a new breed of software and web applications are making the interactive prototyping possible. These include elements such as rollover buttons, working form elements, the ability to update common page elements quickly, and simple animation.

Interactive prototyping resources

Following are some prototyping and wireframe software resources. Most of these programs are available in trial versions, so you can compare and evaluate them based on your needs.

Microsoft SketchFlow
SketchFlow is an application designed specifically for prototyping. In addition to a built-in library of interactive controls, it also allows you to add animated components and data-driven user-interface elements. SketchFlow also features a feedback system that allows team members and clients to add comments to a prototype and then deliver that feedback to the creator. Sketchflow is currently included with the Expression Blend software. If you are a full time student, you can obtain a free copy of the Expression software at *DreamSpark.com*.
www.microsoft.com/expression/products/Sketchflow_Overview.aspx

Adobe Fireworks
Adobe Fireworks is a vector-and-bitmap image editor that also includes features for creating wireframes and prototypes. For example, it includes a Pages feature that builds multi-page documents and generates multi-page HTML elements that are specifically for the web. It also includes templates for wireframes, mobile devices, and grid systems, among others.
www.adobe.com/products/fireworks/

EightShapes Unify
For designers who have a print background and are using Adobe InDesign, EightShapes offers a free set of components and templates. This is a complete system that allows you to build wireframes and prototypes using standard print layout techniques.
http://unify.eightshapes.com/

Be creative during the planning process

The planning stage can be a fun part of the site creation process, because this is where you can propose those crazy ideas that may never make it onto the final site. You want to avoid limiting yourself, as there will be time for a reality check once the designing and coding begins! Keep in mind that in the early stages of site development, collaboration is important. Whether it involves user testing or receiving feedback from a wireframe, if you learn how to collaborate and incorporate good ideas into your design, your final product will benefit.

- **Early sketches should be drawn quickly**

  It's OK for the early sketches of your web pages to be loose, lacking in detail, and incomplete. It's more important to capture your initial ideas in some form. Sketches are cheap and disposable, so don't focus on the quality of a sketch; focus on the ideas behind it.

- **Failure *is* an option!**

  You are unlikely to get concepts right the first time. In fact, you may not be trying hard enough if you aren't discarding some ideas for layout, imagery, or themes for your site.

- **Accept criticism**

  Web design can be a tough field, and your designs and ideas will at some point be questioned or knocked-down. Try not to take it personally when this happens. That mockup you worked on all day really may not be a good fit for the project. If you can keep an open mind, and collaborate with others, your design will ultimately be stronger. You may even find that ideas rejected from one project might be a good fit for some future site.

Self study

1 Using a paper and pencil, come up with your own version of how the SmoothieWorld site might be organized. Research popular recipe websites. How do they organize their large collection of recipes?

2 Find a partner and conduct the usability test outlined earlier in this lesson. What did you learn that you might apply to a site like SmoothieWorld?

Review

Questions

1 What is the difference between a wireframe, mockup, and prototype?

2 Define *information architecture*.

3 What is usability testing and how does it relate to web design?

Answers

1 A wireframe is a diagram or sketch of a web page that focuses on structure and layout, not visual elements such as color or graphics. A mockup is a visual representation of a page that includes font choices, colors, layout, and images. A prototype may contain elements of wireframes or mockups but is primarily concerned with demonstrating the interaction between a user and the site.

2 Information architecture is the process of organizing a website's content and defining the navigation of the site.

3 Usability testing is the procedure in which a user is given a task or series of tasks relating to a website, such as purchasing an item, and then asked to determine where any confusion or difficulty in navigating appears. A web designer would take this feedback and improve the site design as needed.

What you'll learn in this lesson:

- Fundamentals of web page technology
- The roles of HTML, CSS, and JavaScript
- The evolution of web standards

Fundamentals of the Web

In this lesson, you'll learn the fundamentals the Internet and the World Wide Web work and how designing for web differs from other methods of communication.

Starting up

You will work with several files from the web02lessons folder in this lesson. Make sure you have loaded the weblessons folder onto your hard-drive from *www.digitalclassroombooks.com/webdesign*. See "Loading lesson files" in the Starting Up section of this book.

See Lesson 2 in action!

Use the accompanying video to gain a better understanding of how to use some of the features shown in this lesson. You can find the video tutorial for this lesson at www.digitalclassroombooks.com using the URL provided when you registered your book.

How web pages work

You'll benefit from understanding the structure and function of systems that deliver the work you design across the Internet. This lesson focuses on understanding the structure and function of the Internet and the World Wide Web. Understanding these systems will help you deliver your web design projects more effectively. You will now take a quick look at how websites are hosted and how the pages you create end up on visitor's computer screens and mobile devices around the world.

The Internet and World Wide Web domain names

The Internet is based on the fundamental concept that all computers should be able to reach each other using an address. Much like your home, apartment, or school has a street address where the post office or Fed Ex can reach you, or you have a phone number where someone can call you, all Internet connected computers have an address known as a TCP/IP address. The TCP/IP stands for Transmission Control Protocol/Internet Protocol, but that's not critically important. What you need to know is that TCP/IP allows packets of digital information, such as your website, to be sent across networks and then reassembled once it reaches its destination. TCP/IP addresses are commonly referred to as IP addresses.

Sending

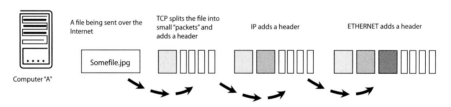

Receiving

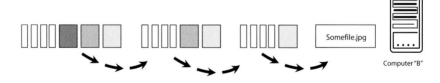

A simplified diagram of how files are sent over the Internet.

In the early 1990s, Sir Tim Berners-Lee took advantage of the Internet's linked nature and created a method for his colleagues to remotely access data that he stored on his computer. A user anywhere in the world who had access to the Internet could connect to a server and request a page, which would then display on the user's computer. Berners-Lee dubbed it the World Wide Web, and his program was a simple version of the first web browser. Web browsers and the information available have evolved greatly, but the technical concepts have not changed. One computer with a TCP/IP address is able to request information, such as a web page, from a computer located at another TCP/IP address.

Researchers such as Berners-Lee appreciated the instant access to documents, and the World Wide Web was used at first primarily by academics for research purposes. Commercial uses of a web browser displaying text and graphics quickly evolved. In 1994 there were a mere handful of websites in existence, and a short five years later, there were over six million websites in existence.

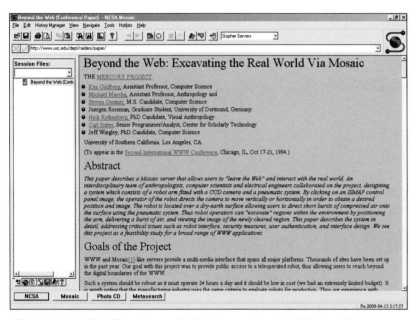

Although not technically the first web browser, the Mosaic browser released in 1993 triggered the popularity of websites worldwide.

Domain names and hosting

Domain names help users find their way around the Internet. You already know domain names because they are commonly surrounded by *www* on the front and *.com* on the end. Domains can also include various endings such as *.org*, *.edu*, and *.gov*.

Domain names exist because it's not very convenient for you to use or remember IP addresses. Domain Name Servers (DNS) translate easy-to-understand domain names into IP addresses. A DNS converts a familiar string of letters, the "domain name," to the numbered IP address. Instead of typing the IP address 72.32.147.166 into a web browser, you can type the domain name, such as *www.digitalclassroombooks.com*. A DNS on the Internet converts your requested domain into the appropriate IP address, which routes your request to the appropriate web server.

The web server is a computer that is much like a desktop PC. It generally runs either a version of Microsoft Windows Web Server or UNIX, but it may have additional processing power and redundant systems to handle traffic from thousands of users at the same time. Web servers maintain a constant connection to the Internet, so your websites are available 24 hours a day.

Because most companies want their web servers to be available all day, every day, they are often maintained by web hosting companies. These firms are paid to maintain your web server so that it is always accessible and running. If you run a small website, they may put your site on a server that is shared with other sites. For more demanding sites, or sites with sensitive information, a business will pay higher fees for a dedicated server. Even large companies will often turn to hosting businesses to maintain their web servers, although some companies may elect to place their web servers within their own company.

The language of the web

Hypertext Markup Language, or HTML, uses tags that enclose plain text. The tags describe how the text should appear and the function of the text. The web browser looks at the tags and displays them accordingly. A simple example of HTML text is:

```
<p>Do you want to have lunch?</p>
```

The text to be displayed, `Do you want to have lunch?`, is wrapped by two tags indicating that it is a paragraph. The first tag is the opening tag `<p>` and the second is the closing tag `</p>`. These tags are generally not displayed in the browser, which reads the text from the web server and formats the text as a paragraph to display on the viewer's screen.

HTML also lets designers create hyperlinks. Hyperlinks are areas of text, images, buttons, or other parts of a page where the viewer can click to navigate to additional content. Clicking a link can open a new web page, site, document, video, or animation.

The evolution of the web and web standards

HTML is interpreted by web browsers, such as Internet Explorer, Firefox, Safari, and Chrome. Web designers have discovered that the same HTML code might be displayed differently on various web browsers. Because web browsers can interpret HTML code differently, you will need to consider browser testing in your design considerations, which we cover in more detail in Lesson 10.

In the early days of the web, some browser developers created proprietary HTML tags. They created tags that were supported by only their browser, as they hoped that the unique capabilities might draw more users.

Soon designers discovered they could not rely on the same HTML code for all browsers. Designers added "hacks," extra code, to pages, making certain that layouts worked in different browsers. Some designers would go so far as to create two versions of a site, and the appropriate version would be displayed based upon the browser being used by the viewer. Other designers would add badges to their sites, letting viewers know that the site performs best with a particular browser. To this day you can still see some sites with notices such as "This site is optimized for Internet Explorer" or some other browser.

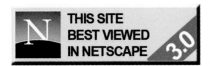

Web pages that were designed to work only in a single browser were taking the web in the wrong direction.

Designers, businesses, and the companies developing browsers eventually discovered that inconsistency and proprietary tags that worked only with their browser were hurting the user experience and harmful to the vitality and growth of the web. The various browser manufacturers have started to recognize the importance of consistency, and most are working with the World Wide Web Consortium (W3C) and independent testing bodies to validate the compliance of their browser with accepted standards. Browser developers now promote their compliance with standards and speed at displaying standards-based pages.

Now that you understand some of the history and concepts behind the web, you'll start to examine some of the HTML code that powers web pages.

Separating structure, style, and interactivity

Modern websites often consist of pages with HTML or XHTML for the page structure and content, Cascading Style Sheets (CSS) for the style, and JavaScript, Flash, or Silverlight for the interactivity. In this exercise, you will look at three examples of source code. Each page has the same content, but has a different appearance and functionality. If you have not done so already, be sure to copy the lesson folders for this book onto your local system.

1   Open your web browser—it doesn't matter if it is Internet Explorer, Firefox, Chrome, Safari, or another browser. Choose File > Open and browse to the web02lessons folder, choose the file plain.html, and then click Open. The page loads into your browser.

   The page displays in your browser. The HTML defines the structure of this page and contains content such as the text and images.

Some browsers may not display the menu bar. In this case, you can use your operating system to navigate to the web02lessons folder and double-click the file to open, or use your keyboard and press Ctrl. + O (Windows) or Command + O (Mac OS).

A local HTML page can be previewed in your web browser.

2   In your web browser, choose File > Open and browse to the document plain_with_styles.html located in the web02lessons folder, and click Open. Your browser displays a more highly formatted web page. It includes a two-column layout, and background colors for the page. The content on this page is identical to the previous document; however, the style is being provided by a number of style rules in a Cascading Style Sheet or CSS.

3   In your web browser, choose File > Open and browse to the document plain_with_styles_js.html located in the web02lessons folder, and click Open. This page includes a collapsible panel which you can activate by clicking the title to expand the content section. JavaScript makes this interactivity possible by registering the mouse click which triggers the expansion or collapse of the panel.

As you can see, the same HTML content can be enhanced and modified using CSS and also by adding interactivity, in this example it was through the use of JavaScript. As you work through this book, you'll learn different ways to have HTML work in concert with CSS and interactive elements and even multimedia to create the page and message you need for the sites you create.

Designing for the web

The best designed websites are those that meet the expectations of a user, are easy to use, and meet the objective of the publisher—whether a business, organization, or individual. There are several considerations that should always be a part of your decision-making process when starting to create a design.

Know your audience

A bank site provides a sense of safety, stability, and professionalism. The kind of image you want from someone that will hold on to your money. It also provides easy access to log-in to your account if you are a user, and has easy-to access links to move to the parts of the site offering various services. The design and navigation is easy to follow, regardless of the age or technical skill of the user.

A banking site and an entertainment site will be designed with their target audiences in mind.

An entertainment site that targets a teenage audience includes a more visual approach, updated news, and links to social networking sites that might be used by the audience. Information about shows and personalities is front-and-center. The site manages to be trendy and still provides easy access to information that viewers are likely to be seeking.

Know that your site's viewers are impatient

The viewers coming to your site are impatient. A recent study of retail websites found that if users reach a website and the page does not load within four seconds, they are likely to leave the site, never waiting for the page to load. The same study found that more than one-third of online shoppers would abandon a site immediately if they have a poor online experience. The majority of those who said they would abandon a site indicated they would not return.[1] As a designer you can help provide a great experience on your sites by keeping the following in mind:

- Use images only when they add value to the page.

- When using images, optimize their size for online use so they load faster. This is covered in detail in Lesson 5.

- Use a common Cascading Style Sheet to standardize layout, navigation and colors.

- Separate long content into multiple pages so it loads faster.

- Only add multimedia such as video, audio, Flash, and Silverlight.

Designing for the screen

When designing websites, consider where they will be viewed. If your audience will primarily be on a desktop or laptop computer, the pages should be horizontal rather than vertical. This keeps users from needing to scroll unnecessarily. Similarly, if your audience is primarily working on mobile devices, consider reducing the content and designing for a smaller, vertical screen.

Displays are available in different sizes, and can display varying amounts of information. The amount of information that can be displayed on screen is known as the resolution of a display, and it is measured in pixels. The word pixel is derived from "picture element" and is the smallest unit of measurement on the screen (when used for web graphics there are often 72 pixels per inch). Two of the most common monitor resolutions on the web are 1024 pixels wide × 768 pixels high and also 1280 pixels wide × 800 pixels high. As you can see in the table below, the same page displayed at various resolutions provides different experiences for the viewer.

The same layout on a 1024×768 monitor (left) and a 1280×800 monitor.

---

1 Report published by Akamai available at www.akamai.com/html/about/press/releases/2006/press_110606.html)

As screen sizes get larger and display resolutions increase, there are a greater number of discrepancies that can occur, making it even more important to design for all the displays on which your site will be viewed and we discuss how to tackle this dilemma in Lesson 7. While it is impossible to design a site that looks the same in every browser at every resolution, you can still create designs that work across various devices and displays.

A fixed layout designed for a 1280 × 800 monitor (left) will be cropped on a 1024 × 768 monitor.

Understanding how your audience will read your web content

Most web users gain information they are seeking through reading. But writing for a website should differ from writing for brochures or other printed documents.

Web readers are more likely to "scan" stories rather than read them in full detail. Effective content is organized, edited, and structured so it works well on a site; it isn't merely copied and pasted from printed brochures. You'll discover that you want to create headings that clearly mark the separation of a story from other content, or format text so it does not span the entire width of a monitor.

You've discovered several key concepts about how the web works, the technical underpinnings of websites, and some key design considerations. We wrap up this section with some self-study ideas and review questions before jumping into the next lesson.

Self study

1 Identify three websites you use frequently and compare how well they are formatted for the screen and note if they work equally well on your monitor. Make a list of the visual elements that contribute to your overall experience of the site.

2 Have you had the experience where you've considered "abandoning" a site because of a poor experience? If so, try to remember the elements that led to this and how your favorite sites might do things differently.

Review

Questions

1 What is an IP address and what role does it play in web design?

2 What elements contain structure, style, and interactivity for a website?

3 When designing for the screen, what is one of the most important considerations for designers?

Answers

1 An IP address is a unique series of numbers that identify the identification and hosting address of a website (or sites). IP addresses are associated with a website's domain name since humans have an easier time working with names (*www.agitraining.com*) rather than numbers (72.32.147.166).

2 HTML provides the structure of the page. The style is provided by CSS and the interactivity is often provided by JavaScript, Flash, or Silverlight.

3 Designers need to be sensitive to the fact that there are users who have different size monitors and will view content at various display resolutions.

What you'll learn in this lesson:

- Creating and editing HTML using a text editor

- Introduction to using Dreamweaver and Expression Web for site design and management

- Using web browsers for testing and troubleshooting

Web Design Tools

Web design tools range from simple utilities to complex and robust software packages. Your choice of tools may be based upon personal preference, the scope of the project, or the tools purchased by your employer. This lesson provides an overview of some of the most common web design tools.

Starting up

You will work with several files from the web03lessons folder in this lesson. Make sure you have loaded the weblessons folder onto your hard-drive from *www.digitalclassroombooks.com/webdesign*. See "Loading lesson files" in the Starting Up section of this book.

See Lesson 3 in action!

Use the accompanying video to gain a better understanding of how to use some of the features shown in this lesson. You can find the video tutorial for this lesson at www.digitalclassroombooks.com *using the URL provided when you registered your book.*

This lesson provides a general overview of web design tools and also includes step-by-step exercises. The web editors used in this lesson are available as fully functional trial versions at no cost. If you haven't decided which tools to use, you'll want to download and install the software tools used in this lesson. You'll need a text editor, such as TextWrangler (Mac) available at *www.barebones.com/products/textwrangler* or Visual Web Developer Express available at *www.microsoft.com/express/Web*. You'll also need a program with a visual design surface such as Dreamweaver, available at *www.adobe.com/cfusion/tdrc/index.cfm?product=dreamweaver*, or Expression Web available at *www.microsoft.com/expression/try-it*.

Web editors versus WYSIWYG tools

HTML and CSS use text as their foundation. Because of this, even the most simple text editor, such as TextEdit on the Mac or Notepad on the PC, is capable of creating web pages. These basic text editing tools, however, lack features that help with web design and development such as checking code syntax, organizing your site folders, and uploading files to web servers. In addition to text editors, there are also fully featured web editors and design tools, such as Adobe Dreamweaver and Microsoft Expression Web. These are WYSIWYG tools ("What You See Is What You Get") that provide a visual layout environment, code editing, along with website management tools. Robust text editors and coding tools that handle web markup and programming languages such as HTML, CSS, JavaScript, and PHP provide another set of tools for creating websites. In this overview you'll look at the advantages and disadvantages of each category of web design tools.

Plain text editors

Plain text editors such as Notepad and TextEdit are included with the Mac OS or Windows operating systems, so you likely already have one installed on your computer. While they are widely available and free, they are not optimized for web design. Working with plain text editors requires excellent knowledge of the language you are coding, because they provide no guidance when writing code. The basic text editors also lack functionality for previewing your pages in a web browser, or the ability to check pages for correct syntax or broken links.

Writing HTML and CSS in a plain text editor provides little guidance.

These default text editors for the Mac OS and Windows can be used if you have no other choice, but it is unlikely you will want to use them as your primary web design tool.

Using Notepad or TextEdit as a web editor

Windows Notepad can be found on any Windows system in the Accessories panel. You can create an HTML document by following these steps:

1   Choose Start > Programs > Accessories > Notepad, and when the Notepad window appears, choose File > New.

By default, the file is saved in the text (.txt) format and so any HTML tags that the file contains cannot be interpreted by a web browser.

2   In Notepad, select File > Save As. Change the file extension from .txt to .html in the file name field.

3   Specify "All Files" in the Save as type field. Set the Encoding value to UTF-8 instead of ANSI; this is the necessary encoding for HTML pages.

4   Click the Save button.

If you work on a Mac OS computer, you can use the TextEdit application to create or modify HTML and CSS files.

1   On your Mac, open the Applications folder and locate the TextEdit application.

By default, TextEdit is designed to open and save documents as .rtf (rich text format) files. In order to use it successfully for HTML, you must change the application preferences.

2   Choose TextEdit > Preferences. The Preferences dialog box opens.

3   In the New Document tab, click to select the Plain text radio button. With this option selected, TextEdit creates only plain text without any formatting applied to the text.

4   Click the Open and Save tab and select the radio buttons for both *Ignore rich text commands in HTML files* and *Ignore rich text commands in RTF files*. With these options selected, TextEdit will open and create HTML files. You also need to deselect the *Add ".txt" extension to plain text files* option as you will be specifying the .html extension when you save.

5   In the HTML Saving Options group, set the document type to XHTML 1.0 Transitional, make sure the Styling menu is set to Embedded CSS, and make sure the Encoding menu is set to Unicode (UTF-8).

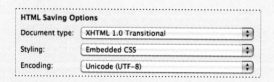

6   Close the Preferences dialog box and exit TextEdit by selecting TextEdit > Quit TextEdit. Then restart TextEdit by double-clicking the icon in the Applications folder. When you restart the program, the new preferences will be used.

Text editors for web design

There are several text editors with more advanced capabilities. These type of editors provide several benefits that make it easier to work with code. We'll look at some of the benefits here.

Code coloring

Whether you are writing a new HTML or CSS page from scratch or opening a pre-existing page, code coloring visually separates your HTML and CSS syntax from the content on your page. Tags that include attributes and values are assigned different colors. This code coloring makes it easier for you to locate specific code, and it can help you spot and correct errors. Forgetting to add a closing bracket or a quotation mark, for example, causes content to be colored differently than if tags were applied correctly. After you become accustomed to using colored syntax, you can use the colors to quickly spot errors in HTML. Most modern text editors also allow you to customize the color of your syntax.

```
<!DOCTYPE html PUBLIC "-//W3C//DTD XHTML 1.0 Transitional//EN"
"http://www.w3.org/TR/xhtml1/DTD/xhtml1-transitional.dtd">
<html xmlns="http://www.w3.org/1999/xhtml">
<head>
<meta http-equiv="Content-Type" content="text/html; charset=UTF-8" />
<title>Untitled Document</title>

</head>

<body>
    <h1>SmoothieWorld</h1>
    <p>Smoothies are the stuff of life. they get you going in the morning, refresh you when you'
Smoothieworld we want everyone to feel the power of Smoothies. We're called Smoothieworld becaus
Smoothies can change the world.</p>

    <img src="images/blueberry_smoothie.jpg" alt="Blueberry Smoothie" width="125" height="200">

    <p>All content on this site is the
    copyright of SmoothieWorld</p>

</body>
</html>
```

Code coloring visually separates the tags from the content.

Line numbers, invisible characters, and other visual aids

Most text editors provide line numbers in documents opened for editing. Line numbers help you orient yourself within your code and also help when collaborating with other designers or developers. These tools also make it easier to see invisible characters such as line breaks or carriage returns.

Code completion

Most text editors can automate a number of certain tedious tasks, such as typing brackets or common tags. Although the methods and shortcuts for each program are different, most full-featured text editors have this capability. Some text editors automatically trigger code completion as you begin to type, while others require you to trigger the code completion and choose the code from a list of options. Code completion is useful, as it removes some of the burden of having to remember every detail of the syntax you are using, whether HTML, CSS, or another language.

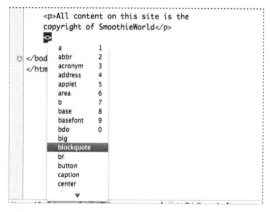

In TextMate (Mac OS), you can trigger code completion manually by pressing the Option + Esc keys. Similar capabilities exist in Windows text editors such as Visual Studio from Microsoft.

Automation features

Most text editors have some capability for automating repetitive tasks. Whether they are called macros, snippets, clips, or by some other name. These automation tools give you the ability to add reusable pieces of code to your pages and can save you a great deal of time.

In Coda (Mac OS), the Clip feature provides a way to save and re-use code across projects. In this example, the basic HTML structure of a page is selected.

Finding and replacing code

Most text editors used for coding also have robust tools for searching and replacing code. Although this can be helpful on a single page, it is indispensable on larger projects where you need to make changes on a large number of pages across a site.

Much more!

Advanced text editors are designed to scale, and accommodate advanced users. Developers and programmers who regularly code in more sophisticated languages such as PHP (originally an acronym for 'Personal Home Page'), ASP (Active Server Pages), and Ruby on Rails (a framework for web applications) often use the advanced features of text editors to help them build their sites. In many ways, the line between text editors and WYSIWYG editors is beginning to blur. Some text editors have built-in functionality that allows you to build local site folders that keep track of site elements such as hyperlinks between documents, and media such as images and videos. They may also have an internal page preview feature or some form of FTP client that allows users to publish their pages to the web.

An overview of text editors

The following is a brief list of popular text editors for both Mac OS and Windows computers. These editors offer capabilities such as automatic code completion, code coloring, and code checking.

BBedit and TextWrangler (Mac) These text editors are similar and are developed by the same company. TextWrangler is free and has fewer features than BBedit. *www.barebones.com*

Coda (Mac) is a text editor that also provides site management, browser preview, and built-in web publishing. *www.panic.com/coda/*

TextMate (Mac) Along with being a text editor, its functionality can be extended by bundles that extend the capabilities of TextMate; for example, there are bundles that make adding JavaScript to your web pages much easier. *http://macromates.com*

E Text Editor (Windows) E Text Editor is a Windows-based text editor that supports many of the features of TextMate such as bundles and snippets. *www.e-texteditor.com*

Microsoft Visual Web Developer Express (Windows) provides a full featured text editor for web coding that supports HTML, CSS, and functionality for .NET programming. It also provides a basic visual layout environment for website design and development. *www.microsoft.com/express/Web/*

WYSIWYG editors

The concept behind WYSIWYG web editors is that you create web pages in design view and the program writes the HTML and CSS code behind-the-scenes. These tools claim to provide a visual way to create web pages without needing to understand HTML or CSS code. To effectively use any web design tool, you still need an understanding of HTML and CSS, and these design tools all include methods for working with code. Editing code is often required when using WYSIWYG editors, despite their visual layout capabilities and marketing claims. If you are just starting out as a web designer, it's useful to know that many web professionals perceive WYSIWYG tools as inappropriate for professional use. While this sentiment is not universal, there is a large population of web designers and developers that dislike all WYSIWYG editors because they do not always produce the best code for a situation.

WYSIWYG applications generally cost more than text editors, and the time required to learn many WYSIWYG applications can be as much as learning HTML and CSS code. Despite the higher cost and time to learn, the use of WYSIWYG editors is widespread. Additionally, they can speed your design work with some projects.

Most popular WYSIWYG editors also include features to help you code your pages when entering code. These include capabilities similar to text editors, such as code completion, code coloring, and automation. Two of the most popular WYSIWYG editors are Adobe Dreamweaver and Microsoft Expression Web. Both applications have similar capabilities. Dreamweaver is available on both the Mac OS and Windows platforms while Expression Web is only available for Windows computers. Expression Web is available at no cost if you are a student, see the note about the Microsoft Dreamspark program, and has a suggested retail price of $150 for business users. Adobe Dreamweaver is $150 if you are a student, and $300 if you are a business user. You can obtain fully functioning trial versions of these products to evaluate them for your own use at *www.microsoft.com/expression* or *www.adobe.com/dreamweaver*.

Microsoft Dreamspark provides no-cost software from Microsoft to full-time students. If you are enrolled as a student, you can obtain Microsoft Expression Web as part of the complete Microsoft Expression Studio package by enrolling at www.Dreamspark.com.

Design and layout tools

Both Dreamweaver and Expression Web use icon-based menus and panels to format text, insert images, and add media such as video files, Flash movies, or Silverlight objects. Adding elements such as hyperlinks, tables, `div` tags, and form elements involves dragging them onto a page.

The Dreamweaver Insert panel features objects in several categories that let you easily add images, web forms, and media to your page.

Expression Web makes it easy to add page elements with the Toolbox panel.

Site management and file transfer protocol

Both Expression Web and Dreamweaver include site management tools, including file transfer protocol (FTP) capabilities so you can upload files to a web server from your local machine. They also support reusable objects, such as page templates and library items, and can check links to make sure they go to valid pages or objects. The site management tools are helpful, as they make certain that links that are created while working on your computer function correctly when the site is moved to a web server.

Coding environment and text editor

Both Dreamweaver and Expression Web offer a code-only view of web pages which can be used for modifying HTML or CSS code, or a design view to work on pages visually, or a split view that displays the code and the visual layout at the same time.

Both programs support popular coding and scripting languages, such as JavaScript, and several server-side languages, including ColdFusion, PHP, and ASP. Specialized menus and code panels help you build pages and applications in the language of your choice. Expression Web offers particular strong capabilities for designers working on sites that use Microsoft's ASP scripting language.

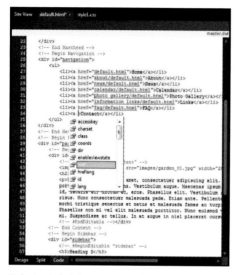

Code view in both Dreamweaver and Expression Web
provides features comparable to a stand-alone text editor.

Scripting languages, such as those used to build interactive web pages or e-commerce sites, fall into two categories: client-side and server-side. Client-side languages, such as JavaScript, run in the web browser, while server-side languages, such as ColdFusion or ASP require special software to be installed on the web server.

Templates and reusable elements

Dreamweaver and Expression Web both provide templates which are essentially *parent* master pages that link to any number of *child* pages. A master page controls the structure and appearance of multiple attached pages, so any change made to a master page is automatically applied to the child pages. This provides a consistent appearance across websites and ensures that site changes are applied quickly and globally across a site. Templates also allow you to make certain sections of a web page non-editable so that other users don't manipulate certain content or design elements. For example, the content of a News page could be designated as being fully editable, but the navigation bar could be marked as being off-limits.

Both Dreamweaver and Expression Web support the same template file format, which uses the .dwt extension. Expression Web also has an alternative template system called ASP.NET Master Pages. The ASP.NET template system is designed for .asp websites, whereas the .dwt template can be used for any HTML-based site.

Defining sites in Dreamweaver or Expression Web

Both applications use site folder definitions for the local and remote storage locations where a website resides. Once you define a site folder, the program keeps track of the files being used. When you add, remove, rename, or reorganize your asset files, both Dreamweaver and Expression Web update any related hyperlinks. The files on your local drive can also be synchronized with the files on your remote web server using integrated FTP capabilities.

In the following two exercises, you will walk through the initial steps of creating a new site in Dreamweaver and Expression Web. These exercises are designed to get you up-and-running in either (or both) of these popular web design applications. If you will only be working in a text editor, you can skip to the "Using design tools in the browser" exercise, or if you already plan to use only one visual editor or the other, you need to only complete the section relating to that WYSIWYG editor.

Obtaining Expression Web or Dreamweaver

Remember that Expression Web is available at no cost for students at www.dreamspark.com or for other users at *www.microsoft.com/expression/try-it* and you can download a trial version of Dreamweaver from Adobe's website at *www.adobe.com/products/dreamweaver.*

Creating a new site in Dreamweaver

You can create a new site from scratch without any templates or pre-existing HTML pages, or you can import a pre-existing site, such as one you have inherited from a colleague or a previous designer. In this first example, you'll create a new site from scratch, using Dreamweaver CS5. Later in the exercise, you'll work with a pre-existing site.

1   Launch Dreamweaver and then choose Site > New Site. In the Site Name text field, type **SmoothieWorld**. Next, you need to define a local folder where Dreamweaver stores the files for the site.

2   In the Local Site Folder field a directory path is provided, which shows the location of the folder on your hard drive. This path is often the Documents folder.

3   Click the Folder icon (📁) to the right of the Local Site Folder field; you are prompted to choose a root folder, which will be the primary folder for this site. This folder can be an empty folder that you have previously created, or a new folder.

Navigate to your desktop and click the New Folder icon. Name this folder **SmoothieWorld** and then click Choose (Mac OS) or Select (Windows). The Local Site Folder field is updated to show the path to the folder you created. Keep this window, you'll need it in the next part of this lesson.

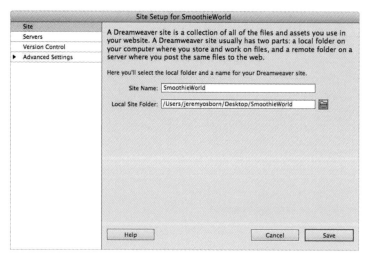

The Local Site Folder field shows the path on your system to the root folder where your files are stored for a site.

Next you'll take a quick look at some of the other options in the Site Setup window.

4 Along the left side of the Site Setup window, click the Servers tab. Use the Servers section to define the details of the remote server where your website will be hosted. You do not need to complete the web server information to begin creating a website; it is only necessary when you are ready to upload the content you've created on your computer to a web server. You will not be uploading this site, so the information can remain blank for this exercise.

5 Continuing to work in the Servers tab, click the + button and the Basic site settings window appears. This window contains fields for Server Name, Connect Using, FTP Address, Username, Password, and other options. These settings allow you to choose both a destination and a method, such as FTP, for Dreamweaver to transfer files to a web server. These details will vary depending upon the web server being used. If you are using a web hosting provider, they can provide this information to you.

6 Click Cancel to close the site settings panel. Then press Save to save the settings for the entire site. The lower-right corner of the Files panel displays the root folder information you just entered.

7 Choose File > New and from the New Document window choose the Blank Page option. Make sure that the Page Type is set to HTML and the Page Layout is set to <none>, then click Create.

8 Choose File > Save and name this file **index.html**. Because you defined a root folder, the new document is automatically set to save in the location you specified when you set-up the site. By defining a site you reduce the risk of saving files into an incorrect location. Click Save and the Files panel updates to include the index.html file.

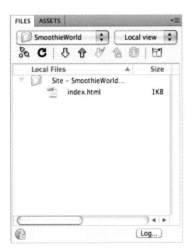

The Files panel automatically updates to include new pages that are created.

9 Choose Insert > Image to add an image to your site. In the Select Image Source window, use the menu to browse to the web03lessons folder and choose the blueberry_smoothie.jpg image, then click OK. A warning appears indicating that the image is outside the root folder. Click Yes to copy the image into the folder with the other content for this, then click Save.

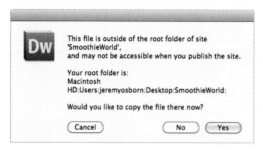

Dreamweaver offers to keep your site organized by placing a copy of images that are outside your site's folder with the other items used in the site.

The Image Tag Accessibility Attributes window will also appear. In the Alternate Text field type "Blueberry Smoothie" and then click OK. Alternate text (commonly referred to as an "alt tag") improves accessibility of your page for devices such as screenreaders. The image is displayed on the page and the file is copied to the root folder for this site.

Importing an existing site into Dreamweaver CS5

Importing pre-existing sites into Dreamweaver is similar to creating a new site. Instead of pointing to an empty root folder, you will identify the path to the folder containing the existing assets for the site.

1 Choose Site > New Site. In the Site Setup window, type **Lesson 03 site** for the site name.

2 Click the Folder icon to the far right of the Local Site Folder field, the Choose Root Folder window appears. Navigate to the web03lessons folder, then click Choose (Mac) or Select (Windows), then click the Save button.

A site cache is created. In the Files panel, you can see the directory of the site.

3 Double-click the index.html document to open it. Next you will rename the images folder in the Files panel to see how Dreamweaver updates links.

4   In the Files panel, click to highlight the label of the images folder and click again to make it active for editing. Then type **smoothieimages** and press Return (Mac) or Enter (PC). The Update Files panel appears because the folder name has been updated, asking if you'd like to update any links to files in this folder. If the links aren't updated, they will become broken because of the new folder name.

A list of files that will be updated appears in the window. Click Update to update the links. Dreamweaver updates the hyperlinks to reflect the new folder name.

Update Files	
Update links in the following files?	(Update)
/index.html	(Don't Update)
	(Help)

Modifying a folder name in your Files panel prompts
Dreamweaver to update any linked files.

5   Choose Site > Manage Sites. The Manage Sites window appears. It provides access to any sites you have defined. Use this window to create new sites or edit the settings of existing sites. You won't be making any changes, so click Cancel to close the window without making any changes.

You can use the Export button to save your site settings as an XML file with the .ste extension. These settings can be imported into Dreamweaver to easily move sites between machines, different versions of Dreamweaver, or share settings with other users.

6   In the Files panel, click the drop-down menu. In the menu list that appears, the directory of your computer is displayed along with a list of your defined sites. You can use this to switch from site to site if you manage several sites. This feature is very useful to designers as it allows them to quickly access assets such as images or code that may be located in another site.

Creating a new site in Expression Web

Site folders in Expression Web are similar to Dreamweaver. As you will see, if you are familiar with creating sites in one program, you are well prepared for doing so in the other.

1   Launch Expression Web then choose Site > New Site. In the window that appears, you can create a one-page site, a new site with no pages (empty), or import an existing site.

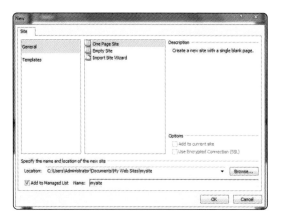

2   Select the One Page Site option. In the Name field at the bottom of the window, type **SmoothieWorld2**. The Location field displays the default path for your site. This is typically a path to a subfolder named My websites within your Documents folder. You will define the location for this folder as the desktop, so keep the window open.

3   Click the Browse button and navigate to your desktop, then click the New Folder icon to create a new folder on the desktop. Name this folder **SmoothieWorld_site** then click Open, and then click OK. The new site is created and appears in the Site View panel the Folder List panel.

4   Choose Site > Site Settings. You can use the site settings window to modify the site name and provide access to the settings for connecting and uploading files to your web server.

5   Click the Publishing tab. You'll look at this tab for informational purposes only, as we are not connecting to a web server. If necessary you could input FTP information for connecting Expression Web to your web server.

Click the Add button to examine the publishing options, then click Cancel and click Cancel again in the Site Settings window to close it.

Web design and development tools in the browser

Modern web browsers do more than display web pages; they also include tools for developing and troubleshooting web pages. Some browser tools for testing and debugging sites include:

Internet Explorer developer tools

Microsoft Internet Explorer includes built-in developer tools. You can access these tools by choosing Tools > Developer Tools or by using the keyboard shortcut F12.

Safari

The Apple Safari browser includes built-in developer tools that are not enabled by default. To enable the developer tools choose Safari > Preferences. In the Preferences menu, select the Advanced menu and then select the check box labeled *Show Developer menu in menu bar.*

The Firefox Firebug extension

The Firebug extension is an option for extending the Mozilla Firefox browser. You can download it at *http://getfirebug.com.*

Chrome

The Google Chrome browser includes built-in developer tools. To access these tools, click the Page menu at the top-right corner of the browser window, then choose Developer > Developer Tools. You can also right-click on any element and select Inspect Element.

They include tools for inspecting your site's HTML and CSS as they exist inside the browser, instead of just viewing the original source code. This is particularly helpful with dynamic sites, complex sites, and sites that use frameworks such as ASP or PHP.

Inspecting HTML elements

You can inspect HTML elements by clicking on them. The code for a selected element is highlighted in a content pane. Use this to quickly identify the exact code that references an element so you can quickly understand information such as the width and height of an object on the page, such as an `image` or `div` element.

Inspecting CSS properties

Quickly access CSS styles that are associated with a selected element to see the exact CSS rules associated with your selection and examine the cascade of rules so you understand whether a style is associated with an internal style or external style sheet. This can make it easier to debug.

(continues)

Web design and development tools in the browser (continued)

Editing source code

You can experiment with styles directly in the browser by editing HTML attributes or CSS properties by clicking on them and typing new values. The change takes effect immediately so you can quickly test changes. This editing does not modify your source, rather, it allows for testing and debugging without needing to switch back to a text editor, saving the file, then previewing the change.

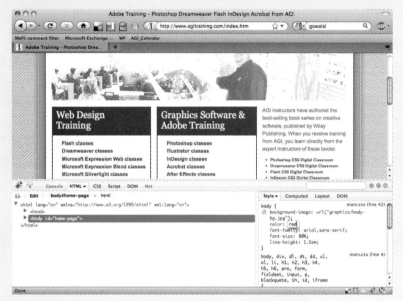

Experiment with styles by modifying style rules.

Review

Questions

1 How is the root folder useful when creating a site on your local computer, before transferring files to a web server?

2 What are some of the features found in WYSIWYG applications such as Dreamweaver or Expression Web that are not found in most text editors?

3 In what three views do both Dreamweaver and Expression Web allow you to view and edit documents?

Answers

1 A root folder stores all resources for a website in a common location, ensuring that the links you create to images or other pages in the site will work when the site is uploaded to a server.

2 WYSIWYG applications provide a preview of your web page in a Design view, allowing you to create web pages or make changes to your page without accessing the HTML or CSS code directly. Additionally, WYSIWYG applications have site management tools for keeping files organized and uploading content to a web server.

3 Design, Split, and Code views are accessible when working with Dreamweaver or Expression Web. Design view displays the layout of the page; Code view displays the code but not the layout; and Split view displays both the layout and the code.

What you'll learn in this lesson:

- The structure of HTML
- The difference between HTML and XHTML
- The fundamentals of CSS

Fundamentals of HTML, XHTML, and CSS

In this lesson, you'll discover the fundamentals of HTML, XHTML, and CSS. Together, these form the structure and style of your web pages.

Starting up

You will work with several files from the web04lessons folder in this lesson. Make sure you have loaded the weblessons folder onto your hard-drive from *www.digitalclassroombooks.com/webdesign*. See "Loading lesson files" in the Starting Up section of this book.

See Lesson 4 in action!

Use the accompanying video to gain a better understanding of how to use some of the features shown in this lesson. You can find the video tutorial for this lesson at www.digitalclassroombooks.com *using the URL provided when you registered your book.*

We used the text editor Coda to create the markup in this lesson, but you can use any of the text editors covered in Lesson 3 to achieve the same results.

Web languages

In this lesson you will discover two languages: HTML and CSS. Although they have different syntax and rules, they are highly dependent on each other. By the end of this lesson, you will understand how to create simple HTML pages, add images, create hyperlinks from one page to another, and add simple styling to pages using CSS.

This lesson covers a lot of ground, and many of the core principles introduced in this lesson are reinforced throughout the remaining chapters.

Web page structure is based on HTML

Hypertext Markup Language (HTML) documents use the .html or .htm extension. This extension allows a web browser or device such as a smartphone to understand that HTML content is on the page, and the content of the page is then rendered by the browser or device according to the rules of HTML.

Markup tags are used to define the content on an HTML page. Markup tags are contained between greater than (<) and less than (>) symbols, and they are placed at the start and end of an object or text that is used in an HTML page. Here is an example of two heading 1 tags for text. The tags are not seen by the viewer of the web page, but every web browser knows that the text between the tags is a heading 1.

```
<h1>New Smoothie Recipe!</h1>
```

In this example, the <h1> is the opening tag and the </h1> is the closing tag. So this entire line of code is an *element*. More specifically, it is referred to as the heading 1 element.

HTML and XHTML are closely related. There is a list of rules defined by the World Wide Web Consortium, or W3C that specify the perimeters of HTML and XHTML.

HTML code as rendered in the browser

To help you understand the relationship between the HTML code and what you see in your web browser, the following illustration will show you the connection between the two.

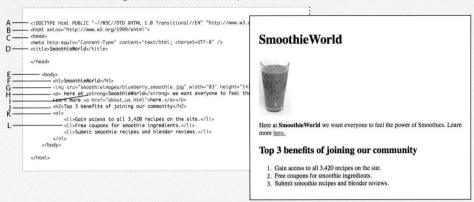

A. Doctype. This line instructs the browser to interpret all the code that follows according to a unique set of rules.

B. HTML element. This element nests all the following elements and tells the browser to expect an HTML document.

C. Head element. This section includes information about the page, but nothing is rendered on the page itself.

D. Title element. Any content inside the title tags show up at the top of the browser. This is what is used when a user bookmarks a page in the browser.

E. Body element. All content within the body can be rendered in the browser's main window.

F. Heading 1 element. The first of six heading elements, content that is a heading 1 is rendered very large and bold.

G. Image element. Links to a graphic file and displays it on the page.

H. Paragraph element. By default the browser adds space before and after this element which often contains multiple lines of text.

I. Strong element. Formats the enclosed content as bold by default.

J. Heading 2 element. Compare the size of second largest heading to the first one.

K. Ordered list element. Defines the enclosed list items as numbered.

L. List element. Multiple list items will automatically be numbered by the browser.

The details of XHTML syntax

There is little fundamental difference between HTML 4.0 and XHTML 1.0—the two standards previously released by the W3C (World Wide Web Consortium). As XHTML was defined, it was created so that pages written in XHTML also work in browsers that render current HTML. The tags and attributes of XHTML and HTML remained the same, but the syntax of XHTML code is more strict. The most significant differences between XHTML and HTML are as follows:

- In XHTML, all tags must be lowercase.

- XHTML requires all tags to be closed—meaning that there must be a tag at the start and end of the element being tagged—such as a headline, paragraph, or image.

All tags in XHTML must close, even special tags that technically don't require an open and close tag. For example the <br> tag which creates a line break, uses a special self-closing syntax. A tag that self-closes looks like this (with a space and a forward slash):

<div align="center">

`<br />`

</div>

- XHTML requires proper nesting of tags. In the following example, the <em> tag to emphasize text opens within the <h1> headline tag. As such, it must be closed before the <h1> is closed.

```
<h1>Smoothies are <em>great!</em></h1>
```

We've used XHTML-compliant code throughout this book as we provide HTML5 examples, which helps make your designs compatible with modern browsers and mobile devices.

Doctype lets the web browser know what to expect

The start of every web page should include a Doctype declaration, telling the Doctype declaration tells the web browser a little bit of information about what it is going to see on the page. Because there are different specifications for XHTML and HTML the web browser knows which language it's about to see and render. Because a browser renders the page starting at the top line and then moves down, placing your doctype on the first line makes a lot of sense. While it's not required, it's good form to always use Doctype at the start of your HTML pages. The doctype for HTML 4.0.1 looks like this:

```
<!DOCTYPE HTML PUBLIC "-//W3C//DTD HTML 4.01 Transitional//EN"
"http://www.w3.org/TR/html4/loose.dtd">
```

When a web browser sees a doctype declaration, the browser expects that everything on the page that follows will use that language. If the page adheres to the specifications perfectly, it is considered valid.

The W3C and page validation

You may recall from Lesson 2 that the W3C is the World Wide Web consortium—a non-profit group that helps guide the evolution of the web. The W3C provides guidelines and rules for specifications including HTML and XHTML. One way to determine the validity of the HTML or XHTML code you generate is to use W3C's free online validation service.

You will need access to the Internet for this exercise. If you do not have Internet access, you may read through the exercise to understand the validation process.

1   Open your web browser and navigate to *http://validator.w3.org*.

2   Click the Validate by File Upload tab.

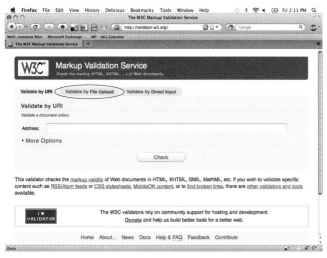

The W3C validator allows you to check your HTML code for errors.

3   Click Browse (depending on your browser, this may also read "Choose File"), and navigate to your web04lessons folder, and select the w3_noncompliant.html file. Click the Check button to validate the code.

4   The W3C site returns several errors. Scroll down the page and you can see in-depth information on the errors. Don't worry about the errors at this point. You will now upload a nearly identical file without errors.

5   Click the Browse button, navigate to your web04lessons folder, and select the w3_compliant.html file.

6 Click the Revalidate button. You now see a Congratulations message that the page has been checked and found to be compliant as XHTML 1.0 Strict.

Although the page is valid it may not look good to a viewer. This example uses a page that has missing styles and missing images to emphasize this point. It's important to understand that having valid code is only one step in a series to make certain your web pages can be viewed by the widest possible audience.

You can validate web pages that you've already placed online. Do this by using the Validate by URL option. You can also paste HTML code directly into the validator by choosing the Validate by Direct Input option.

7 In your web browser, choose File > Open, navigate to the web04lessons folder, and select the same w3c_compliant.html document that you just confirmed was valid. If you are using Internet Explorer, navigate to the web04lessons folder on your computer and drag and drop w3c_compliant.html into it.

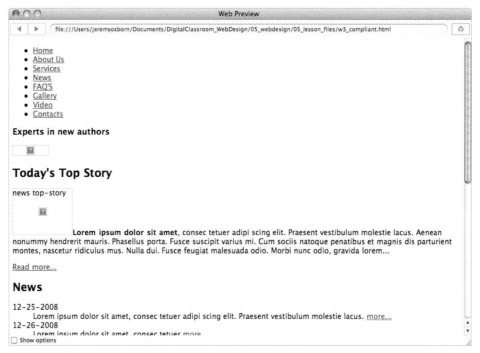

A "valid" page can have links to images that don't exist and may have a poor visual design.

Because we know that the page uses valid XHTML, we know that whatever problems there are with the page, they are not due to improper XHTML code. We know that there are no missing tags or misspelled tags. This can be useful for troubleshooting, allowing you to quickly identify any syntax problems.

Other benefits of standards-based design

W3C page validation is the most tangible aspect of standards-based web design, but there are also other benefits to creating well-structured pages, including:

Less code: Using HTML and CSS allows you to create similar pages with fewer lines of code—less work for you and faster download times for the viewer.

Ease of maintenance: Less code means a website that is easier to maintain. This helps you, the author of a page, as well as any members of a team working on maintaining or revising a website.

Accessibility: Web documents marked up semantically, meaning those that use the best HTML tag for the job, can be easier to navigate by users with visual impairments and the information they contain is more likely to be found by a visitor to the site.

Search engine optimization: Web pages with clear and logically named sections, both within the code and also within page content, are easier for search engines to index and categorize because content that is organized and well-labeled is easier for search engines to evaluate content and relevance of content on the page.

Device compatibility: Websites that separate the structure from the style are more easily repurposed for mobile devices and other browsers. CSS also allows for alternative style sheets that optimize the appearance based on the device being used to view the page.

HTML structure

One of the most important concepts to understand when designing web content is the nested structure of HTML documents. Elements are often nested within each other. You will often start with the HTML structure first and then begin to style it with CSS.

As an example, let's look at the basic elements that are in virtually every web page:

```
<html>
    <body>
    </body>
</html>
```

In this example, the <body> element is nested within the <html> element. In other words, <body> is placed between the opening <html> tag and the closing </html> tag, so nested tags are those that are placed between other opening and closing tags. These two elements <body> and <html> form the structure of all web pages; when a browser opens an HTML document, it looks for this structure.

Content within the body tag is visible on the page as it is displayed within the web browser.

```
<html>
    <body>
    Nobody knows who invented smoothies, but the world wouldn't be
    the same without them!
    </body>
</html>
```

In HTML documents, some of the content is displayed to the viewer in their browser, but there is also other code on the page that is hidden from view, but useful for the browser, search engine, or site developer. Examples of this hidden code include scripts to add interactivity, code to help search engines categorize the document, and the styles that define the appearance of the page. This code is often found inside of the <head> element, and the <head> element is nested within the <html> tags. An example of this is:

```
<html>
    <head>
    </head>
    <body>
    Nobody knows who invented smoothies, but the world wouldn't be
    the same without them!
    </body>
</html>
```

In the above example, there is no content in the <head> element just yet. Notice that the <head> element is nested within <html> but is not nested within <body>. The <head> element opens and closes before the <body> element starts.

The <body> element contains text but it is lacking context so neither you nor a search engine can determine if it is a heading, list, quotation, or some other type of content. To define the text as a paragraph the <p> tag is used:

```
<html>
    <head>
    </head>
    <body>
    <p>Nobody knows who invented smoothies, but the world wouldn't be
    the same without them!</p>
    </body>
</html>
```

The paragraph element is now nested within the <body> element, which, in turn, is now nested within the <html> element. You will now open this document in a text editor and add to the file:

1 Choose File > Open and navigate to your web04lessons folder. Depending on which text editor you are using, you may need to select "All Files" instead of "Text Documents" in order to see the file. Choose the index.html file and then click Open.

To get a better understanding of the structure of HTML and nesting of tags, you will add a hyperlink to this document linking the word *SmoothieWorld* to an external website.

2 In the last paragraph that reads "All content on this site is the copyright of SmoothieWorld," click once before the word SmoothieWorld and then type the following code: **<a>**. This <a> is the opening for the anchor element, which you use to link to other pages in your site or elsewhere on the Internet.

3 Click to the right of the word SmoothieWorld and type **</a>**. This is the closing tag for the anchor tag and is required in XHTML.

If you are using Dreamweaver, it may be set to automatically complete closing tags. To change this preset, choose Edit > Preferences (Windows), or Dreamweaver > Preferences (Mac). Under Category, click Code Hints and select Never under Code Hints, and choose OK.

To finish the job of creating a link, you need to add the destination of the link with the `href` attribute.

4 Click between the letter a and the closing bracket (>) in the opening tag. Press the spacebar once to add a space and type **href=""**. The complete code should now read `<a href="">`.

You now have an anchor tag and the href attribute. To finish the job of creating a hyperlink, you need to add the value of the attribute. In this case the value will be a URL — a web address.

5 Click inside the quotation marks and type **http://www.digitalclassroombooks .com/smoothieworld**. This completes the destination and with all the pieces in place, you now have a complete hyperlink.

```
    <p>All content on this site is the
    copyright of <a href="http://www.digitalclassroombooks.com/smoothieworld">SmoothieWorld</a></p>

</body>
</html>
```

Creating a hyperlink using the <a> tag and href *attribute.*

6 Choose File > Save and then preview the page in your web browser by either opening your browser and choosing File > Open and navigating to the file you just saved, or by Ctrl + clicking (Mac OS) or right-clicking (Windows) the file and directing your operating system to open the file with a web browser. The link has the standard blue underlined appearance of a hyperlink that you have not yet visited.

7 Close your browser and return to your text editor.

Placing images in HTML

To add images to an HTML document, use the <img> tag. Like the anchor tag, the image tag does nothing by itself. The image tag relies on attributes and values that specify the image to display. Here you will insert an image into the HTML code.

1 Click once after the closing paragraph line </p> that follows the text indicating the site content is copyrighted. Press Return to go to the next line. Type **<img />**.

The image tag is in a special category of HTML tags that are self-closing. You do not need a pair of tags with the image tag; one tag is sufficient. However, it is important that you type this tag correctly. There is a space between the img and the /. This satisfies the requirements of XHTML syntax, and you will specify the exact image to use in the space between the img and /.

```
<body>
    <h1>SmoothieWorld</h1>
    <p>Smoothies are the stuff of life. they get you going in the morning, refresh you when you're h
    
    <p>All content on this site is the
    copyright of <a href="http://www.digitalclassroombooks.com/smoothieworld">SmoothieWorld</a></p>
    <img />
```

Adding an image to to your page with the <img> tag.

2 Click once to the right of the text img, press the spacebar, and then type **src=""**.

src is the source attribute, and you will specify a value, which is the location (URL) of an image which will display on the page.

3 Click between the quotation marks that follow the src= code and type **images/blueberry_smoothie.jpg**.

Your img code should now look like this:

```
<img src="images/blueberry_smoothie.jpg" />
```

This code tells a web browser to look inside the images folder and display the file blueberry_smoothie.jpg. In the next few steps, be sure to maintain the extra space between the last quotation mark and the closing tag. You will be adding an alt tag.

This alt attribute represents the text equivalent for the image and is required if you want your page to be valid. Alt attributes help those who use screen readers to navigate the web. They also appear in browsers if the image is broken or missing for some reason.

4 Click to the right of the last quotation mark that follows the blueberry_smoothie.jpg file name and press the spacebar. Type **alt=""**.

5 Click inside the quotation marks you added in step 4 and type **Blueberry smoothie**.

Both the src attribute and the alt attribute are required for fully valid XHTML. There are also optional attributes that you should consider. We'll look at two of these options attributes: height and width.

6   Click to the right of the last quotation mark following the `alt` attribute, press the spacebar, then type **width="180" height="320"**. These attributes tell the web browser how large the image should be displayed on the page. The values used are pixels. Keep this document open as you will be working with it in the next exercise of this lesson.

```
<p>All content on this site is the
copyright of <a href="http://www.digitalclassroombooks.com/smoothieworld">SmoothieWorld</a></p>
<img src="images/blueberry_smoothie.jpg" alt="Blueberry Smoothie" width="180" height="320" />
```

Adding Width and Height values to your image is not required but is a good idea.

Using Optional Attributes

Many of HTML's optional attributes fall under the category of best practices. *Best practices* is an umbrella term used to describe the accepted way of doing something in web design. There are generally logical reasons behind best practices; for example, setting the width and height creates a placeholder for the images even if they haven't loaded due to a slow Internet connection. Without the placeholder created by the width and height values, the page layout will change as the images load.

7   Choose File > Save and then preview your page in the browser to see your image.

The result of an embedded image as displayed in the browser.

The role of CSS

Cascading Style Sheets (CSS) use a separate language from HTML. CSS allows you to apply consistent styling of elements across all pages on your site, so that all headings, lists, and paragraphs look and act the same on every page of a site.

How we refer to CSS syntax in this book

Before you begin to work with CSS, we need to explain how we will refer to the various parts of CSS syntax throughout this book. This is not as easy as it sounds because there is a gap between the official specification of the CSS language and the way designers often refer to CSS in the "real world." Nevertheless, here are the fundamentals: all the following code is what we refer to as a rule in CSS:

```
h1 {
    color:blue;
    margin-top:1em;
}
```

There are various components to this rule, as follows:

```
A——┌──┐
     h1  {
B———————————————┐
            color:blue;
C———————————┐
            margin-top:1em;
                         └──┘——D
     }
```

A. Selector. B. Declaration. C. Property. D. Value.

We will refer to each of the various components from time to time throughout the book, so if we ask you to change the value "blue" to "red" you should know what to do. Or if we ask you to locate and change the h1 selector to a h2 selector, it should make sense.

On a day-to-day basis, most designers aren't always so specific however. For example the rule above might be referred to as a "style," "style rule," "the h1 rule," or "the CSS rule for h1." Also, as you can see above, the official name for the pair of the property and the value is called a declaration. Again, in everyday use, the use of the term "declaration" is not common and most designers will use the term property or properties interchangeably.

Styling a heading

To get a sense of how CSS works, you'll create a simple CSS rule that changes the style of a heading in your page. In your index.html page, you already have the content "SmoothieWorld" nested inside an `<h1>` tag. Perhaps one of the best ways to begin thinking about how CSS works is to consider how the default style of this heading is rendered in the browser.

1   Examine the heading of the file you previewed in the last step of the previous exercise. The style and formatting instructions are being provided by the browser. The size, color, and font are provided by the browser because exact formatting instructions are not specified. The browser only knows that this is a headline. You will redefine this style with a CSS rule.

2   In your code, locate the `<title>` tag on line 5, click once at the end of the line, following the closing tag, then press return to add a new line of code. Type the following:

`<style type="text/css">`

3   Press Return three times and then type **`</style>`**, This is a style element which you will use to place your rule for the style of the `<h1>` element.

```
<!DOCTYPE html PUBLIC "-//W3C//DTD XHTML 1.0 Transitional//EN" "http://www.w3.org/TR/xhtml1/DTD/xhtm
<html xmlns="http://www.w3.org/1999/xhtml">
<head>
<meta http-equiv="Content-Type" content="text/html; charset=UTF-8" />
<title>Untitled Document</title>
<style type="text/css">


</style>
```

The `<style>` element is nested within the head section of the page, and is where the CSS rules will be placed.

The `<style>` element is nested within the `<head>` tags of your page. In HTML, everything nested inside the `<head>` section is not rendered by the browser on the page. For example, there is also a `<title>` element inside this section; this title appears at the top of the web browser, not on the actual page.

4   In the empty line below the opening `<style>` tag, type the following:

`h1 {`

This is your selector. The selector is the HTML element you want to style, in this case the Heading 1 element.

5   Press Return and then press Tab to place your cursor below the curley bracket. The tab is optional but it helps make your CSS more readable. As you will soon see, the number of lines in this rule will grow and it's worthwhile keeping the code easy to read.

6 Type the following code below the h1 {:

color:purple;

The word *color* is referred to as a property in CSS syntax and the word *purple* is a value. The combined pair of a property and a value is called a *declaration*.

```
<title>Untitled Document</title>
<style type="text/css">
h1 {
    color:purple;

</style>
```

The combination of the property (color) and the value (purple) is often referred to as style rule.

7 Press Return again and on the next line, type **}** which is the right curley bracket character.

This closes the curley bracket you added in step 4.

You now have three lines in this rule:

```
h1 {
    color:purple;
}
```

8 Choose File > Save and then preview your page in the browser. The head is now a light purple color and you have successfully created your first CSS rule. Close your browser and return to your text editor.

Your H1 color is now being styled by a CSS rule.

9   In the HTML file, select the word `purple` and type the following for the color value: `#800080`. This hexadecimal color is the equivalent of purple. You can use either named colors or hexadecimal colors when defining colors using CSS.

Save your file and then preview it in the browser. The color remains the same. Hexadecimal colors are a more common method for describing colors.

Hexadecimal colors

Color in both HTML and CSS color is referred to by a six-character code preceded by a pound sign. This code is called hexadecimal code, and is the system used to identify apply color to elements. You can reproduce almost any color using a unique hexadecimal code. For example, the following code is dark-red: `a#CC0000`.

The first, middle, and last pair of digits in the hexadecimal code correspond to values in the RGB spectrum. For instance, white, which is represented in RGB as R:255 G:255 B:255, is represented in HTML as #FFFFFF (255|255|255). A program like Photoshop will allow you to choose a specific RGB color in the Color Editor and give you the equivalent hexadecimal color for use in your code.

There are also online references you can use to locate or "mix" hexadecimal colors such as: *www.w3schools.com/Html/html_colorvalues.asp*

The rule you just created uses what is officially known as a "type selector" since it targets every instance of the `h1` element type in your document. Type selectors assign CSS properties to an existing HTML tag. In this case the `<h1>` tag. All `<h1>` tags on this page will be displayed as purple. Type selectors are more commonly known as tag selectors. It is rare that you will actually hear someone use the phrase "type selector" but that is the official name for it, so we mention it here.

You will now get an introduction to another category of CSS styles known as a class. You will also work with the `<span>` element which separates and controls inline content, such as a sentence within a paragraph, or an individual word within a sentence.

Understanding class styles and <span>s

Tag selectors are frequently used, but they can only be applied to HTML elements. When you want to style something that does not map directly to a tag, for example, change the color of a single word within a paragraph, standard HTML tags are not a good option. In this case, you can use a class selector, which is a CSS rule that you can apply to any number of items on a page. Class selectors have flexible naming options, but you should choose names that describe what they do. For example, you may wish to name class selectors as `caption`, `imageborder`, or `redtext`. In this exercise, you will create a class style that applies the color purple to the word Smoothies in your paragraph.

1 Place your cursor on the line immediately below the closing curly bracket for the `h1` rule, then type the following:

```
.purple {
    color:purple;
}
```

Note the period at the beginning of the class selector. The text following the period is the class name. You can use any name you wish, but the period is required at the start to identify it as a class. The rule is the same as in the last exercise, only here the selector is not the `h1` element. The class name can be anything you want, but it must have the period at the beginning to identify it as a class. Next you'll apply this class to the word Smoothie in order to style it purple. To do this, you will use an HTML tag `<span>`.

2 In the paragraph within the `<body>` tag, locate the word Smoothies, click once to the left of it, and then type:

<span>

```
<body>
    <h1>SmoothieWorld</h1>
    <p><span>Smoothies</span> are the stuff of life. they get you going in the morning, refresh you

    <p>All content on this site is the
    copyright of <a href="http://www.digitalclassroombooks.com/smoothieworld">SmoothieWorld</a></p>
    <img src="images/blueberry_smoothie.jpg" alt="Blueberry Smoothie" width="180" height="320" />
```

The <span> tag allows you to define the portion of a paragraph you'd like to style.

3 Click to the right of the word Smoothies and add a closing span tag **</span>**.

Your code should look like this:

```
<p><span> Smoothies</span> are the ...
```

Save your file. If you were to preview the page in the browser you would see no change. The `<span>` tag in HTML is an empty tag; it does nothing on its own and needs to be paired with a style. The `<span>` tag defines the beginning and end of where the style will be applied within the paragraph, but it does not apply the style on its own, and does not define the style.

4   Close the browser and return to your text editor. Locate the opening `<span>` tag you inserted before the word Smoothies. Click once after the word span but before the `>` bracket, then type the following:

`class="purple"`

The code should now read

`<span class="purple">Smoothies </span>`

5   Locate the word Smoothies in the second sentence

`<span class="purple">` and after the word `Smoothies` type: **`</span>`**.

6   Save your page and preview it in your browser. The text is now styled purple. Keep the document open in the text editor, as you will be working with it in the next exercise.

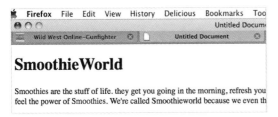

The word Smoothies is styled using an HTML span tag and a CSS class style.

Three ways to use styles

In this exercise, your styles were located within the head section of the page. This type of style is called an *internal style sheet*. In addition to internal (or embedded) style sheets, there are external style sheets and inline styles.

An *external style sheet* is a separate document with the file extension .css. When using an external style sheet, all styles reside inside the style sheet document and you link it to your HTML pages. While internal style sheets affect only the page on which they exist, external styles can be applied to multiple pages.

Inline styles are used infrequently. With inline styles, the style rules are nested inside the HTML tags. An example of an inline style that colors a heading purple would look like this:

`<h1 style="color:purple">Smoothies</h1>`

Inline styles are powerful because they override both internal and external styles, although they only apply to a single tag at a time. This embedded nature of inline styles means they are not easily re-used. In the simple example illustrated above you can see the style for the color purple is nested inside the `<h1>` tag. If you had 50 `<h1>` elements throughout your website and were using inline styles, you would add this style code 50 times. If you decided to change the color to green, you would need to locate and modify all 50 uses of the style. Inline styles are useful for single overrides or when an internal or external style sheet may not be available; a good example of this is HTML-based e-mail.

You will not be using inline styles very often in this book, which is a reflection of the current state of web design. Working with a combination of internal and external styles is the most common practice of web designers today.

Internal versus external style sheets

Internal style sheets are CSS rules contained directly within a document, using the `<style>` tag. The entire style sheet is contained within the opening and closing `<style>` tags.

External style sheets are CSS rules saved in a separate document with the file extension .css. With internal style sheets, CSS rules apply only to the HTML in the current document. For example, if you had a 20 page website and were using internal style sheets, you would need to create a separate style sheet in each of the pages. A change to the style would require you to update the internal styles in each of the 20 separate pages.

External style sheets place all the CSS rules for a site in a single document. You can attach the .css file to an unlimited number of HTML pages. This provides more flexibility. If a style rule is changed in the external style sheet, all paragraphs across the site are modified with a single step. You will make an external style sheet and then attach it to a new HTML page.

Creating an external style sheet

An HTML page does not have to be limited to just one style sheet, and many large websites will break-up their styles into separate pages, making them easier to organize and maintain. You can even use style sheets for specific functions such as printing a page or for displaying a site on mobile devices. In Lesson 9, you will see that specific style sheets can even be used to make sites compatible with older web browsers when they are used to visit sites you create.

In this exercise, you will create a new external style sheet, move the style rules from your current document to the external style sheet, and then attach the style sheet to a new HTML page.

1   Choose File > New Text Document.

The text editor you are using may have a different menu command. You may need to choose the equivalent command.

2   Choose File > Save. Name the document **styles.css** and save the styles.css file into the same folder as the HTML document you worked on in the previous exercise. An external cascading style sheet has a specific .css file extension but it is simply a text file.

3   Switch to the HTML document from the last exercise, but keep the style sheet open as well.

4 In the HTML document locate the rules you created within the `<style>` tags and then select them. Do not select the style tags themselves, just the rules that start with `h1` and end with the closing bracket }.

```
<style type="text/css">
h1 {
    color:purple;
    }

.purple {
    color:purple;
    }

</style>
```

Select just the style rules, not the `<style>` *tag.*

5 Choose Edit > Cut, then switch to the styles.css file and choose Edit > Paste to paste the rules into the external style sheet document. Choose File > Save to save your style sheet.

The entire external style sheet acts as a substitute for the `<style>` tags in the HTML document. Now that you have moved the rules to this document you need to link it to your HTML page so that a web browser knows where to find the style rules that apply to the HTML.

6 Switch back to the index.html page and choose File > Save. You will add the `<link>` tag, pointing to the styles.css document. If you do not link to the external styles, the HTML page will have no styles.

7 Place your cursor *after* the closing style tag `</ style>` then press return to start a new line. Now type the following:

`<link rel="stylesheet" type="text/css" href="styles.css" />`

You have added the `rel`, `type`, and `href` attributes. You may recall the `href` attribute from when you added the hyperlink in an earlier exercise. In order for your external style sheet to work properly, the name of the file, and the path to where it is located must both be accurate.

8 Choose File > Save and then preview the HTML page in your browser. The page should not change, as the same style is being used; it is simply being applied from outside the document.

9 Close the browser and return to your text editor. You'll now create a new HTML document, and add the same link to the external CSS file, seeing how the rules are applied.

10 Choose File > Open and locate the file test.html in the web04lessons folder. This is an empty HTML document.

11 Continuing to work in your text editor, switch back to the index.html file and select the entire `<link>` element you typed in step 7:

`<link rel="stylesheet" type="text/css" href="styles.css" />` and then choose Edit > Copy.

12 Switch back to the test.html document and then click below the `<title>` element and Choose Edit > Paste to place the `<link>` element, then save the the file by choosing File > Save.

```
<!DOCTYPE html PUBLIC "-//W3C//DTD XHTML 1.0 Transitional//EN" "http://www.w3.org/TR/xhtml1/DTD/xhtm
<html xmlns="http://www.w3.org/1999/xhtml">
<head>
<meta http-equiv="Content-Type" content="text/html; charset=UTF-8" />
<title>Untitled Document</title>
<link rel="stylesheet" type="text/css" href="styles.css" />
</head>
```

Attaching an external style sheet using the `<link>` element.

The external style sheet is now attached to this HTML document. Any HTML tags you add to this new document will be styled if there is a corresponding rule in the CSS file. For example, the `<h1>` tag has a style of the color purple.

13 Click inside the `<body>` element and type:

`<h1>The Benefits of Smoothies </h1>`

Save the file and preview it in your web browser.

> **Firefox** File Edit View History Delicious Bookmarks To
> Untitled Do
> Untitled Document +
>
> # The Benefits of Smoothies

The `<h1>` tag gets its style from the external CSS style sheet you created.

The heading is purple because the style rule for the `<h1>` element is `color:purple` and because this rule is located in an external sheet and linked in two places: the index.html and test.html pages. Because of this, you can control the style from of both HTML documents a central location.

What makes styles cascading

You've seen three different places where CSS rules are found: inline, internally, and externally. If there are conflicting definitions of styles between inline, internal, and external styles, the inline style will be used because it is closer to the HTML source. The internal style sheet takes precedence over an external style sheet, and definitions used in an external style sheet are used only if they don't conflict with either inline or internal styles.

> *In this lesson, you've discovered many ways to format text. When you want to style text, it is almost always best to use actual text rather than an image of text. Using actual text rather than a picture of text created in programs like Photoshop or Illustrator makes your sites more accessible to the widest audience of users, devices, and search engines.*

Self study

1 In this lesson, you discovered three categories of styles: internal, external and inline. You also created an element style, and a class style and then move them into an external style sheet. Additionally, you explored how to link an external style sheet to a new HTML page.

Review

Questions

1 What is a doctype and how does it relate to page validation?

2 In the following XHTML code what is the attribute and what is the attribute value? What other attributes would you often find in an img element such as this?

```
<img src="images/blueberry_smoothie.jpg"/>
```

3 Define the purpose of an external style sheet and one of the benefits of using an external style sheet.

Answers

1 A doctype is a declaration at the start of your HTML document. It is used by a web browser to determine what markup language and version is used on the page. Page validation tests the syntax of your code against the specifications of your doctype. Page validation is a good way to check your page for problems such as missing tags or typographical errors in your code.

2 In this line of code `src` is the attribute and the attribute value is `images/blueberry_smoothie.jpg`. Nested inside the `<img>` tag is the `src` attribute and its value. It links to an image that is then rendered on the page. Other examples of image attributes are the `alt` attribute, which provides a text version of an image to devices such as screen readers and the `width` and `height` attributes which define the size of the image on the page.

3 An external style sheet is a text document with the extension .css. This document contains CSS rules that define the appearance of HTML elements. Because external style sheets can be linked to multiple HTML pages, they provide one central location for your styles. One benefit to this is the ability to update the style of an entire site with a single change to a CSS rule. Other benefits include the ability to use multiple style sheets for organizational purposes, and to specify specific style sheets for printing or optimize the display for mobile devices.

What you'll learn in this lesson:

- Locating free resources that you can use for image editing

- Determining the optimum file size

- Deciding on the best format

- Exporting optimized images from Photoshop

- Slicing images in Photoshop

Graphics, Color, and Transparency

In this lesson, you'll learn how to optimize images so they have a small file size and still look great in a viewer's browser. By learning about the different image formats and the features they offer, you will be able to export files that contain accurate colors and partial or full transparency. You'll learn about image slicing and how it allows you to choose different formats for different parts of a single image so the final result both looks great and downloads quickly.

Starting up

You will work with several files from the web05lessons folder in this lesson. Make sure you have loaded the weblessons folder onto your hard-drive from *www.digitalclassroombooks.com/webdesign*. See "Loading lesson files" in the Starting Up section of this book.

See Lesson 5 in action!

Use the accompanying video to gain a better understanding of how to use some of the features shown in this lesson. You can find the video tutorial for this lesson at www.digitalclassroombooks.com *using the URL provided when you registered your book.*

The examples throughout this lesson use Adobe Photoshop, but there are other applications you can use for cropping, scaling, saving, and retouching images. The following links contain free software and resources that can help you do most tasks in this lesson:

GIMP

www.gimp.org

Adobe Photoshop (free trial version)

www.photoshop.com

Windows Live Photo Gallery

http://explore.live.com/windows-live-essentials

Picasa (photo-editing application from Google)

http://picasa.google.com/

Optimizing graphics for the web

Optimizing refers to the preparation of images for use on the web. The goal of optimization is to reduce the file size of the image for faster downloading, without compromising the quality of the image. Ultimately, you may have to reduce the quality of your images so they are small enough to be downloaded and viewed quickly; in many cases, it is more important to have a speedy download than to make the user wait for beautiful (but large) image files.

Before you start adjusting the file size of your images, you should have a general idea of how you will use them, and how big they will be.

Resizing the image

Many web designers mistakenly believe that if an image has a resolution of 72 dpi (dots per inch), it's ready for the web. However, the *total pixel dimensions* of the image is much more important.

This example uses Adobe Photoshop, and the image is ready to be resized. In your workflow, all retouching, adjustments, and other editing must be completed before you begin optimizing an image for the web.

1 In Adobe Photoshop, choose File > Open. Navigate to the web05lessons folder and open the file named web0501.jpg. An image of several people enjoying smoothies appears.

The designer has planned well and knows the approximate size that this image will be on the web page. You will now open the rough comp that the designer created to plan the size of the image within the page.

2 Keep the file web0501.jpg open, and choose File > Open. In the dialog box that appears, navigate to the web05lessons folder.

3 Locate the image named web0502.jpg and click Open. The rough comp appears. (The designer created this document using the SketchFlow feature in the Microsoft Expression Blend application.)

The rough design for this web page.

The designer has decided that the final web page will be approximately 800 pixels wide. For more information, see the following sidebar, "Images and Browser Window Size." The images you will work on are represented by the two solid squares on the right.

In this case, you have a mock-up that helps to determine the size of the final images. Even if you do not have a mock-up prepared, before optimizing your images, you should know the approximate size of your final images based on the final size of the web page.

Images and Browser Window Size?

According to the website Counter.com, over 50 percent of users have monitors with a resolution of 1024×768 pixels. Thirty percent have 1280×1024-pixel monitors. This does not mean their browser window opens to that size; in fact, their browser window usually varies from 800×600 pixels to 960×600 pixels.

To determine how wide a web image should be, separate the total number of screen pixels into sections, and specify the percentage of the screen you want the image to occupy. For example, if you want the image to occupy half the screen (remember, browser windows are typically about 900 pixels across), type **480** into the Width text field in the Pixel Dimensions section of the Image Size dialog box; for one-quarter of the screen, type **240**, and so on. You should also remember that the pixel size will not change, regardless of what the ppi resolution of your image. So, 200 pixels in a 300-ppi image occupy as much window space as 200 pixels in a 72-ppi image.

At this point, you can determine the approximate size of the optimized images. In this example you will use the grid feature, separated into percentages, to help you determine the size of the images.

4   With web0502.jpg open, choose View > Show > Grid. A grid appears in the image area. You will now adjust the grid size.

5   Choose Edit > Preferences > Guides, Grids & Slices (Windows), or choose Photoshop > Preferences > Guides, Grids & Slices (Mac OS).

6   In the Grid section of the Guides, Grids & Slices dialog box, type **100** in the Gridline Every text box and choose percent from the drop-down menu.

7   In the Subdivisions text box, type **8** and click OK.

Each of the eight grid subdivisions represents 100 pixels; you can use this value to determine the size you want to optimize your image to.

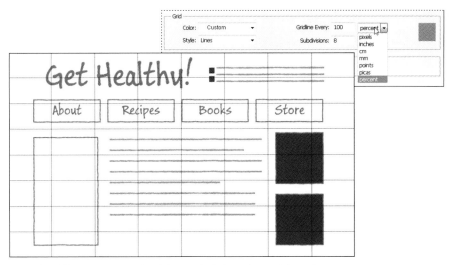

Set up the grid lines to appear in eight subdivisions (top); the resulting grid (bottom).

Adjusting the image size

By looking at the grid on your mock-up, you can see the images on the right occupy more than two grid divisions in both width and height, which means that this image is approximately 225 pixels wide by 150 pixels high.

If you have Photoshop Extended, you can select an area in your image, choose Window > Measurement, and then click the Record Measurements button to see the pixel dimensions of your selection. This is a helpful feature when trying to rebuild from existing compositions.

You will now optimize this image to fit the allotted space; first, you'll check the file size of this image.

1 Return to the web0501.jpg file and select Image > Image Size. The Image Size dialog box appears, indicating that this file is 849 by 565 pixels.

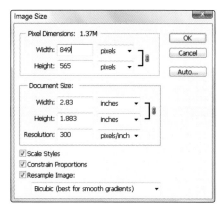

The Image Size dialog box.

Remember that the top part of this dialog box is for on-screen resizing and the bottom part is for resizing an image for printing. On-screen images cannot accommodate more dots per inch in the same space; they occupy space on the monitor based on their pixel count. This particular image would use about 90 percent of a browser window as calculated from the pixel dimensions, not from the resolution. In the following steps, you will only consider pixel dimensions.

2 After looking at the pixel information in the Image Size dialog box, click Cancel. Since you must determine a specific width and height, you will use the Crop tool.

3 Click the Crop tool (◻) to select it in the Tools panel.

4 In the Options bar, type **225px** in the Width text box and **150px** in the Height text box.

Fixing the crop size.

5 With the Crop tool still selected, click and drag the image to select the area you want to include in the final image. Notice that you cannot control the proportions of your crop; you are forced to use the same proportions as the pixel amounts you entered.

Cropping the image to a fixed pixel size.

6 Once you determine the crop area, press Return or Enter, or click the check mark icon (✔) in the upper-right corner of the Options bar.

 If you want to cancel a crop, press the Esc key or click the Cancel Current Crop Operation button (◎), also in the upper-right corner of the Control panel.

7 Choose Image > Image Size; in the Image Size dialog box, you see that the image area is now cropped to the required dimensions.

Applying the Unsharp Mask filter to an image

We strongly recommend that you sharpen an image after you resize an it Photoshop because it can become blurry. The Unsharp Mask filter is a great tool for sharpening images. The following figure shows the image before and after you apply the filter. The Unsharp Mask feature sharpens the image based on levels of contrast, while keeping the areas that don't have contrasting pixels smooth.

The image before (left) and after (right) you apply unsharp masking.

Follow these steps to apply the Unsharp Mask filter:

1   Choose View > Actual Pixels or double-click the Zoom tool (🔍).

When you're using a filter, you should view your image at its actual size to see the results more clearly.

2   Choose Filter > Sharpen > Unsharp Mask.

The Unsharp Mask dialog box displays three options:

- **Amount**: The Amount value ranges from 0 to 500. The amount you choose depends upon the subject matter. For example, you can sharpen a car or appliance at 300 or 400, but with a portrait, every wrinkle, mole, or hair will become more defined. If you are unsure about the value to use, start with 150 and gradually increase the amount until you find a value that looks good.

- **Radius**: The Unsharp Mask filter creates a halo around the areas that have enough contrast to be considered an edge. For print images, you can use a value between 1 and 2, but if you're creating a billboard or poster, increase the size.

- **Threshold**: The Threshold value is the most important one in the Unsharp Mask dialog box because it determines the parts of the image that should be sharpened. This value can range from 0 to 255. Apply too much, and no sharpening appears; apply too little, and the image becomes grainy. For example, if you leave it at zero, noise appears throughout the image, much like the grain you see in high-speed film. A value of 10 causes the filter to apply when the pixels are ten shades or more away from each other. Start with a value of 10, and gradually increase it until you find a value that works well.

3 For this exercise, set the Amount to **250**, Radius to **1**, and Threshold to **10**.

You can compare the original image with the resulting image in the Preview pane of the Unsharp Mask dialog box by clicking and holding the image in the Preview pane; this shows the original state of the image. When you release the mouse button, you preview the Unsharp Mask filter again.

4 Click OK to apply the filter. The image is sharpened.

5 Choose File > Save; keep the file open for the next part of this lesson.

In some images, stray colored pixels may appear after you apply the Unsharp Mask filter. If this occurs in your image, choose Edit > Fade Unsharp Mask immediately after applying the Unsharp Mask filter. In the Fade dialog box, select the Luminosity blend mode from the Mode drop-down list and then click OK. This step applies the Unsharp Mask filter to the grays in the image only, thereby eliminating sharpening of colored pixels.

You can also choose Filter > Convert for Smart Filters before you apply the Unsharp Mask filter. Smart filters allow you to undo all or some of any filter, including sharpening filters that you apply to a layer.

Selecting the best image format

When saving an image that you will use on the web, you need to consider two factors: the quality and size of the image file. When you are saving a file, you must find a balance between the quality you want and the download speed your viewers demand.

In this section, you will look at different file formats and decide on a format for the picture you just resized; the following example uses the Save for web & Devices feature in Adobe Photoshop.

Choosing the right file format

The most popular formats for web images are JPEG, PNG, and GIF. Each one of these formats has benefits and drawbacks, as shown in the following table.

File Formats

FILE FORMAT	LOSSY	SUPPORTS ANTI-ALIASING	SUPPORTS TRANSPARENCY	SUPPORTS ANIMATIONS	SUPPORTS VARYING AMOUNTS OF TRANSPARENCY	HAS LIMITED COLORS	IS BEST FOR PHOTOS	IS BEST FOR SOLID COLORS
JPEG	●	●					●	
PNG-8	●				●	●		●
PNG-24	●	●	●		●		●	●
GIF			●	●		●		●

Choosing the best file format for your image

Throughout this lesson, you will have the opportunity to save images in each of the major file formats: JPEG, PNG, and GIF. You will also see the differences between the formats and when to use each.

Saving images as JPEGs

The JPEG file format helps you keep the file size down, but some loss in image quality occurs when you save the image file. Since the JPEG format supports anti-aliasing, we recommend it for photographic images and illustrations with a lot of gradients; anti-aliasing is a technique used in computer graphics that helps smooth out the naturally jagged edges of objects such as text or any area where a transition in tonal values is needed. When saving an image as a JPEG, you can also choose varying levels of quality.

Choosing the quality of a JPEG

In the following steps, you will complete the optimization process by saving your image as a JPEG.

1   With web0501.jpg still open, choose File > Save for Web & Devices. The Save for Web & Devices window appears.

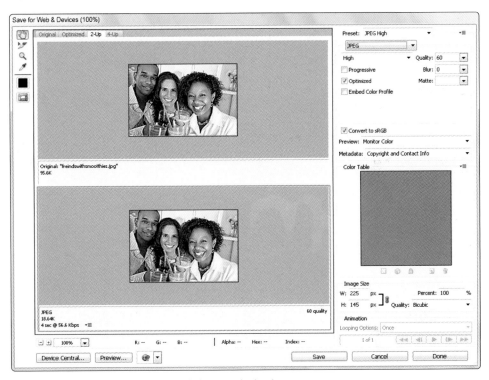

The Save for Web & Devices window shown with the 2-Up tab selected.

The Save for Web & Devices window allows you to preview changes that you make in the settings, such as file type and size. The section in the upper-right corner of the window is where you determine the file format and file compression settings. In this example, JPEG is selected.

The Save for Web & Devices feature is used here to create an image for the web, but you can also use this feature to prepare and preview files for use on mobile devices by clicking the Device Central button.

Above the Format drop-down menu is the Preset drop-down menu. This menu contains pre-configured settings for many file formats; later in this lesson you will learn how to store your own presets here.

In the upper-left corner is a toolbar with tools you can use to select sections (or slices) of an image, zoom into, and sample colors from an image.

The large preview window allows you to compare different file formats and compression settings. You can compare up to four file formats and see the approximate download times and file sizes.

2 Select the 2-Up tab at the top of the preview window.

3 Click to select the second image preview to assign settings.

From the Preset drop-down menu, select JPEG High. Note that the image preview shows an image of the file in that format and displays information about the JPEG settings in the lower-left corner.

Download information appears under the preview.

In this example, the file is reduced to 18.64K and it will take about 4 seconds to download at the speed of about 56.6 kbps (kilobits per second).

You can change the speed and recalculate the download time by clicking the Select Download Speed button (▾≡) located to the right of the download speed.

Since most viewers are not willing to wait for a download, this file size might be too large for the viewer. You will lower the image quality in the following steps to reduce the file size.

4 Click the Compression drop-down menu located below the Format drop-down menu and choose Medium; note that the settings change along with the download information. The JPEG image format uses lossy compression to save a file. Lossy means that the image is compressed by discarding part of the data in the file.

5 Click the Compression drop-down menu and choose Low. The visual quality changes and the download time decreases.

For this example, the Low quality is too low and the download time for Medium quality is too long. Toggle between the two settings to see that the Quality text box indicates that Low is set to 10 and Medium is set to 30. These presets are helpful, but you can manually adjust the settings.

6 Click Quality to display the Quality slider and drag it to the right, increasing the value to **20**.

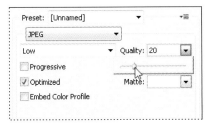

Customize the quality of your image using the Quality slider.

Previewing your image

The Save for Web & Devices window allows you to preview an image file in a browser before saving it. You must first ensure that a browser can be recognized from this window.

1 Click the Preview the Optimized Image in a Browser button (🖼 ▾) and choose Edit List.

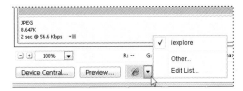

To choose a web browser click on the Preview the Optimized Image in a Browser button.

2 When the browser window appears, click Add. In the dialog box that appears, navigate to C:\Program Files (Windows) or Macintosh HD\Applications (Mac OS) and locate the browser in which you want to preview your images; click Open and then click OK in the browser window.

3 Click the Preview button to view your image in the browser. If you want to change the quality, close the browser window and return to the Save for Web & Devices window.

4 If you want a better image quality, change the JPEG setting to Very High. Preview the image directly in the Save for Web & Devices window.

5 Click Save in the Save for Web & Devices window. In the dialog box that appears, navigate to the web05lessons folder.

6 Name the file **web0501_optimized**, and make sure that Images only is selected in the Format drop-down menu.

7 Make sure Settings are configured to Default Settings, and then click Save. Remember that when creating a website, you should save this image file into the appropriate site folder.

You are now back to your image in Photoshop. We strongly recommend that you keep a copy of your image in an uncompressed format. If you have Photoshop, save this file as a PSD image. If you do not have Photoshop, save as a TIFF or PNG file. Avoid saving a file multiple times as a JPEG, because the quality is reduced every time you save your file in this lossy format.

8 Choose File > Save As and navigate to the web05lessons folder. In the File Name text box, type **WEB0501_done**. Choose the Photoshop (PSD) format, and click Save.

9 Choose File > Close to close the file.

Creating a transparency effect in a JPEG image

Transparency doesn't exist in the JPEG format, but you can simulate the transparency effect.

In following steps, you will use the Matting feature to match the background color of your web page and then preview the image in your browser.

1 In Photoshop, choose File > Open. In the dialog box that appears, navigate to the web05lessons folder, select the image named web0503.psd, and click Open. An image of a smoothie with a transparent background appears.

When you save an image for the web, file size is a big concern. Since this is a photographic image, JPEG is the best format to use to keep the file size small. However, the web page has a pale yellow background, and by default, the JPEG will appear with a white background. The solution is to use the Matte control, which becomes available when you optimize this file.

2 Choose File > Save for Web & Devices. In the Save for Web & Devices window, choose JPEG Medium from the Preset drop-down menu.

3 Click the Matte drop-down menu and choose Other. The Color Picker appears.

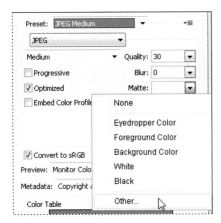

Changing the matte color.

4 In the Hexadecimal text box (located to the right of the # sign), type **FFFFCC**; then click OK. The color appears immediately in the preview window.

5 Click the Preview button to preview the image in the browser with the new matte color applied.

Preview your image in a web browser with the background color applied.

6 Close your browser window and return to the Save for Web & Devices window.

Saving your settings

You can store your customized settings for future use. through the Optimize Panel menu in the upper-right corner of the Optimize section of the Save for Web & Devices window. Follow these steps to store your settings:

1 With the Save for Web & Devices window still open, click the Optimize Panel menu in the upper-right corner of the Optimize section, and select Save Settings. The Save Optimization Settings dialog box appears.

Saving your custom settings.

You are automatically directed to the Optimized Settings folder for your application. To share this setting, browse to a location on a server or removable device.

2 In the Save As text box, type **JPEG_ffffcc**, and then click Save. You now can select these settings from the Preset drop-down menu at the top of the Optimize window.

Now that you have saved your settings, you will save your optimized image file.

3 In the Save for Web & Devices window, click Save. In the dialog box that appears, navigate to the web05lessons folder and in the File Name text box, type **web0503_optimized**. Ensure that the Format menu is set to Images Only and that the Settings menu is set to Default Settings.

To test a file, click Done instead of Save. This keeps your settings and does not save the file.

Saving images as GIFs

GIF is a popular web format that has some limitations in terms of color and appearance. This file format is lossless, so the clarity of the image is not compromised by GIF compression. You can compress the file size of a GIF by reducing the image's pixel dimensions and the number of indexed colors that it uses, which makes GIF the best format for images with a lot of solid colors, such as logos and illustrations. The compression algorithms for GIF files work best on large spans of color, thereby reducing the file size when optimized. However, a photographic image or an illustration with a lot of tonal values will result in a much larger file size than a same-sized image with solid colors.

The GIF format works best with images that have large spans of solid colors. In this example, an image with a lot of tonal values are saved as a GIF with 32 colors.

When saving as a GIF, your image file can contain up to 256 indexed colors, but you should reduce the number of colors to the minimum. You can reduce an image to four colors, but it requires testing to find the best-looking file with the smallest file size.

You can animate GIF files and include transparent pixels to blend the image with different-colored backgrounds. The pixels in a GIF image must be fully transparent or fully opaque, so you cannot fade the transparency as with a PNG image, which is discussed later in this lesson.

In the following steps, you will open an image that contains multiple shades of solid color, and you will save it with a transparent background. You will then animate the image.

 You should use animations conservatively because many viewers do not like the distraction.

1   Choose File > Open. In the dialog box that appears, browse to the web05lessons folder and open the file named web0504.psd. A colorful logo appears.

The logo you will optimize.

This logo contains a lot of solid color, and has an image behind it. In such situations you must determine the part of the image on which you want to focus; in this case, you will focus on the logo type, not the image behind it.

You will now remove the background. When you have a solid background, you can remove it using the Magic Eraser tool, which has a tolerance option to control the pixels to delete to transparency.

2   Select the Magic Eraser tool (✐), which is hidden under the Eraser tool (✐) in the Tools panel.

3   In the Options bar at the top of the window, confirm that the number 32 is in the Tolerance text box. Also, make sure that the Contiguous option is checked.

Tolerance determines how much of a selected pixel color is deleted when you use the Magic Eraser tool: the higher the value, the more shades of that color are deleted. The lower the value, the fewer shades of that color is deleted. Selecting the Contiguous option ensures that only touching pixels are deleted to transparency.

Click the Contiguous button to select only pixels that are connected to each other.

4 Click the White background. The Background layer converts to Layer 0 and the background becomes transparent.

5 Choose File > Save as, and in the dialog box that appears, navigate to the web05lessons folder. Name the file **web0504_work**, and keep it in the Photoshop .psd format. Click Save. Keep the file open for the next part of this lesson.

Optimizing the GIF image

In the following steps, you will determine the best settings for optimizing your GIF image. You will use a color table to affect the appearance of the final optimized image.

1 With the web0504_work image still open, choose Image > Image Size. In the Image Size dialog box, change the Width to **200** pixels and click OK.

2 Your image might appear smaller on the screen than it actually is. Double-click the Zoom tool ($\mathbb{Q}$) to view your image at 100 percent.

3 Choose File > Save for Web & Devices. The Save for Web & Devices window appears.

4 Choose GIF 64 No Dither from the Preset drop-down menu, and check the Transparency check box. Notice in the GIF preview that the image size is now about 10K.

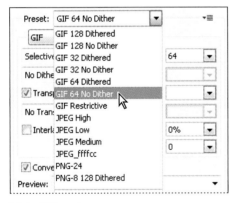

Select a GIF preset.

Understanding Dithering

Dithering is the attempt to approximate a color from a mixture of other colors when the required color is not available. Dithering produces a pattern or grainy appearance in images, and should only be used to help define tonal values.

Original image (left), and with dithering applied (right).

5 Keep this window open for the next part of this lesson.

Using the color table

By selecting GIF 64 No Dither, you have indicated that you want to use 64 colors in your optimized image. Note that the color table in the optimization section displays a table of these indexed colors.

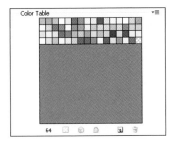

Use the color table to keep the most important colors in your image.

You can delete, change, or lock the colors in this table to preserve the look of your image. In this section, you will learn to lock critical colors to make sure important colors are not deleted when you reduce the number of colors in the table.

1   With the image still open in the Save for Web & Devices window, select the Eyedropper tool (🖋)and click the orange color surrounding the text in the optimized GIF preview of the image. The Eyedropper samples the color and selects that color in the color table to the right. This tool is useful when you need to ensure that a specific color appears as close as possible to the print color. For example, the logo for this exercise might be for a company where the branding department wants to ensure the specific orange used appears as close as possible to the print color (PMS 173 for this example).

Using the Eyedropper tool to select a color from the optimized image.

The Pantone Color Matching System (PMS) is a standardized color reproduction system used mostly in print, but whose colors can also be used online. By standardizing colors, corporations can ensure their colors stay as consistent as possible regardless of where the colors are reproduced.

2   Locate the selected color in the color table and double-click it to open the Color Picker. You can use the Color Picker to enter a new value for the selected color.

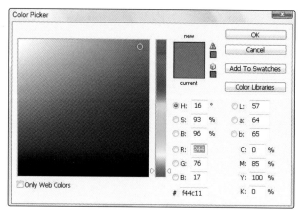

Double-click on the color to open the Color Picker.

In the Color Picker window, you can specify colors in any color space; for example, you could choose an RGB or Hexadecimal value. For this lesson, you will closely match a Pantone color a client has provided to you.

Type Hexadecimal values in the text box to the right of the # sign.

3   Click the Color Libraries button to open the Color Libraries window. The Pantone solid coated library is selected by default. Each color in this library represents a specific Pantone color on coated paper. The color is automatically matched with the most similar Pantone color.

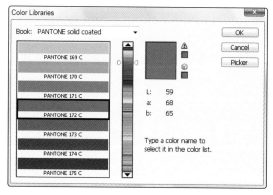

Opening the Color Libraries section of the Color Picker.

Return to the standard Color Picker by clicking the Picker button.

4   In this example, the client has specified that the orange should match PMS 173. Click the color value Pantone 173 C, and then click OK. The color changes to match the value of PMS 173 and has a white square icon in the lower-right corner with a diagonal line through it. This indicates that the color is locked and has been mapped to a color other than the original. You will now lock additional colors.

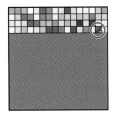

This color has been locked
and mapped to a specific value.

5   Click any color in the color table, and then click the padlock icon (🔒) at the bottom of the color table. For this part of the exercise, select four additional colors you would like to retain in this image, and lock them as instructed in the previous steps.

You will now reduce the number of color values in the optimized image even further.

6   From the Colors drop-down menu, choose 8. This is a significant reduction in the number of colors, and although your important colors are locked and the file size has been reduced, the image quality is poor. So you will need to increase the number of colors used to improve the quality.

Reducing the color values in the color table.

7   Using the Colors drop-down menu, increase the number to 32. Keep this window open for the next part of the lesson.

Adding a matte to a GIF

When placing images over a colored background, you might see a pixelated edge. You can avoid this edge by applying matting to the image in the optimization stage. Matting lets you to find pixels that are almost transparent. However, unlike pixels in PNG images, pixels in a GIF image are either transparent or not. In the following steps, you will apply matting that matches the background color of the web page where the image will be placed.

1   With the Save for Web & Devices window still open, click the white section in the Matte drop-down menu. The Color Picker appears.

Select a custom matting color.

2   In the Color Picker window, type **3366CC** into the Hexadecimal text box (located to the right of the # sign). Click OK. Notice that the graphic now has a thin, dark-blue border around the edge. If you choose to use this image on a page with a different background, remember to change the matting color to match the new background.

Matting applied to the GIF image.

3   Test your image by clicking the Preview button at the bottom of the Save for Web & Devices window. The preview window matches the matting color you selected so you can see the image in the same background color in the browser.

4   Once you are done previewing your file, close the browser, return to the Save for Web & Devices window, and click Save. In the Save As dialog box, browse to locate the web05lessons folder. Name the file **web0504_optimized.gif**, and then click Save.

5   Choose File > Close to close the web0504_work file.

Animating a GIF

Where appropriate, animated GIFs add interest to a web page. In the following steps, you will create an animated GIF.

1   In Adobe Photoshop, choose File > Open. In the Open dialog box, locate the image named web0505.psd in the web05lessons folder. The original image file for the last image you worked on is now open.

2   Choose Window > Animation to open the Animation window. If you are using Photoshop Extended, the Animation (Timeline) panel appears. Click the convert to frame icon in the lower-right corner. The Animation panel changes to Frames mode.

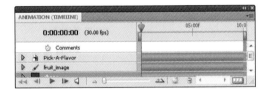

The Animation panel in the Timeline mode.

The Animation panel in the Frames mode.

In Photoshop, frames are like a flip book. Each frame appears for the amount of time you specify, creating a simple animation.

3 In the Animation panel, select the duplicates selected frames icon (⬛) to duplicate your frame.

4 Select the Move tool, and then select the Pick-A-Flavor layer. Click and drag the Pick-A-Flavor logo to the bottom of the image area.

Click and drag the Pick-a-Flavor layer to reposition it in the second frame.

Click the first frame in the Animation panel; the original position is intact in this frame. Click the second frame; the logo appears repositioned to the bottom of the image area.

Changing the timing of an animation

The timing of the animation is important. In the following steps, you will change the speed at which the frames are viewed, and also change the number of times they rotate through the flip.

1 Select both frames by clicking the first frame and Shift + clicking the second frame in the Animation panel.

2 Click the arrow in the lower-right corner of either frame to open the frame delay time. Choose 0.1 second. You will now change the number of times your animation will play.

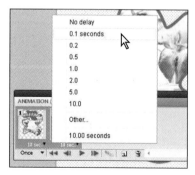

Change the timing of the animation frames.

3 Click the Selects Looping Options button in the lower-left corner of the Animation panel and change the value to 3 times. The animation will now play three times and then stop.

Changing additional properties in an animation

You will now change the opacity value of the Pick-A-Flavor layer. A layer which has a value of 100% opacity is completely visible. A layer which has a value of 0% opacity is not visible. You will now set different opacity values for the first two frames in order to create an "off/on" visual effect.

1 Select the first frame in the Animation panel, and then select the Pick-A-Flavor layer in the Layers panel. Click and drag the Opacity slider from 100 percent to 0 percent.

Change the opacity of the frames.

2 Click the second frame, and with the same Pick-A-Flavor layer selected, drag the Opacity slider to the right until it reaches 100 percent.

3 Test the animation by clicking the Play button (▶) at the bottom of the Animation panel. A flashy animation plays three times. In the following steps, you will use the Tween feature to create a better transition between the frames.

Tweening

In the following steps, you will build a better transition between the frames. Tweening automatically creates new frames between two existing frames. The process saves you the time and the effort from having to make each frame manually.

1 Select any frame, and then click the tweens animation frames icon (⁙) at the bottom of the Animation panel. The Tween window appears.

2 In the Tween window, type **3** into the Frames to add text box. Leave the others settings as they are, and click OK. Three frames are added in between the existing frames.

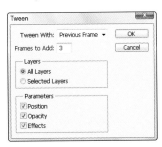

Create a smooth transition by using the Tween feature.

3 Click the plays animation icon (▶) to test your animation.

4 Choose File > Save for Web & Devices and make sure the setting for Preset is GIF 64 No Dither. Then press Save.

5 Choose File > Save to save this file and then choose File > Close.

Saving as a PNG

Some characteristics, such as the ability to display variable levels of transparency, are uniquely supported by the PNG format, but you cannot reduce the file size such as you can with JPEG and GIF formats. You can use the PNG format to benefit from its unique characteristics more than for a need to reduce file size.

In the following steps, you will create a navigation bar.

1 Choose File > Open, and in the Open dialog box, select the file named web0506.psd. You will use this image at the top of a web page.

The initial artwork.

2 Choose Window > Layers. The Layers panel appears with three layers already created. You will first group these layers, and then apply a mask to all three layers to allow the image to fade from 100-percent to 0-percent opacity.

Three layers exist in the Layers panel.

3 Select the bottom layer (baseimage) and Shift + click the top layer (Get Healthy). All three layers are now selected.

4   From the Layers panel menu, choose New Group from Layers. The New Group from Layers dialog box appears. Type **banner** in the Name text box, and then click OK.

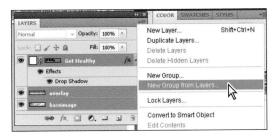

Choose to group the layers.

5   Click the Add Layer Mask button at the bottom of the Layers panel. A mask is added to the entire group of layers you created.

Add a mask to the banner group.

6   Select the Gradient tool (■) from the Tools panel and press D. This restores the foreground and background colors to their defaults (black and white).

7   Click the Gradient Picker in the Options bar and make sure you have the Foreground to Background gradient selected.

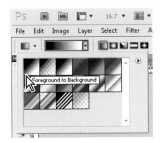

Makes sure that the Foreground to Background gradient is selected.

8 Using the Gradient tool, click and drag from the right side of the image to the left, and release the mouse when you reach the **y** in the word **Healthy**.

Click and drag with the Gradient tool across the image area.

By creating a mask for the group and applying a gradient to it, you have created a gradient mask that fades the banner layers to 0-percent opacity.

9 Choose File > Save for Web & Devices. When the Save for Web & Devices window appears, choose PNG-24 from the Preset drop-down menu. PNG-24 supports varying levels of transparency in the image.

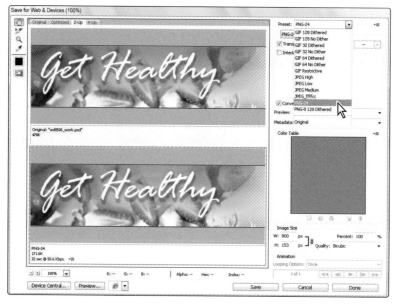

Select PNG-24 to use the fade to transparency feature.

10 Click the Preview button at the bottom of the Save for Web & Devices window to see a preview of your PNG file in a browser.

11 Once you have previewed your image, close the browser window and return to the Save for Web & Devices window.

12 Click Save. In the dialog box that appears, browse to the web05lessons folder, name the file **web0506_banner.png**, and click Save. Choose File > Close to close the file.

PNG-8 versus PNG-24

Many software packages allow you to save an image in PNG-8 or PNG-24 format. The 8 and 24 represent the number of bits each file format contains. The one you choose depends on the type of image and how you want it to appear. The PNG-8 format uses an indexed color palette similar to GIFs, which makes this format ideal for images with areas of solid, even colors. Use the PNG-24 format when you want variable transparency or many gradients in your image.

Slicing an image

In this section, you will learn to slice an image in Adobe Photoshop. A slice is a part of an image, cut from a larger image. These pieces are held together by an HTML table or Cascading Style Sheets (CSS). In this example, you will use CSS to create the final navigation bar.

An example of a sliced image.

Slices are useful when your web page contains large images, because downloading several smaller packets of information on the web is faster than downloading one large packet. Slices are also helpful when you need to save parts of an image in different formats. In this exercise, you will use existing layers to create slices. Note that you can also use guides to determine where the slicing of your image occurs.

Viewing the completed file

Before starting this lesson, you'll use your browser to view the completed image with navigational links that you will create in this section.

1 Open your web browser.

2 Choose File > Open, or the Open file command appropriate for your specific browser.

This page is created using CSS; you can export pages built from tables of CSS from the Photoshop Save for Web & Devices window. Find out more about CSS at w3.org/Style/CSS/.

3 In the Open dialog box, navigate to the web05lessons folder and open the sitefolder located inside. Choose to open the index.html file. An image created to help viewers navigate a website appears.

You have reached the Index page

The completed navigation bar in a web browser.

4 Click the ABOUT, RECIPES, BOOKS, and STORE text links; these links take you to generic pages with related titles. As you can see, each slice can have its own independent attributes, such as file type and link.

You will create this web page from start to finish, including adding the links, and export the page using CSS.

5 You can keep the finished web page open in the browser for reference, or choose File > Close.

6 Return to Photoshop.

Creating slices

You will now use the existing layers in this image to create layer-based slices using Adobe Photoshop.

You will start by saving a work file.

1 Choose File > Open and browse to the web05lessons folder. Open the file named web0507.psd. The navigational banner appears.

2 Choose File > Save as. In the dialog box that appears, browse to the web05lessons folder. In the Name text box, type **web0507_work.psd**.

3 Choose Window > Layers to open the Layers panel.

4 Select the Slice Select tool (⌀), which is hidden under the Crop tool.

5 Select the About Shape layer, hold down the Shift key, and click the Store Shape layer. All four shape layers are now selected.

6 Choose Layer > New Layer Based Slices. The shape layers are now defined as slices.

7 Choose File > Save; keep this file open for the next section.

Changing the attributes of the slices

In the following steps, you will change the individual slice attributes to add alternative text and individual hyperlinks.

1   Using the Slice Select tool, which is hidden under the Slice tool, make sure no slices are active by clicking between any two slices.

You cannot have any slices selected before
changing individual attributes of the slices.

2   Using the Slice Select tool (🔪), select the About Slice, and then click the Set Options for the Current Slice button (📄), which is located in the upper-right corner of the Options bar. The Slice Options window appears.

3   In the Name text box, type **about**.

4   In the URL text box, type **about.html**. To create a link to an existing page, you would type the URL address here. To allow the user to navigate to an external link, you would enter a full address. For this exercise, you are linking to a local page located inside the same folder where you will be saving this sliced image.

5   In the Alt Tag text box, type **About**. The text in the Alt Tag text box is visible to users when they place their mouse cursor over the link, or choose to not have the graphics on the web page visible. An accurate Alt tag also gives search engines more information about your web page. Click OK.

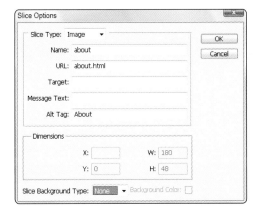

Changing the first slice's options.

6   With the Slice Select tool, click the Recipes slice, and then click the Set Options for the Current Slice button (📄).

7 Type **recipes** into the Name text box, **recipes.html** into the URL text box, and **Recipes** into the Alt Tag text box. Click OK.

8 Continue this process by double-clicking the third slice, Books. (Double-clicking a slice is another way to open the Slice Options dialog box.) In the Slice Options dialog box, type **books** in the name text box, **books.html** in the URL text box, and **Books** in the Alt Tag text box; then click OK.

9 Repeat this process for the Store slice, typing **store** in the Name text box, **store.html** in the URL text box, and **Store** in the Alt Tag text box; then click OK.

10 Choose File > Save to save this file. Keep it open for the next part of this lesson.

You are now ready to optimize these images and create your HTML page.

Saving slices out of Photoshop

In this section, you will learn to optimize your sliced images and save them to an HTML file that contains the code needed to create the final navigation bar on a web page.

1 With the web0507_work.psd file still open, choose File > Save for Web & Devices.

2 In the Save for Web & Devices window, choose the Slice Select tool from the toolbar in the upper-right corner, and click each slice once. Note that you can choose a different optimization setting for each slice. This is useful for images that have a lot of gradients in one section and solid colors in another.

3 Click the About slice, and then Shift + click the Recipes, Books, and Store slices. All the slices are now selected.

4 Choose PNG-8 from the Optimized File Format drop-down menu, since this image only has a few solid colors.

5 Choose Perceptual for the Color reduction algorithm, which creates a custom color table by giving priority to colors for which the human eye has greater sensitivity.

6 Choose No Dither from the Specify the Dithering Algorithm drop-down menu. Dithering scatters different colored pixels throughout an image to make it appear as though there are more colors than there are, this can result in a grainy appearance in your solid spans of color.

7 Choose 16 from the Colors drop-down menu. The image used for this exercise appears to have two colors, blue and white, but it has more. Transparency is a color, and the transition between the white text and the blue background contains many shades of color. If you reduce the colors too much, you will have a pixelated result.

8   Select the Transparency check box.

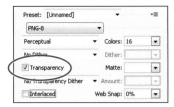

A portion of the Save for Web & Devices dialog box.

9   Click Save. In the Save Optimized As dialog box, navigate to the web05lessons folder and double-click to select the site folder located inside.

10   In the File Name text box, type **index**. This page will be the initial start page for the test website.

11   In the Format drop-down menu, choose HTML and Images, leave the Settings at Default Settings, and leave Slices set to All.

As a default, Photoshop exports your slice images formatted in an HTML table tag. To export your slice images in CSS (Cascading Style Sheets) containers, choose Other from the Settings dialog box, and then click and hold HTML to select the Slices option; you can then select the Generate CSS radio button.

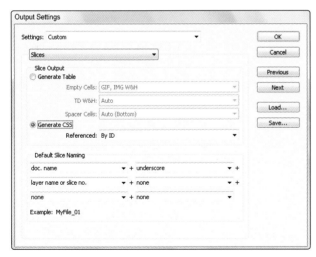

You can export your code as a table or in CSS.

12   Click Save. Open your browser and choose File > Open and navigate to index.html to view your menu.

In Internet Explorer, you can display your File menu by pressing F10.

Self study

1   Now that you have experience resizing and optimizing an image for the web, go through the steps on your own to optimize the image of the children making smoothies (image web0508, located in your web05lessons folder). In its final form, the image should maintain as much quality as possible and be 225 pixels wide and 150 pixels high.

Review

Questions

1   Which is the more important factor to pay attention to when resizing a web image: pixel size or resolution?

2   What is the best format for an *animated* graphic that contains many gradients?

3   What format can you save in that allows you to fade an image and see through to the objects underneath it on a web page?

Answers

1   Pixel size is more important for web images (resolution is more important for printed output).

2   The GIF format is currently the *only* format that supports animation.

3   The PNG-24 format allows you save an image with varying levels of transparency.

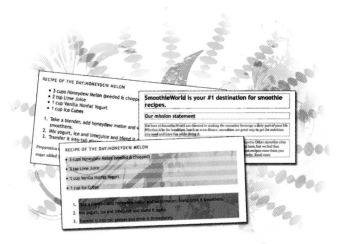

What you'll learn in this lesson:

- Using the `font-family` property
- Setting the size of your text
- Working with the em measurement
- Changing text properties
- Using HTML lists

Formatting Text with CSS

In this lesson, you'll learn how to control the appearance of text on your web pages using CSS styling.

Starting up

You will work with several files from the web06lessons folder in this lesson. Make sure you have loaded the weblessons folder onto your hard-drive from *www.digitalclassroombooks.com/webdesign*. See "Loading lesson files" in the Starting Up section of this book.

See Lesson 6 in action!

Use the accompanying video to gain a better understanding of how to use some of the features shown in this lesson. You can find the video tutorial for this lesson at www.digitalclassroombooks.com *using the URL provided when you registered your book.*

Although this lesson uses the TextWrangler text editor to create the markup, you can use any of the text editors covered in Lesson 3 and get the same results.

The importance of typography on the web

> Typography is two-dimensional architecture, based on experience and imagination, and guided by rules and readability. And this is the purpose of typography: The arrangement of design elements within a given structure should allow the reader to easily focus on the message, without slowing down the speed of his reading.
>
> —*Hermann Zapf*

Typography has a starring role in graphic design, including web design. Most user interaction on the web starts with text. Users spend a great deal of time on the web scanning, navigating, and reading text. As a result, it is extremely important that the web designer understands how to control the placement, appearance, and style of text.

For purposes of clarity, it is worth pointing out that the words *typeface* and *font* are mistakenly used interchangeably. A typeface is a more abstract term for the character design of an alphabet; it is a term that preceded the invention of computers and digital typesetting. An example of a common typeface is Helvetica, which also includes different styles including Bold, Condensed, and Light, among others. A font is the digital system file that resides on a computer and is used in print design to set text. In web design, web browsers use a font to display text on the screen (as well as when printing).

The challenges of fonts on the web

When designing for the web, you can format text in a way that is similar to desktop publishing and word processing applications, but there are important differences to keep in mind. When you specify that a specific font be used, that font needs to be installed on the user's computer when the web page is rendered on the viewer's computer or device. If the user does not have this font, the browser replaces it with another font.

Because you don't know what fonts are installed on viewers' computers, and because the web browser of a viewer might substitute fonts, your design intentions for text might not be faithfully reproduced. One option is to use fonts that you are sure will be found on most computers. Unfortunately, only a handful of fonts can reliably be found on virtually all computers around the world.

Web-safe fonts

Following is a list of the most reliable fonts for web use:

- Arial
- Verdana
- Georgia
- Times New Roman
- Courier
- Trebuchet
- Lucida
- Tahoma
- Impact

The list is small because it takes into account both Mac and Windows platforms and assumes that there may still be older computer systems that are active and accessing the web. These older systems had a more limited font selection than today's systems, and so a designer needs to consider this when choosing fonts.

The above list is also limited for stylistic reasons. Both Courier and Impact, for example, are used infrequently because although they are widely available, their distinctive styles limit their everyday use.

One of the solutions to the lack of fonts on the web is to use a *font stack*. In CSS, a font stack is a list of multiple fonts that the web browser uses in an attempt to display text onscreen. The following CSS code shows an example of a font stack:

```
font-family:"Helvetica Neue", Helvetica, Arial, sans-serif;
```

In this example, the browser first looks for the Helvetica Neue font on the user's system. Notice the quotation marks in this example. In most cases when specifying a font, quotation marks are unnecessary, but in some cases, the quotation marks are needed to help the user's computer choose the right version of the font. If the user doesn't have Helvetica Neue, then the browser looks for the more generic version of Helvetica. If Helvetica is absent, the browser uses Arial, which is a font that is extremely similar to Helvetica. If for some reason Arial is not on the system, the last choice is sans-serif, which allows the system to use any sans-serif font it can find on the system. Sans-serif is the generic definition for all fonts that do not have small strokes (called serifs) at the end of each character. Examples of serif fonts are Times New Roman and Georgia.

Setting a `font-family`

In this exercise you will set your `font-family` for an entire page and then set the `font-family` for your headings.

1   In your text editor, choose File > Open and navigate to the web06lessons folder. Locate the 06_fonts.html file and click OK. This file has four blocks of text: a heading 1 `<h1>`, a heading 2 `<h2>`, and two paragraphs `<p>`. Additionally, in the `<style>` section, empty style rules are added to save you time. In this exercise, you will add the CSS properties. You will start by adding the `font-family` property for the body element.

2   In the style rule for the body, type the following line (highlighted in red):

```
body {
     font-family:"Trebuchet MS", Tahoma, Arial, sans-serif;
}
```

3   Choose File > Save and then preview your page in the browser. As noted above, your web browser renders Trebuchet if you have it on your system; if you do not, it displays Tahoma; and if you don't have Tahoma, you still see a sans-serif font.

When you define the font family Trebuchet for the body rule, all your text is set in this font.

All of the text on your page is rendered in Trebuchet because the only style set is for the body. Remember that the HTML body tag defines all of the elements on the page. Now you will set a specific font family for the paragraph element.

4   In the style rule for the paragraph (p), type the following line (highlighted in red):

```
p {
     font-family:Georgia, "Times New Roman", Times, serif;
}
```

5   Save your document and preview it in your browser. Now that there is a specific rule for paragraphs, they are styled as Georgia. The two headings are still using Trebuchet, which you defined in the body style.

6 In the style rule for heading 2 (h2), type the following line (highlighted in red):

```
h2 {
    font-family:Zapfino;
}
```

7 Save your document and preview it in your browser.

Styling the heading 2 as Zapfino will only show up if that font is on a user's system.

If you have the Zapfino font on your system, you see a calligraphic script for your heading. The Zapfino font is installed with Adobe applications such as Photoshop, so it is very likely that designers will have this font on their system. However as noted earlier, many users on the web do not have this font on their system and so setting it is not a good idea.

8 Select the entire `font-family` line in your h2 rule and delete it.

The promising future of web fonts

The lack of choices for using fonts on the web has been a source of frustration for web designers for many years. The situation is improving as several companies have created solutions to enable your pages to display on a browser with the fonts you've specified as a designer.

Some of the methods use paid services, but free options are also available. Here are some resources to get you started:

- *http://code.google.com/webfonts*
- *http://typekit.com/*
- *http://fontdeck.com/*
- *www.fontsquirrel.com/fontface*

Sizing text with CSS

When using CSS to style text for the web, you have a few options for the unit of measurement. The CSS property that controls the size of your text is named `font-size`.

You can control the `font-size` property in a few different ways:

- **Absolute-size:** A set of keywords that indicate predefined font sizes. Named font sizes scale according to the user's font setting preferences. Possible values include `xx-small`, `x-small`, `small`, `medium`, `large`, `x-large`, and `xx-large`.

- **Length:** A number, followed by an absolute units designator (`cm`, `mm`, `in`, `pt`, or `pc`) or a relative units designator (`em`, `ex`, or `px`).

- **Percentage:** An integer, followed by a percent sign (`%`). The value is a percentage of the font size of the parent object.

- **Relative-size:** A set of keywords that are interpreted as relative to the font size of the parent object. Possible values include `larger` and `smaller`.

Choosing the unit of measurement for the `font-size` in a web page is an important decision and not as easy as it is in print design. The main difficulty in selecting a size has to do with monitor resolution. Text on smaller monitors looks different than text on larger monitors; however, with a bit of forethought you can correct for this. In addition to the monitor resolution issue, you must also consider the way that different web browsers interpret how text is rendered. For example, unlike print, the web allows users to resize their text manually. Furthermore, there is a growing audience that browses the web with mobile devices, which makes sizing your text even more important.

Pixels and points are not the best choices

Setting font size in points might come naturally to you if you have worked in print design or if you have created web graphics you might be comfortable measuring using pixels. The `font-size` property in CSS allows you use both forms of measurement. In the following example, the first CSS selector shows you a paragraph rule for points, while the second one shows you a paragraph rule for pixels:

```
p {
    font-size:12pt;
}
```
Points

```
p {
    font-size:12px;
}
```
Pixels

Even though points are supported, it is bad practice to use them and not advised for web design. Points are a system of measurement designed for print, and although available for use, they indicate an absolute unit of measurement and they don't translate well to the screen.

Pixels, on the other hand, are the unit of measurement often used for screen-based graphics. Monitor resolution sizes are measured in pixel units. In an ideal world, designers could reliably use pixel sizes for their fonts because they are relative units and are designed to scale natively. Unfortunately web browsers such as Internet Explorer 6 and 7 do *not* resize pixel-based text if the user chooses to override the default settings.

Web browsers include a text resize option. This option is often found in the View menu. In some modern browsers, the text-resize option is located in a submenu called Zoom. *Many browsers also use the keyboard shortcut* Ctrl + + *(plus) and* Ctrl + − *(minus) to increase and decrease the text size, respectively. On the Mac OS, these shortcuts are* Command + + *[plus] (and* Command + − *[minus].)*

Using a combination of percent and the em measurement

Here you will create reliable font sizing using a combination of percent and ems. To get a sense of how these work, you will apply some CSS styling to a page of text for the SmoothieWorld site.

1   In your text editor, choose File > Open and navigate to the web06lessons folder. Locate the 06_sizing.html file and click OK. This file has four blocks of text: a heading 1 <h1>, a heading 2 <h2>, and two paragraphs <p>. The font-family styles are included from the last exercise as well. You will start by setting different properties for the body to see their effect.

2   Before making any changes, you should know what the page looks like in its default state. Preview the page in your default browser. Browsers need to set some default size for the text if there is no rule defined; in most cases 16 pixels is the value used for the body (in this case, the paragraphs are inheriting the body's value). Close your browser and return to your text editor.

Some browsers allow you to view the default font and font size and even to change it. In Firefox 3 and later, for example, this setting is found in the Content section of the preferences.

3   In the style rule for the body, type the following line (highlighted in red):

```
body {
    font-family:"Trebuchet MS", Tahoma, Arial, sans-serif;
    font-size:10px;
}
```

4 Save your file and then preview your page in the browser. Note that all your text is smaller. This is because the body style defines the baseline size for text on your page.

Remember that the HTML body tag contains all the rendered content on the page, so this style is simply targeting your entire page.

5 Return to your text editor and change the following value (highlighted in red) in your `font-size` property:

`font-size:`**`small;`**

6 Again, save your file and preview the page in your browser. All your text is slightly larger than the 10-pixel value you set in step 3. As noted above, the value `small` is an absolute-size unit of measurement called a *keyword*. Web browsers have pre-defined sizes assigned to keywords, and though keywords can be useful because they avoid the whole issue of using units, they often don't offer the level of control that designers prefer.

7 Return to the text editor and change the following value (highlighted in red) in your `font-size` property:

`font-size:`**`100%;`**

8 Save your file and preview the page in your browser. You might notice that there is no difference between this size and the size of the text at the beginning of the exercise (when no `font-size` was defined). This step explicitly defines the `font-size` for the body to be the same size as the browser-defined `font-size`.

You will have to take a small leap of faith here and realize that the technique you are learning addresses some particular resizing problems in two popular web browsers (IE6 and IE7). Taking care of these problems now will mean fewer problems in the future.

9 In the style rule for the paragraph, type the following line (highlighted in red):

```
p {
    font-size:1em;
}
```

The unit of measurement called an *em* is very similar to pixels in that it is designed to scale; the main difference is that ems are not tied to the monitor resolution while pixels are related to the monitor resolution. Ems may not be intuitive at first, but understanding how to use them will pay off in the future.

10 Save your file and then preview the file in your browser. Depending on which browser you are using, you will probably not see any changes in your page. This is because an em value of 1 is tied to the `font-size` of 100% that you defined in the body.

It may help to understand this relationship in an equation form: **1 em = 100% = 16 pixels**. Here, the paragraph size is the `1em` value, the `font-size` for the body is 100%, and the default `font-size` for the web browser is 16 pixels. Once you understand this relationship, you can begin to change the value of the em in order to enlarge or reduce the size of your text.

11 Close your browser and return to the text editor. In the rule for the paragraph, change the following value (highlighted in red):

```
font-size:0.875em;
```

12 Save your file and preview the page in your browser. Your paragraph text is now smaller. The reason for using the precise 0.875 value is because it is the font-size equivalent to 14 pixels.

If you're starting to think that web design is all about math, don't worry too much. It all gets easier from here. However, if you are interested in understanding the math more deeply, you multiply the em value (0.875) by the browser's default pixel value (16) to arrive at the 14-pixel number.

13 You will now size your headings using ems as well. For the `h1` property, add the following line (highlighted in red):

```
h1 {
    font-size:1.5em;
}
```

This scales the top heading to 1.5 times the size of your body text; in this case, it is the equivalent of 24 pixels. Save your file and preview the page in your browser to see the effect.

Your heading 1 element is set to 1.5em, the equivalent of 24 pixels.

Now the `h1` is approximately the same size as the `h2`, which isn't particularly logical, so you will reduce the size of the `h2` heading as well.

14 For the `h2` property, add the following line (highlighted in red):

```
h2 {
    font-size:1.25em;
}
```

This scales the top heading to 1.25 times the size of your body text, which is the equivalent of 20 pixels.

15 Save your file and preview it in the browser. You now have text proportioned as needed.

Remember that one of the main reasons why ems are used is to adjust for users who resize the text in their browser. You can simulate this by going into your browser and enlarging the text size. You can see that the text responds well to this enlarging and reducing. When you are finished, be sure to return the text size to the default setting. Most browsers have a command to allow you to do this.

The issue of browsers resizing text is a bit more complicated because some browsers use a zoom feature that increases or decreases magnification of the entire page. Zoom-enabled browsers may also have a text-only resize option.

There is another benefit of using ems, and this has to do with the scaling relationship between all elements that use ems.

16 In your body property, modify the following value (highlighted in red):

```
font-size:85%;
```

17 Save your file and preview your page. All your text is now smaller, even though you just changed one value! This is because of the linked relationship the em has to the body element. Some designers adjust this base size if, for example, a client wants larger or smaller text across the entire site. Rather than modifying all the individual properties, having one rule control multiple font-sizes makes it easy to do.

18 Return the `font-size` value to the original 100% value (highlighted in red):

```
font-size:100%;
```

Save your document.

Pixels-to-em conversion table

The following chart can help you make easy conversions from pixels to ems. Keep in mind that this chart is based on two constants: that your default browser text size is 16 pixels and that your body `font-size` is set to 100%.

Pixel font-size	Em equivalent
11	0.689
12	0.750
13	0.814
14	0.875
15	0.938
16	1.000
17	1.064
18	1.125
19	1.188
20	1.250
21	1.313
22	1.375
23	1.438
24	1.500
25	1.563
26	1.625
27	1.688
28	1.750

There are also free em-to-pixel calculators to help you with on-the-fly conversions:

- http://pxtoem.com/
- http://jameswhittaker.com/projects/apps/em-calculator-air-application/

Using margins to modify the space between your text

In this exercise, you will work with the CSS `margin` property in order to change the amount of space between your various text elements. Understanding how the `margin` property works and how to control it is key to understanding CSS, and in fact is the first step toward CSS layout. In order to better understand all the effects of using margins for text, you will first add the `margin` property to your body style.

1 In the body style, add the following line (highlighted in red):

```
body {
    font-family:"Trebuchet MS", Tahoma, Arial, sans-serif;
    font-size:100%;
    margin:0 20%;
}
```

This `margin` property sets the margins of the page in shortcut form. The 0 value is for the top and bottom margins. The 20% value is for the left and right margins.

2 Save your page and preview it in your browser. You can see that your text is centered in your browser window. Change the width of your browser window and you see the text reflow.

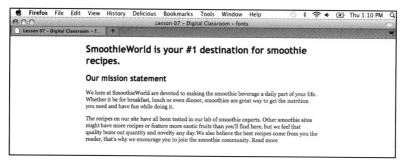

The result of changing the left and right margins of the body to 20%.

Return to your text editor.

You will now work further with margins in order to begin controlling the space between your elements. First, you will add temporary borders to your text elements in order to better understand how margins work.

3 In the style for your paragraph element, add the following line (highlighted in red):

```
p {
    font-family:Georgia, "Times New Roman", Times, serif;
    font-size:0.875em;
    border:thin red solid;
}
```

This is the CSS `border` property, which allows you to add borders around your elements. You will eventually use borders as decoration in your layout, but here they are being used to help you understand how elements such as headings and paragraphs interact with each other. You will now add this same code to your h1 and h2 elements.

4 Select the `border:thin red solid;` code from your paragraph rule and press Ctrl + C (PC) or Command + C (Mac) to copy the code.

5 Click inside the h1 style and press Ctrl + V (PC) or Command + V (Mac) to paste the code. Repeat this step for the h2 style.

6 Save your file and preview it in your browser. With the red borders applied, you can now see the space between the elements more clearly.

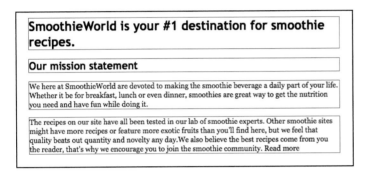

Applying borders to your elements helps you see the default margins more clearly.

This space between your paragraphs and headings is a result of the default margins as defined by your web browser. You have learned about browser defaults before in the `font-size` exercise, and this is very similar. HTML elements have default styles associated with them that include properties such pixel size, margins, bold styling, italic styling, and many others. You need to set specific rules to override the default styles for these properties. In this case, you will adjust the space between the heading 2 and the first paragraph.

7 Return to your text editor and add the following line to your h2 element (highlighted in red):

```
h2 {
    font-size:1.25em;
    border:thin red solid;
    margin-bottom:0em;
}
```

The `margin-bottom` property affects the margin spacing on the bottom of the h2 element only. However, this is not enough to affect the spacing between your heading and the paragraph. You also need to set the top margin of the paragraph.

8 Add the following code to your p element:

```
margin-top:0em;
```

9 Save your file and preview it in the browser.

> **SmoothieWorld is your #1 destination for smoothie recipes.**
>
> **Our mission statement**
>
> We here at SmoothieWorld are devoted to making the smoothie beverage a daily part of your life. Whether it be for breakfast, lunch or even dinner, smoothies are great way to get the nutrition you need and have fun while doing it.
>
> The recipes on our site have all been tested in our lab of smoothie experts. Other smoothie sites might have more recipes or feature more exotic fruits than you'll find here, but we feel that quality beats out quantity and novelty any day. We also believe the best recipes come from you the reader, that's why we encourage you to join the smoothie community. Read more

With the bottom margin of the heading and the top margin of the paragraph set to 0, the space between them has collapsed.

You can now see that the space between your heading 2 and the first paragraph has collapsed. To increase space between elements, you can increase margin values. For example, you will now increase the space between your paragraphs.

10 Add the following code to your paragraph (p) element:

```
margin-bottom:1.5em;
```

Remember that 1 em in this style sheet is equal to 16 pixels, so setting a value of 1.5 ems is the same as adding 24 pixels.

11 Save your file and preview it in the browser.

You can now see the space between your paragraphs increase. At this point, the borders around the elements have served their purpose; however, you don't want to lose them completely so you will comment them out. Commenting is a process that deactivates a style without removing the code.

12 Add the following code (highlighted in red) to the border rule in your paragraph element:

```
/*border:thin red solid;*/
```

The forward slash and the asterisk at the beginning and end of the code will disable this rule. However, the original code is always available in case you want to enable these borders again.

13 Repeat step 12 by adding the commenting code to the two other `border` properties in your `h1` and `h2` styles.

14 Save your file and view the page in your browser to see your page without any borders.

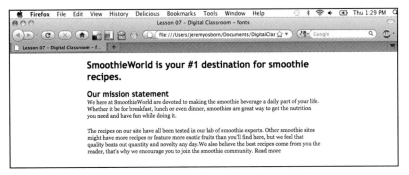

The final result of modifying your margins by deactivating the borders.

Setting paragraph `line-height`

To improve readability of your text, you can change `line-height`, which is the amount of space between lines. In the world of print design this is called *leading*, but the concept here is the same: changing the amount of space between sentences can affect the readability of your text. A `line-height` that is too small results in cramped text, while a `line-height` that is too high risks losing the reader's focus. However, you can't just set a universal `line-height` value and be done with it; `line-height` is connected to a number of factors including the amount of text and the width of the text block, as well as the color, size, and choice of font. In this exercise you will set the `line-height` of your current paragraphs.

1 Add the following code (highlighted in red) to your p element:

```
p {
    font-family:Georgia, "Times New Roman", Times, serif;
    font-size:0.875em;
    /*border:thin red solid;*/
    margin-top:0em;
    margin-bottom:1.5em;
    line-height:1.75em;
}
```

2 Save your file and preview it in your browser. You now have extra space between the lines in your paragraph.

SmoothieWorld is your #1 destination for smoothie recipes.

Our mission statement

We here at SmoothieWorld are devoted to making the smoothie beverage a daily part of your life. Whether it be for breakfast, lunch or even dinner, smoothies are great way to get the nutrition you need and have fun while doing it.

The recipes on our site have all been tested in our lab of smoothie experts. Other smoothie sites might have more recipes or feature more exotic fruits than you'll find here, but we feel that quality beats out quantity and novelty any day. We also believe the best recipes come from you the reader, that's why we encourage you to join the smoothie community. Read more

---

Increasing the line-height values will increase the amount of space between paragraph lines.

Line-height works on any multiple-line body of text. For example, if your heading 1 **SmoothieCentral is your #1 destination for smoothie recipes** is broken over multiple lines, you can set the line-height.

3 Add the following code to your h1 element:

```
line-height:1.5em;
```

4 Save your file and preview it in your browser.

Depending on your monitor resolution, you may need to narrow the width of your browser in order to force the heading to break. The type in the heading is much larger than the paragraph, so it wouldn't do as well with the same line-height value.

You can feel free to override the browser defaults in order to control the look of your page.

Transforming text with CSS

As discussed earlier, the lack of choices when it comes type on the web is a bit constraining; however, you have other options. There are a number of CSS properties that allow you to control the appearance of your text in visually interesting ways. In this exercise you will work with several styling techniques to create unique headings for your page, including font-weight, text-transform, and letter-spacing.

The first setting you will modify is the font-weight for your main heading in order to decrease the thickness of the characters.

1   Add the following code (highlighted in red) to your h1 element:

```
h1 {
    /*border:thin red solid;*/
    line-height:1.5em;
    font-size:1.5em;
    font-weight:normal;
}
```

2   Save your file and preview the page in your browser.

By setting the font-weight to normal, you have decreased the thickness of the heading. The default browser styling for a heading 1 is actually bold, so you are essentially resetting this bold style to normal. The default browser styling for all headings is bold, and you can see this by comparing the styles of your heading 1 to your heading 2. The heading 2 has thicker letterforms and even though it is smaller in size, it appears more dominant on the screen.

There are additional values for the font-weight property. Here you'll lighten the value for the heading 2 and then add a new text-transform property.

3   Add the following code to your h2 element:

```
font-weight:lighter;
text-transform:uppercase;
```

The value *lighter* for the font-weight reduces the thickness of the letterforms further, and the value for text-transform converts your text to uppercase.

4   Save your file and preview the page in your browser.

Your heading is now in uppercase. This is a good example of how CSS controls style. The HTML code shows that the source text is still lowercase; however, the display of the characters is controlled by the CSS.

5   Return to your text editor and add the following code to the same h2 style:

```
letter-spacing:0.2em;
```

Letter-spacing controls the amount of space between characters. In print design this is called *kerning* and *tracking*. Save your page and preview the page in your browser. By increasing letter-spacing, you can add a bit more space around the letters in condensed headlines. However, you should be careful about adding too much letter-spacing, as it can make headlines harder to read.

It is even possible to set negative values for most of these CSS properties (letter-spacing: -0.4em, for example), although you will not be doing this as often. Experiment with different combinations of fonts and styles, and you might be surprised with what you can come up with.

Often times, experimenting with styles such as `text-transform` and `letter-spacing` will require you to return to your initial `font-size`. In your heading 2, for example, using all capital letters makes the heading look bigger, so you will reduce the size a bit.

6 Modify the `font-size` value (highlighted in red) of your h2 style as follows:

`font-size:`**`1.125em;`**

7 Save and close your file.

Working with HTML lists

Lists are found on many web pages and it is important that you learn how to control their appearance. Examples of where you might find lists include recipes, frequently asked questions, and navigation menus. In this exercise you will learn the three categories of lists and how to control their styles. The three categories are *unordered lists, ordered lists,* and *definition lists.*

Unordered lists are also called bulleted lists because the default style adds a bullet to the left of each item in the list. Ordered lists are also called numbered lists because the default style adds a number to the left of each item in the list. Definition lists have two default styles: a bold style for a definition term and an indented style for the definition description.

1 In your text editor, choose File > Open and navigate to the web06lessons folder. Locate the 06lists.html file and click OK. This file has the styled text from the previous exercise, as well as three new paragraphs that you will be converting to lists.

Before starting on the exercise, note a few changes that are made to the new <h3> style. In this example, you want all the attributes of the h2 without having to write them again, so a comma and the code h3 are added to the h2 selector. However, because the h3 element needs to be smaller, a new `font-size` property of `0.875em` is set. To adjust the `letter-spacing`, this property is set to `0.1em`. Because these are the only two properties for h3, they override the properties for h2.

2   Preview the page in your browser to see the default paragraph styling. Keep this formatting in mind as you begin converting the paragraphs to lists. Close your browser and return to your text editor.

SmoothieWorld is your #1 destination for smoothie recipes.

OUR MISSION STATEMENT
We here at SmoothieWorld are devoted to making the smoothie beverage a daily part of your life. Whether it be for breakfast, lunch or even dinner, smoothies are great way to get the nutrition you need and have fun while doing it.

The recipes on our site have all been tested in our lab of smoothie experts. Other smoothie sites might have more recipes or feature more exotic fruits than you'll find here, but we feel that quality beats out quantity and novelty any day. We also believe the best recipes come from you the reader, that's why we encourage you to join the smoothie community. Read more

RECIPE OF THE DAY: HONEYDEW MELON
3 cups Honeydew Melon (seeded & chopped) 2 tsp Lime Juice 1 cup Vanilla Nonfat Yogurt 1 cup Ice Cubes

Take a blender, add honeydew melon and watermelon; blend until it smoothens. Mix yogurt, ice and limejuice and blend it again. Transfer it into tall glasses and drink it immediately.

Preparation time 10 Minutes Number of servings (12 oz) 2 Calories per serving 250. 295 if 1 tbs sugar added 315 if 1 tbs honey added

---

You will convert the last three paragraphs to lists.

3   In the first paragraph in the list of ingredients, change the opening `<p>` and closing `</p>` paragraph tags to an opening `<ul>` and closing `</ul>` to change this element to an unordered list.

You now need to separate the ingredients into list items. The `<ul>` tag is rarely used by itself as the whole purpose of lists is to have separate items.

4   Add an opening `<li>` tag at the beginning of the first line and a closing `</li>` tag (both highlighted in red) at the end:

```
<ul>
    <li>3 cups Honeydew Melon (seeded & chopped) </li>
    2 tsp Lime Juice
    1 cup Vanilla Yogurt
    1 cup Ice Cubes
    <em>Optional:</em> 1 tbl Honey or Sugar
</ul>
```

Preview this page in your browser and note the bullet point on the first line. Close your browser.

5 Repeat step 4, and add the list tags to the next three ingredients. Each list item will have its own bullet point.

Now you'll convert the next paragraph, which describes the steps for making the smoothie, into an ordered list.

6 In the next paragraph, change the opening `<p>` and closing `</p>` paragraph tags to an opening `<ol>` and closing `</ol>` to change this element to an ordered list. Then, as in steps 4 and 5, add `<li>` tags (highlighted in red) to create three list items:

```
<ol>
    <li>Add honeydew melon cubes to blender; blend until smooth.</li>
    <li>Add yogurt, ice and lime juice and blend it again.</li>
    <li>Transfer into tall glasses and garnish with melon slice.</li>
</ol>
```

7 Save your file and then preview it in the browser. The ordered list now displays numbers for each list item.

RECIPE OF THE DAY: HONEYDEW MELON

- 3 cups Honeydew Melon (seeded & chopped)
- 2 tsp Lime Juice
- 1 cup Vanilla Nonfat Yogurt
- 1 cup Ice Cubes

1. Take a blender, add honeydew melon and watermelon; blend until it smoothens.
2. Mix yogurt, ice and limejuice and blend it again.
3. Transfer it into tall glasses and drink it immediately

Preparation time 10 Minutes Number of servings (12 oz) 2 Calories per serving 250. 295 if 1 tbs sugar added 315 if 1 tbs honey added

The second paragraph has been converted to an ordered (or numbered) list.

Close the browser and return to your text editor.

One of the advantages of ordered lists is that the numbers are rendered in the browser. This allows you to add or remove list items in your HTML and not have to worry about keeping track of the numbers.

8 Add the following line between list items 2 and 3:

```
<li> Sample your smoothie and add honey or sugar if needed. Blend
again.</li>
```

Save the file and preview it in your browser. Note that the steps have automatically been renumbered. Close your browser and return to your text editor. Now you'll convert the last paragraph into a definition list.

9 In the last paragraph, change the opening <p> and closing </p> paragraph tags to an opening <dl> and closing </dl> to change this element to a definition list.

Definition lists are used less often than ordered and unordered lists. One way to think of them is to visualize a listing in a dictionary. A dictionary is just a big list of words; however, for any given word there may be a number of different definitions. A definition list has two types of list items: the definition term <dt> and the definition description <dd>.

10 Add the following code (highlighted in red) to separate this list into terms and descriptions:

```
<dl>
    <dt>Preparation time</dt>
    <dd>10 Minutes</dd>
    <dt>Number of servings (12 oz)</dt>
    <dd>2</dd>
    <dt>Calories per serving</dt>
    <dd>250</dd>
    <dd>295 if 1 tbs sugar added</dd>
    <dd>315 if 1 tbs honey added</dd>
</dl>
```

Save the file and preview it in your browser. The definition terms act as a type of a heading with the definition description indented below. Note that you may have multiple descriptions, as you can see in the last definition term for Calories.

Styling HTML lists

You can easily modify the styling for lists with CSS. The indentation and spacing of a list (as well as the list items) are controlled by margins and padding. There are also a few CSS properties that are unique to lists; for example, later in this exercise, you will learn how to customize the bullet appearance in the unordered list. First, however, it's important to understand the default styles of both the parent list and the list items. A specific goal of this exercise is to make you aware of the differences between margins and padding; these two properties are often confused by beginners and your future as a web designer will be much happier if you avoid this confusion!

One thing you may have noticed is that all your lists are bigger than your paragraphs and they also have a different font family. This is because you have not set any rules for them yet, so they are inheriting their style from the body. As you go through styling each list, you will add font-size and other properties as needed.

1 Type the following code to add a `font-size` as well as a new background color to the unordered list style:

```
ul {
    font-size:0.875em;
    background-color:#E5DAB3;
}
```

2 Save the file and preview it in your browser. You can see that the background color defines the area of the unordered list. Although you can use background colors to make your lists more attractive, here you are using a background color to illustrate how lists work. Close your browser. You will now style the list items.

RECIPE OF THE DAY: HONEYDEW MELON

- 3 cups Honeydew Melon (seeded & chopped)
- 2 tsp Lime Juice
- 1 cup Vanilla Nonfat Yogurt
- 1 cup Ice Cubes

Using a `background-color` *helps you see the boundaries of the* `ul` *element.*

3 Add this code to the empty list item style:

```
li {
    background-color:#AA6C7E;
}
```

Save the file and preview it in your browser.

You can see that the background color of the list items overrides the color of the unordered list, but it's not a complete overlap; the list item `background-color` stops at the bullet points (and at the numbers in the ordered list). Equally important is the fact that both the unordered list and the ordered list use `<li>` tags so they are all styled equally. If you want to specifically change the color of the list items in the unordered list, you must target them with a more specific rule.

4 Add this entire section of code to create a specific rule for list items in an unordered list only:

```
ul li {
    background-color:#ABC8A5;
}
```

This rule is known as a *descendant selector* because the list item is a descendant of the unordered list in your HTML. Because this rule is more specific, the rules of CSS state that it will override the more general rule for the `<li>` element.

5 Save the file and preview it in your browser. The background color for the list items in the unordered list is green because of that `ul li` rule, while the background color for the ordered list is purple based on the `li` rule.

RECIPE OF THE DAY:HONEYDEW MELON

- 3 cups Honeydew Melon (seeded & chopped)
- 2 tsp Lime Juice
- 1 cup Vanilla Nonfat Yogurt
- 1 cup Ice Cubes

1. Take a blender, add honeydew melon and watermelon; blend until it smoothens.
2. Mix yogurt, ice and limejuice and blend it again.
3. Transfer it into tall glasses and drink it immediately

Only the list items in your unordered list are colored green.

6 Close your browser and return to your text editor. You'll now focus on controlling the spacing of your lists. However, first you'll correct the fact that your ordered list is bigger than your unordered list by adding a `font-size` property.

7 Add the following code to make the ordered list the same size:

```
ol {
    font-size:0.875em;
}
```

In order to add space between the unordered list and the ordered list, you can add a bottom margin (highlighted below in red) to the unordered list:

```
ul {
    font-size:0.875em;
    background-color:#E5DAB3;
    margin-bottom:2em;
}
```

This works much like the earlier exercises where you controlled the space between your headings and paragraph. However, it is also important that you understand the role of padding when it comes to lists.

8 Add the following code to your `ul` style:

`padding-left:0em;`

Save the file and preview the page in your browser.

RECIPE OF THE DAY:HONEYDEW MELON

- 3 cups Honeydew Melon (seeded & chopped)
- 2 tsp Lime Juice
- 1 cup Vanilla Nonfat Yogurt
- 1 cup Ice Cubes

The unordered list with a left padding of 0 places the bullet points outside the box by default.

By zeroing-out the left padding, you collapse the default padding, all the list items shift to the left, and the bullet points are now hanging outside the unordered list! Close the browser and return to your text editor. Using a CSS rule, you can force the bullet points to be inside the unordered list.

9 Add the following code to your ul style:

`list-style-position:inside;`

This causes the bullets to be nested within the unordered list.

10 The spacing of lists is also determined by the margins and padding of the individual list items. Here you will modify both properties of the unordered list in order to see the difference. First you will add a top margin value (highlighted in red):

```
ul li {
    background-color:#ABC8A5;
    margin-top:1em;
}
```

Save the file and preview it in your browser. `Margin-top` adds 1 em of space to the top of each list item. Because the margin value adds space on the outside of an element, you see the `background-color` of the unordered list.

Now you'll add padding to the ordered list.

12 Add the following code:

```
ol li {
    padding-top:10px;
}
```

13 Save the file and preview it in your browser.

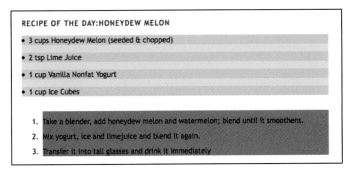

RECIPE OF THE DAY:HONEYDEW MELON

- 3 cups Honeydew Melon (seeded & chopped)
- 2 tsp Lime Juice
- 1 cup Vanilla Nonfat Yogurt
- 1 cup Ice Cubes

1. Take a blender, add honeydew melon and watermelon; blend until it smoothens.
2. Mix yogurt, ice and limejuice and blend it again.
3. Transfer it into tall glasses and drink it immediately

The list items in the first list are spaced using margins, while the list items in the second list are spaced using padding.

`Padding-top` adds 1 em of space to the top of each list item, but because padding adds space to the inside of an element, you do not see the background color.

14 Return to your text editor and comment out all three of your background color properties. For a reminder of how to do this, you can revisit step 12 of the margins exercise on page 126.

15 Save the file and preview it in your browser.

Notice that without the background colors it would be impossible to know that the spacing of the first list used margins and the spacing of the second list used padding. Using margins and padding indiscriminately can lead to problems, especially as your lists become more complicated.

In this lesson you learned the different ways you can set the `font-size` of your text with an emphasis on using the em unit of measurement. You also learned how to control the appearance of your text with CSS properties including `margins`, `padding`, `line-height`, `text-transform`, `letter-spacing`, and `font-weight`. Finally, you learned the three types of HTML lists and how to style them.

This lesson involved the most coding you have done up to this point. If you would like to compare your work with a finished version, open the final page, named 06_final.html, which is located in your web06lessons folder.

Self study

To practice styling lists, create new style rules for the definition list. Here are some ideas to help you get started:

1 Make the entire definition list smaller than the other two lists and create an italic style for the definition definitions `<dd>`.

2 Experiment with some of the other properties you learned in this lesson, such as `text-transform`, `letter-spacing`, and so on.

3 Remember that with definition lists you have an extra item to work with (the `<dt>` element).

Review

Questions

1 What is the em measurement when referring to `font-size`? What are its advantages?

2 Jennifer has defined the paragraph rule in her CSS the following way:

```
p {
    font-family:Baskerville;
}
```

Is this the best way for her to define her paragraph style? Explain your answer.

3 What is the best way to increase or decrease space between two text blocks (for example, the space between a heading and a paragraph)?

Answers

1 The em as it applies to `font-size` in CSS is a relative unit of measurement. A unit of 1 em is equivalent to the default `font-size` of the web browser (traditionally 16 pixels). Because em units are relative, they scale well when resized in a browser. They also allow the designer to link elements such as paragraphs and headings to a specific value in the body. This allows for easy resizing of text if needed.

2 This is not the best way for Jennifer to define her paragraph style. Because fonts defined in a style sheet only appear on the user's page if they have the font installed on their system, it is best to use a font-stack. A font-stack lists two or more fonts in the preferred order of display (based on their availability on the user's system). Furthermore, this font-stack should include fonts that are generally accepted as being on most systems.

3 The best way to increase or decrease space between two text blocks is to use `margins`, `padding`, or some combination of the two. All CSS elements are based on a box model, and the space *outside* of the element is controlled by an invisible margin on all four sides. The space *inside* the element is controlled by invisible padding. In the case of a paragraph that is below a heading, you would only need to set the top or bottom values, not the right or left values.

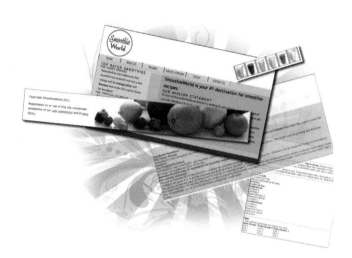

What you'll learn in this lesson:

• Understanding CSS reset files

• An overview of CSS layout options

• How to use margins and padding to add space to your page

• Working with the `float` and `clear` properties

Introduction to CSS Layout

In this lesson, you will learn to control the appearance of text on your web pages using CSS style.

Starting up

You will work with several files from the web07lessons folder in this lesson. Make sure you have loaded the weblessons folder onto your hard-drive from *www.digitalclassroombooks.com/webdesign*. See "Loading lesson files" in the Starting Up section of this book.

See Lesson 7 in action!

Use the accompanying video to gain a better understanding of how to use some of the features shown in this lesson. You can find the video tutorial for this lesson at www.digitalclassroombooks.com using the URL provided when you registered your book.

The examples in this lesson use the TextWrangler text editor to create the HTML markup, but you can use any of the text editors covered in Lesson 3.

Working with a CSS reset file

Before you start building your page layout, you will learn to use a CSS reset file. In Lesson 4, you learned that virtually all HTML elements (such as paragraphs and headings) have default styles rendered by the browser. For example, the heading 1 default style has top and bottom margins of 10 pixels. If you want to style a heading so there is no margin, you must explicitly set the style rules to zero.

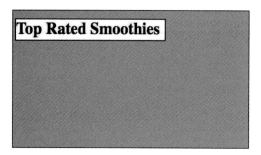 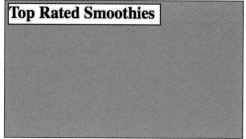

On the left is a heading 1 with default margins of 10 pixels. On the right is a heading 1 with the margins set to zero.

The CSS rule for setting the margins to zero is as follows:

```
h1{
    margin-top:0px;
    margin-bottom:0px;
}
```

All HTML elements have default margins; unfortunately, web browsers use their own rules for rendering content, and interpret the appearance of these margins differently. For example, the 10-pixel margin in browser A might be rendered as 15 pixels in browser B. These differences can introduce inconsistencies in your page layouts. Fortunately, you can use the CSS reset file to remove the default styles from the most commonly used HTML elements. With the CSS styles reset, you have a reliable and consistent foundation on which to base your new styles. To get a better sense of how styles work, open a page that contains a number of default styles and link the CSS reset style sheet to this page.

1 In your text editor, choose File > Open. In the dialog box that appears, navigate to the web07lessons folder, choose the 07_reset.html file, and click Open.

This file has a number of generic HTML elements, such as headings, paragraphs, lists, and forms; it has no CSS styles.

2 Preview the page in your web browser and notice the space between the headings as well as the appearance of the lists and the form. Add a link to your CSS reset style sheet to see how this affects the appearance of these elements. Close your web browser and return to your text editor.

3 Add the following line of code (highlighted in red) to attach the reset.css style sheet located in the web07lessons folder:

```
<head>
    <meta charset="utf-8" />
    <title>Digital Classroom Lesson 07 CSS Reset</title>
    <link href="reset.css" rel="stylesheet" type="text/css">
</head>
```

Save the file and preview it in your browser.

| Heading 1 |
| Heading 2 |
| Heading 3 |
| Heading 4 |
| Heading 5 |
| Heading 6 |

Lorem ipsum dolor sit amet, test link adipiscing elit. **This is strong.** Nullam dignissim conv
Nunc iaculis suscipit dui. Nam sit amet sem. Aliquam libero nisi, imperdiet at, tincidunt nec
eget sapien fringilla nonummy. Mauris a ante. Suspendisse quam sem, This is small conseqc
quis tellus.
HTML and CSS are our tools. Mauris a ante. Suspendisse quam sem, consequat at, commoc
Praesent mattis, massa quis luctus fermentum, turpis mi volutpat justo, eu volutpat enim dia

List Types
Definition List
Definition List Title
This is a definition list division.
Definition
Another dd tag>
Ordered List
List Item 1
List Item 2
Nested list item A
Nested list item B
List Item 3
Unordered List
List Item 1
List Item 2
Nested list item A
Nested list item B
List Item 3

Table
  The caption tag defines the caption of a table
Table Header 1Table Header 2Table Header 3
Cell 1   Cell 2   Cell 3
Cell 1   Cell 2   Cell 3
Cell 1   Cell 2   Cell 3

A page of common HTML elements that have been reset.

Many of the elements on your page have had the margins and padding set to zero. As a result, all the space between them has collapsed. There are a number of other reset styles; for example, your list-styles are set to "none," which removes the default bullet points from unordered lists and the numbers from ordered lists. Close your browser and return to your text editor.

4 Choose File > Open. In the dialog box that appears, select the reset.css file and click Open. Take a few moments to look through the file.

This group of rules removes the default margins, padding, and borders from most of your HTML elements.

You will not change this style sheet, but will attach it to your pages. Remember that reset style sheets are optional. They help standardize your layout across browsers, and some designers also add their most frequently used styles to their reset style sheets.

Extending the reset style sheet

Eric Meyer was the first designer to develop reset style sheets, which he then released into the public domain. You will use his style rules in this exercise. For more information on the reset technique, visit *http://meyerweb.com/eric/thoughts/2007/04/18/reset-reasoning/*.

Many designers customize this reset style sheet to fit their needs. For example, if the most common font-family you use is Verdana, you can add this rule to your body style. If you like more space between the lines in your paragraphs, you can set a standard line-height value that best works for you. The point is to have a consistent set of rules that you can use to quickly start up a project.

Using CSS reset style sheets has some potential disadvantages, especially for beginners: you must constantly remember that the reset style sheet is there and be aware of how it affects the appearance of different elements in your site. If you are using the reset style sheet across the entire site, you might be surprised by some of its effects, especially when using elements you are not familiar with. For example, a CSS reset file strips out the margins and padding for most form elements, and when you start working with forms for the first time, you might be confused as to why your buttons, form fields, and other elements appear the way they do.

A brief history of layout techniques on the web

Although you will be learning how to build your page layout using CSS styles, you should note that this was not always a standard practice. As web design developed in the mid-1990s, the only method available for sophisticated page layout, such as adding multiple columns to a page, was to use the HTML `<table>` tag. The HTML table was originally designed to present data in a logical format, using rows, columns, and cells.

Designers adopted this table element and used it as the foundation for their page structure. At the time, this technique made perfect sense: tables were the only tool available to create the sort of designs required at the time.

Designers often used techniques such as nesting tables. For example, the code for a standard two-column page might start with a table consisting of three rows and two columns.

A three-row and two-column table.

However, because the first row would become a header section, the column being defined would be in the way. The HTML `<colspan>` tag allowed the designer to merge the two cells.

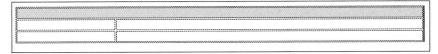

A table with two merged cells in the first row.

In this merged first row, a designer might want an independent three-column section for a logo and other elements, such as navigation or a user login. To add this section, the designer would add a new table (with three columns) into the top row.

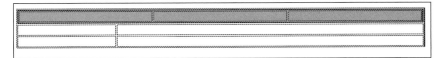

Nesting a new three-column table into the top row of the original table.

To give this table structure, the designer might set the original table to a fixed width and height. Assume the designer also wanted a thin, black border around the entire layout. However, the border property for HTML tables is very basic and does not allow the addition of colors. One common solution was to insert the existing table into another table, which would consist of a single cell with a background color of black. By modifying the padding and background color and merging additional cells, the designer was able to create a table-based layout with some basic styling.

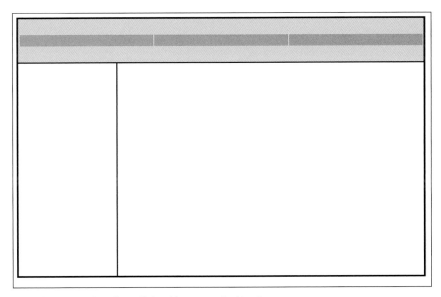

A typical empty "template" for a table-based layout as rendered in a browser.

This review of web layout is relevant today because a vast number of websites were built and continue to be built using the table method. CSS has been replacing the use of tables for page layout, but the process is a slow, gradual one. Table layouts have an advantage of being reverse-compatible with older browsers; however, this advantage has decreased as people update to newer browsers.

CSS layouts were also not well supported (if at all) in early web browsers, and so for web designers, there was no real incentive to discard table layout techniques for CSS layout. However, one of the disadvantages of table-based layouts was the amount and type of code required to build a page. The layout described in the previous paragraphs would have required code similar to the following:

```
<table width="799" border="0" cellspacing="1" cellpadding="1">
    <tr>
        <td bgcolor="#000000">
        <table width="800" height="485" border="0">
            <tr>
            <td height="81" colspan="2" bgcolor="#CCCCCC">
            <table width="100%" border="0">
                <tr>
                    <td bgcolor="#FF9966"> </td>
                    <td bgcolor="#FF9966"> </td>
                    <td bgcolor="#FF9966"> </td>
                </tr>
            </table>
            </td>
            </tr>
        <tr>
            <td width="191" bgcolor="#FFFFFF"> </td>
            <td width="599" bgcolor="#FFFFFF"> </td>
        </tr>
            </table>
            </td>
        </tr>
    </table>
```

This is a relatively simple layout with no content or navigation. However, defining the relationship between all the various elements is very confusing, and it requires multiple lines of code.

If you want to look at this code in your text editor, you can find it in the 07_table.html file within the web07lessons folder.

Remember that one of the main goals of CSS was to separate the style from the structure of HTML. In the table code above, note that values for width and height, as well as the background color and a few other values, are embedded within the HTML. Although this practice was unavoidable before CSS, you can now set these values using CSS.

The HTML table element is slowly returning to its original function of presenting data, and not being used for layout. You might still find examples of these layouts on the web, but you will not learn to build them in this book. Instead, you will learn the basics of layout using CSS.

An overview of page layout options

Before building a page layout, there are a few decisions you should make. The first is the width of the layout. There are two main categories of layout widths: *fixed-width layouts* and *flexible layouts*. Fixed-width layouts are much more common: in a fixed-width layout, all page elements are nested within a container that has an explicit width (in this example, you will use 960 pixels, but the unit of measurement is often in ems as well). A fixed-width layout is useful for the designer because it offers a way to reliably position the various layout elements (such as headers, sidebars, and footers). It also provides a reliable structure for elements, such as the width of a paragraph on a page or the placement of images.

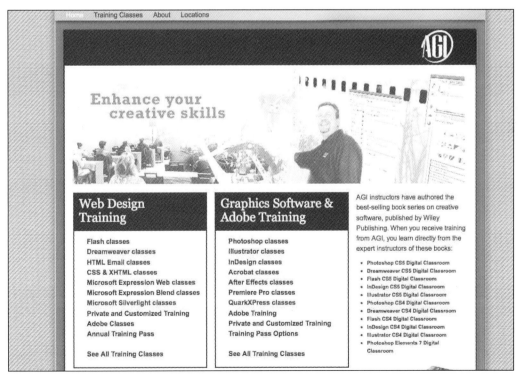

Fixed-width layouts have explicit widths and have a defined space on a web page.

Flexible layouts are so named because they are designed to adapt to the width of the browser window. This style of layout is useful when users have different monitor resolutions, making it impossible to build a fixed-width layout that looks the same on every screen. A properly designed flexible layout can automatically adjust to fit the user's browser window.

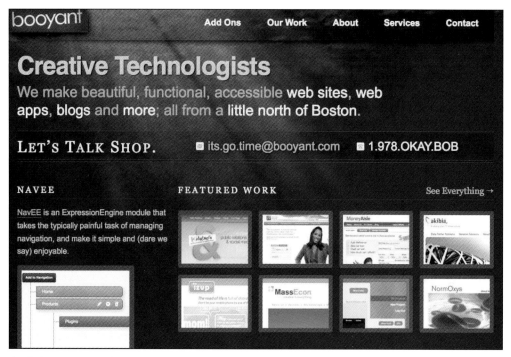

Flexible layouts readjust as the browser window changes size.

You could argue that flexible layouts are more appropriate for the web. It is, after all, not print: both text and images on a web page can reflow. Now that mobile devices make up a substantial proportion of web browsers, a flexible layout might be better suited to these new interfaces than a fixed-width layout.

Flexible-width layouts are much more difficult to build. There are more decisions for the designer to make and more options to consider. For this reason, you will learn how to create a fixed-width layout in this lesson.

Understanding <div>s: creating a two-column fixed-width CSS layout

In this exercise, you will build a fixed-width two-column layout. To begin, you will work with a basic page that has been set up for you. This page uses a series of HTML `div` elements as the basic structure. Think of the `<div>` element as a container into which you'll place logically related elements on a page. Opening and closing `<div>` tags are often placed around other elements on a page, thereby nesting the related items inside the container. You may have multiple `<div>` elements on a page and they are often used to create the layout structure of a page. A `<div>` element often has either a CSS class or ID attribute, which are used to style the container. By using `<div>` elements you can make it easier for others to identify the sections of your pages, and it can make it easier to control and style a section of a page. Here you will combine the `div` element with CSS IDs.

1   In your text editor, choose File > Open. In the dialog box that appears, navigate to the web07lessons folder. Select the 07_layoutstart.html file and click OK.

2   Choose File > Save As and name this file 07_layoutwork.html. This preserves the original structure of the page for you. This page has a series of HTML `div` elements with some placeholder content. Analyze and style this page to understand how it was set up. The HTML page contains several comments to guide you through the file.

The structure of the page was established for you; however, you will go through each section to get an understanding of how it works. The first step is to understand the function of the HTML `<div>` tag and its central role in CSS layout.

3   In your HTML, locate the line `<div id="wrap">`. This is the beginning of a section of your page that will nest all your other page elements. By itself, the HTML `<div>` tag does nothing, which makes the tag unique, since all the other HTML elements, such as paragraphs (`<p>`) and lists (`<ul>`, `<li>`, `<dl>`), have some effect on their content.

The `<div>` tag as well as paragraphs and lists, among others is a block-level element. Block-level elements usually start new lines of text when they are used. The `div` tag is often paired with either a CSS class or a CSS ID. Once you pair the CSS class or ID with a `div` tag, you can begin to add rules to control its appearance. Before doing this, you should take a look at the page before you style it.

4   Preview the page in your browser. The reset.css file you examined earlier is causing the elements on your page to be collapsed.

Top Rated Smoothies
The Funky Orange
Submitted by user iosborn22, this smoothie has recieved over 200 5 star ratings and its **orange juice** and **banana** base make this a great choice for breakfast!
The Tropical KickBack
Submitted by user smoothj282, this smoothie combines the exotic ingredients passionfruit and mango. The result is an invgorating and delicious beverage that is great any time of the day.
SmoothieWorld is your #1 destination for smoothie recipes.
Our mission statement
We here at SmoothieWorld are devoted to making the smoothie beverage a daily part of your life. Whether it be for breakfast, lunch or even dinner, smoothies are great way to get the nutrition you need and have fun while doing it.
The recipes on our site have all been tested in our lab of smoothie experts. Other smoothie sites might have more recipes or feature more exotic fruits than you'll find here, but we feel that quality beats out quantity and novelty any day. We also believe the best recipes come from you the reader, that's why we encourage you to join our smoothie community. Learn more
Footer

This page has a number of pre-built `div` sections and the HTML elements have been reset.

To understand `div` tags, you will style the `wrap` div to begin your fixed-width layout. Close your browser and return to your text editor.

5 Locate the `<style>` tag that was added to your document. Add a style rule (highlighted in read) for the ID named wrap. The following code shows how

```
<style type="text/css">
    #wrap {
            background-color:#E0B3B9;
    }
</style>
```

Save the file and then preview it in your browser. The `wrap` div encompasses all the other content on the page, as shown by the background color you added. Currently, this div stretches from one side of the browser to the other. This is a very basic flexible-width layout. Resize your browser window and notice how the text reflows. You will now define the width of the `wrap` div.

6 Return to your text editor and add the following two lines of code (highlighted in red) to your `#wrap` style.

```
#wrap {
    background-color:#E0B3B9;
    width:960px;
    border:thin solid black;
}
```

Save the page and preview it in your browser. The `wrap` div now occupies 960 pixels of space on your page.

Top Rated Smoothies
The Funky Orange
Submitted by user iosborn22, this smoothie has recieved over 200 5 star ratings and its **orange juice** and **banana** base make this a great choice for breakfast!
The Tropical KickBack
Submitted by user smoothj282, this smoothie combines the exotic ingredients passionfruit and mango. The result is an invgorating and delicious beverage that is great any time of the day.
SmoothieWorld is your #1 destination for smoothie recipes.
Our mission statement
We here at SmoothieWorld are devoted to making the smoothie beverage a daily part of your life. Whether it be for breakfast, lunch or even dinner, smoothies are great way to get the nutrition you need and have fun while doing it.
The recipes on our site have all been tested in our lab of smoothie experts. Other smoothie sites might have more recipes or feature more exotic fruits than you'll find here, but we feel that quality beats out quantity and novelty any day. We also believe the best recipes come from you the reader, that's why we encourage you to join our smoothie community. Learn more
Footer

Your `wrap` *div is now 960 pixels wide and has a thin, black border.*

The border is there to help illustrate the boundaries of the `wrap` div. Resize your browser window again. The text no longer reflows, and if your browser window is narrower than 960 pixels, your content is cropped. When the browser window is wider than 960 pixels, the box defined by the `wrap` div is aligned to the left. There is a simple way to position this div so it will always be centered in the browser window.

7   Return to your text editor and add the following line of code (highlighted in red).

```
#wrap {
    background-color:#E0B3B9;
    width:960px;
    border:thin solid black;
    margin:0 auto;
}
```

This is a margin shorthand rule; the value '0' defines the top and bottom margins of the `wrap` div, and the value `auto` defines the left and right margins. The auto value automatically calculates equal amounts of margin on both sides of the `wrap` div. As a result, the box is always centered.

Save the file and then preview it in your browser to see how the margin shorthand rule works. Close your browser and return to your text editor. You will work with the other `div` elements, but you must first apply a basic style to the header.

8   In your HTML, insert an image into the `masthead` div—in this case, the site's logo. To begin, allow the height of the image to set the height of the `header` div by adding the following code (highlighted in red) to link to the logo image located in the web07lessons folder.

```
<div id="masthead">
    <img src="images/smoothieworld_logo.png" width="200" height="150"
        alt="smoothieworld_logo" />
</div>
```

The `div` tag has no style, even though the height of the `header` div is controlled by the image. This is why you can see the color of the wrapper, for example. However, if you set the background color of the header, it will be visible.

9   Below your rules for #wrap, add the following rule for the `masthead` div:

```
#masthead {
    background-color:#FFF;
}
```

Save the file and preview it in your browser. The entire `masthead` div now has a white background color, and this overrides the background color of the `wrap` div.

Your `masthead` *section now has a logo and a background color.*

10 The navigation section will require some more advanced work later in this lesson. For now, you will set a few basic style rules in order to define this section on the page. Add the following rules below your rules for `#masthead`:

```
#mainnav {
    background-color:#C2C895;
    height:40px;
}
```

Save your page and preview it in the browser.

Your `mainnav` *section with a background color and defined height.*

You have now reached the inner wrap section, which contains the sidebar and the main content sections. You will learn to create columns by positioning them with divs. The current CSS specification does not have a column element; "columns" are styled divs that are often taller than they are wide. To understand how columns are made, you need to understand the concept of the CSS `float` property.

Understanding the CSS `float` property

The `float` property in CSS allows text to wrap around an image. This style was borrowed from print design, where the effect is called text wrap or runaround. CSS achieves this effect by allowing elements following a floated element in the HTML markup to surround the element, effectively changing their position. This behavior also makes it possible to create columns on a page.

In the left image below, there is an inline graphic nested inside a paragraph. This is the default behavior of the graphic, as there is no `float` property. In the right image, nothing changes except that the rule `float:right` has been applied to the graphic. The graphic shifts as far to the right as posssible and the text wraps around the left side automatically.

An image in the default flow of HTML (left). The same image floated to the right (right).

You can also have a float value of `left`. In the above example, this would place the graphic at the left-most margin and wrap the text on the right.

The only values possible for a float are `left`, `right`, or `none`. You cannot center an object using the `float` property.

If you have multiple floated elements within the same element, they align beside each other. This behavior is often used for common web page features such as horizontal menus or image galleries.

Understanding how multiple floated elements interact with each other is crucial to using them effectively. Consider the following example: there are six images inside a div that is 360 pixels wide. Each image is 50 pixels wide, and also has 10 pixels of margin space (5 on the left and 5 on the right). By adding the values, you can see that 6 × 50 is 300 pixels for the images and 6 × 10 is 60 pixels of margin. Consequently, the images plus the margin fit inside the div, with a total width of 360 pixels.

If you have defined an explicit width for the container, adding another image causes the new image to break to the next row.

This behavior might work well for a thumbnail image gallery, but not for navigation.

You will learn more about using floats in the next exercise when you build a two-column layout.

Creating columns with the `float` property

You will apply the `float` property to the `sidebar` and `main` content divs to see how they are affected.

1   Add the following selector and style rules (highlighted in red) below the `#mainnav` rule:

```
#sidebar {
    float:left;
    width:300px;
    background-color:#CCC;
}
```

Save the page and preview it in your browser. The page has become "broken"; however, you must learn to recognize the reasons behind a "broken" page such as this one, because this behavior teaches you how floats work.

When you float an element (in this case, the `sidebar` div), it is removed from the normal flow of the HTML. This is why the sidebar extends over the entire container. The two divs that have content are contained within boundaries of the sidebar.

Top Rated Smoothies
The Funky Orange
Submitted by user iosborn22, this smoothie has recieved over 200 5 star ratings and its **orange juice** and **banana** base make this a great choice for breakfast!
The Tropical KickBack
Submitted by user smoothj282, this smoothie combines the exotic ingredients passionfruit and mango. The result is an invgorating and delicious beverage that is great any time of the day.

SmoothieWorld is your #1 destination for smoothie recipes.
Our mission statement
We here at SmoothieWorld are devoted to making the smoothie beverage a daily part of your life. Whether it be for breakfast, lunch or even dinner, smoothies are great way to get the nutrition you need and have fun while doing it.
The recipes on our site have all been tested in our lab of smoothie experts. Other smoothie sites might have more recipes or feature more exotic fruits than you'll find here, but we feel that quality beats out quantity and novelty any day. We also believe the best recipes come from you the reader, that's why we encourage you to join our smoothie community. Learn more
Footer

The sidebar is floated, but is also overlapping the boundaries of other page elements.

However, this containment can be deceptive because it is affected by the amount of content in each div. To illustrate, you will add more content into the `main` div by duplicating the current paragraph.

2   In your HTML, select the entire paragraph element and press Ctrl + C (Windows) or Command + C (Mac OS) to copy it. Click once after the element and press Ctrl + V (Windows) or Command + V (Mac OS) to paste it.

3   Save the file and then preview it in your browser. When additional content is added to the `main` div, it expands and pushes the `footer` div downwards. Now the `footer` div appears below the sidebar because there is space for the div above it. Close your browser and return to your text editor.

4 These three divs (`sidebar`, `main`, and `footer`) currently appear to be interdependent. Removing (or adding) content from the sidebar also has an effect. In your HTML, select the last paragraph within the sidebar and delete it. Save the page and preview it in your browser. Now that the height of the `sidebar` is shorter than both the `footer` and the `main` divs, they "flow" beneath it. This can lead to some layout problems; you will learn strategies for solving these problems in a later section, but now, you will float the main container as well.

5 Close your browser and return to your text editor. Press Ctrl + Z (Windows) or Command + Z (Mac) to undo the deletion of the paragraph in the sidebar. Additionally, select the paragraph in the `main` div that you duplicated in step 2 and delete that as well.

6 Add the following selector and style rules (highlighted in red) below the `#sidebar` rule:

```
#main {
    width:600px;
    float:right;
    background-color:#ADA446;
}
```

Save the file and preview it in your browser.

Top Rated Smoothies
The Funky Orange
Submitted by user iosborn22, this smoothie has recieved over 200 5 star ratings and its **orange juice** and **banana** base make this a great choice for breakfast!
The Tropical KickBack
Submitted by user smoothj282, this smoothie combines the exotic ingredients passionfruit and mango. The result is an invgorating and delicious beverage that is great any time of the day.

Footer **SmoothieWorld is your #1 destination for smoothie recipes.**
Our mission statement
We here at SmoothieWorld are devoted to making the smoothie beverage a life. Whether it be for breakfast, lunch or even dinner, smoothies are great nutrition you need and have fun while doing it.
The recipes on our site have all been tested in our lab of smoothie experts. sites might have more recipes or feature more exotic fruits than you'll find that quality beats out quantity and novelty any day. We also believe the bes from you the reader, that's why we encourage you to join our smoothie cor more

The `main` div floats to the right, but the footer has moved upwards in the flow of the page.

Floating this div to the right solves the problem of the content appearing below the `sidebar`; however, the amount of content in the `main` div forces it to extend outside the entire container. This is a problem when you consider the `footer` element: footers should appear at the bottom of the page, and this one is not.

To force the `footer` div to the bottom of the page, you will assign a new property called `clear` to this div.

Working with the `clear` property

When you add the CSS `clear` property to an object, you add a rule that says, "No floated elements are allowed to my sides." You can specify whether you want to clear floated elements on the left side, the right side, or both. In the case of the footer, you will choose both.

1 Add a new selector and style rules (highlighted in red) below your `#main` div:

```
#footer {
    clear:right;
    background-color:#BA2B22;
}
```

2 Save the file and preview it in your browser. Your footer is now placed at the bottom of the `main` div. This is because the `clear:right` rule does not allow any floated elements to the right of the footer. The `main` div was floated, and so the footer moves to the next available spot on the page. Close your browser and return to your editor.

As in the earlier examples, the amount of content in your divs can affect your floated and cleared elements. For example, if the amount of text in the sidebar expands to the point of reaching the footer, you have a problem again as the sidebar extends outside. For this reason, elements are often set to clear on both sides.

3 Change the value of your `clear` property as follows (highlighted in red):

```
clear:both;
```

This code ensures that no floated elements are allowed on either side of the footer.

Creating a list-based navigation using `floats`

Now that you have learned the basics of floating and clearing, you will return to your navigation section and add a simple navigation bar based on an unordered list. The list items inside your navigation should be floated to override the default vertical appearance of a list. CSS navigation menus are used frequently in standards-based design because they can easily be updated and modified, and because they are text-based (not images), which improves accessibility in devices such as screen readers and can even help a website's search engine rankings.

1 In your HTML, select the placeholder content inside your `mainnav` div and replace it with the following unordered list and list items (highlighted in red):

```
<div id="mainnav">
    <ul>
        <li><a href="index.html">Home</a></li>
        <li><a href="about.html">About Us</a></li>
        <li><a href="recipes.html">Recipes</a></li>
        <li><a href="submitrecipe.html">Submit a Recipe</a></li>
        <li><a href="forum.html">Forum</a></li>
        <li><a href="contact.html">Contact Us</a></li>
    </ul>
</div>
```

The list items are linking to pages that do not exist yet. Nevertheless, you are linking the items because they need to be hyperlinked to be styled correctly.

2   Preview the page in your browser.

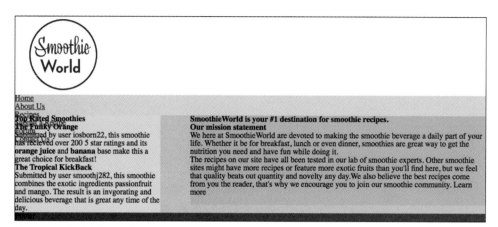

Your list is in the default vertical position and is overlapping your sidebar.

Notice that your page appears "broken" again. This is because your list is overlapping your floated sidebar. Also, the list has no bullet points. Remember that your CSS reset style sheet is attached to this page and one of the rules has a property of `list-style:none`, which removes the bullet points. For this example, the lack of bullet points is acceptable because you are using this list for navigation.

3   Return to your text editor and locate your `#mainnav` rule. Add a new rule between this one and the sidebar by pressing Return a few times to add some space and then adding the following code:

```
#mainnav li {
    float:left;
}
```

This is a new type of CSS rule called a *contextual selector*; it targets *only* list items that are inside the `mainnav` div. If you were to define a new rule just for list items, all the list items on the page would be affected, which would not work for this example.

4   Save the page and preview it in your browser. All the list items are now stacked side by side. Notice that the list inside the main content has not been affected. Add space between the list items and add other styles as indicated in the following step.

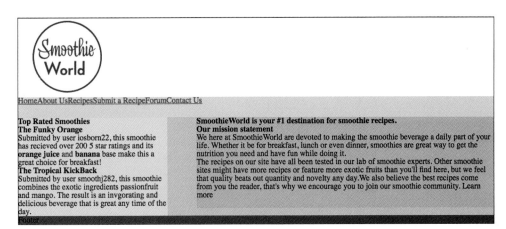

Floating the list items causes them to be stacked side by side.

5   Add the following code (highlighted in red) to your `mainnav li` rule:

```
#mainnav li {
    float:left;
    width:120px;
    height:25px;
    background-color:#CCC;
    text-align:center;
    border-left:1px black solid;
    border-right:1px black solid;
}
```

In this code, you have done the following: defined the box around each list item as 120 pixels wide by 25 pixels high; added a background color; aligned each list item to the center; and added a border to both sides of the item. Save the file and preview it in your browser.

When you define the width and height of the box, the text naturally sits at the top. Unfortunately, while there is a `text-align:center` property that centers the text horizontally, there is no simple way to *vertically* center objects in CSS. In this case, you will use the `line-height` property to move the nav text downwards.

6 Add the following line of code below your `border-right` declaration:

```
line-height:25px;
```

Save the file and preview it in your browser. Your text is now centered within the box. Remember that the line-height number is based on the font size; it will likely change if you change the font size.

Adding line-height to the list items positions them vertically within the navbar.

Adding text styles

Before continuing with your layout, you will import the text styles you worked on in Lesson 6. Until now, you have added your styles to an internal style sheet instead of an external one. When building a layout, using an internal style sheet is a matter of convenience: creating and modifying style rules is easier to do by scrolling up the page than by accessing an external style sheet. Eventually, you will move the layout rules you have created to an external style sheet. For now, you will attach a style sheet that sets the base rules for elements such as your headings, lists, and paragraphs.

1 At the top of your HTML, locate the `<link>` tag for your reset.css style sheet. To add another external style sheet, select this line and then press Ctrl + C (Windows) or Command + C (Mac OS) to copy it. On the next line, press Ctrl + V (Windows) or Command + V (Mac OS) to paste the line. Now replace the value "reset.css" with the following value (highlighted in red):

```
<link href="reset.css" rel="stylesheet" type="text/css" />
<link href="base.css" rel="stylesheet" type="text/css" />
```

2   Save the file and then preview it in your browser to see the effect of the new values.

Your page now uses an external style sheet for the text elements.

3   Return to your text editor and choose File > Open. In the dialog box that appears, navigate to your web07lessons folder, select the base.css file, and click Open. Review the styles in this CSS file. They should be familiar to you from Lesson 6, but the margin and padding styles were removed because these styles made sense in the context of that lesson, but not in the new layout. You can add a style to these elements.

The effect of margins and padding on your fixed-width layout

In this section, you will add space between the sections of text on your page (which have margins of zero from the reset style sheet). You will learn some strategies for controlling the layout; however, the goal of this exercise is not to show you a single method of CSS layout, but to help you understand the different options, which should help you in your future projects to decide which method to use.

In this first exercise, you will add padding to the `sidebar` element.

1 Preview the page in your browser and notice the lack of space between your text and the edge of your sidebar. Also, notice the width of this sidebar: if you measure it based on the navigation bar above, the sidebar ends approximately one-third of the way through the "Recipe" list item.

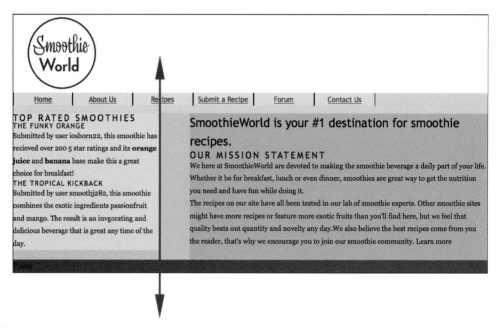

A guide is added in this screenshot to show where the sidebar ends in relation to the navigation bar.

The width of this sidebar is set to 300 pixels; increase the padding of the sidebar by following the instructions in the next step.

2 Return to your text editor, locate the rule in your CSS for the sidebar, and add the following code (highlighted in red):

```
#sidebar {
    float:left;
    width:300px;
    background-color:#CCC;
    padding:0px 20px 0px 20px;
}
```

Remember that this is a CSS shortcut and you should read the values in a clockwise manner. The first value (0px) is the top padding, the second value (20px) is the right padding, the third value (0px) is the bottom padding, and the last value (20px) is the left padding. Save the page and preview it in your browser.

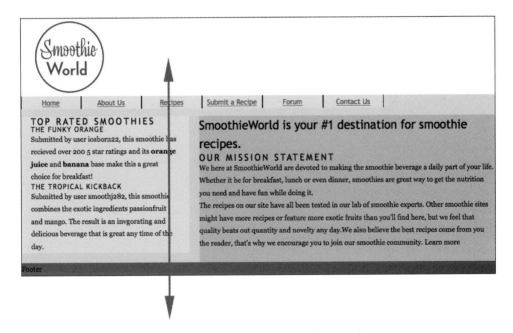

Using the guide as a reference you can see the width of the sidebar has expanded by 40 pixels

By adding 20 pixels of left padding and right padding to the `sidebar` div, you can increase the amount of space inside the column. However, notice the end of the sidebar now lines up at the end of the Recipe item. This is because increasing the padding has increased the width of the sidebar by 40 pixels. This means the absolute width of the sidebar is 340 pixels, where 300 pixels comes from the width property in the `sidebar` rule and 40 pixels comes from the padding that you add.

3 Return to your text editor. Add an equivalent amount of padding to the `main` div because it also needs space for the text.

Locate your #`main` rule and add the following padding (highlighted in red):

```
#main {
    width:600px;
    float:right;
    background-color:#ADA446;
    padding:0px 20px 0px 20px;
}
```

Save the file and preview it in your browser. A new problem arose: the total width of your two columns when you include the padding is wider than the container they are nested in. If you scroll down the page in your browser, you see the `main` div has slid into the only space it is allowed, underneath the `sidebar`.

You can fix this problem in several ways: you could expand the overall width of the `wrap` div, you could reduce the width value of the `sidebar` or the `main` div (or both), or you could reduce the padding values. However, all these methods are based on using padding, and there is an alternative method of adding space to columns that does not rely on padding at all. You will use this method.

4 Return to your text editor and locate the padding rules you added in steps 2 and 3. Select and delete these rules. You can achieve a similar effect by adding margin rules to the text elements inside the columns, as described in the following step.

5 Below the #`footer` rule in your CSS, add the following rule (highlighted in red):

```
p, h1, h2, h3 {
    margin-left:20px;
    margin-right:20px;
}
```

This rule places 20 pixels of margin on the left and right of all paragraph and heading elements on the page. Save the file and preview it in your browser.

TOP RATED SMOOTHIES
THE FUNKY ORANGE
Submitted by user iosborn22, this
smoothie has recieved over 200 5 star
ratings and its **orange juice** and
banana base make this a great choice for
breakfast!
THE TROPICAL KICKBACK
Submitted by user smoothj282, this
smoothie combines the exotic ingredients
passionfruit and mango. The result is an
invgorating and delicious beverage that is
great any time of the day.

Adding margins to the elements within the sidebar increases the amount of space but does not increase the width of the sidebar.

As in the earlier padding example, the result is extra space between the text and the columns. However, a crucial difference is that when you add margins to the text elements, the width of the columns is *not* affected. This can be advantageous, as you no longer have to add width to the padding. You only need to consider the width property for the column.

This technique has its own disadvantages, because the rules you set currently apply to *all* paragraphs and headings 1, 2, and 3 elements on the page. For example, notice that the footer was pushed 20 pixels to the right because the content is a paragraph. In cases where you only want to specify the elements within the sidebar and main, the contextual selector you used earlier for the navigation is useful.

6 Return to your text editor and delete the `margin-left` and `margin-right` properties you added in step 5 (but leave the rule intact). Add the following group of rules (highlighted in red):

```
p, h1, h2, h3 {


}
#sidebar p, #sidebar h2, #sidebar h3, #main p, #main h1, #main h2,
#main h3 {
    margin-left:20px;
    margin-right:20px;
}
```

This is a CSS shorthand to select any paragraph, heading 1, heading 2, or heading 3 element child of the sidebar ID or the main ID and apply left and right margins of 20 pixels.

7 Save the file and preview it in your browser. Scroll to the footer paragraph and notice that it no longer has margins. Close your browser and return to your text editor.

This method of styling requires a bit more attention to detail than the padding method. For example, when new elements are added inside a div, they do not use the same margins. The next step shows an example of this problem and then the solution, which involves adding a heading 4 element to the sidebar.

8 In the HTML of your `sidebar` div after the last paragraph, add the following code:

```
<h4>Submit a Recipe</h4>
```

Save the page and preview it in your browser. This heading 4 uses its zero margins (inherited from the reset.css style sheet) so it is flush against the column. Close your browser and return to your text editor.

9 In your group of rules for the sidebar and main columns, add a new rule (highlighted in red) in the sidebar for heading 4 (h4):

```
#sidebar p, #sidebar h2, #sidebar h3, #sidebar h4, #main p, #main h2 {
    margin-left:20px;
    margin-right:20px;
}
```

Save the page and preview it in your browser. The heading 4 element now has the same margins as the others.

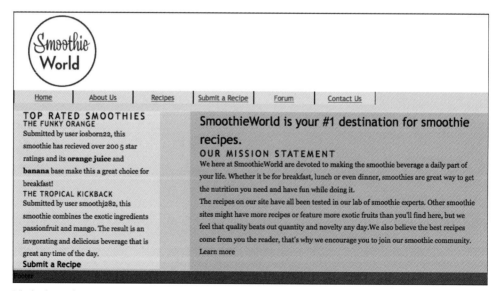

The heading 4 element now has the same margins as the other elements in the sidebar.

You can add a different margin to one of the elements. For example, you might want to move the paragraphs inside the sidebar to the right so they are indented. In this case, add another rule specifically for the p elements in the sidebar, as indicated in the next step. Close your browser and return to your text editor.

10 Add a new rule immediately below your previous rule set for the sidebar paragraph,

```
#sidebar p, #sidebar h2, #sidebar h3, #sidebar h4 #main p, #main h1,
    #main h2, #main h3{
    margin-left:20px;
    margin-right:20px;
}
#sidebar p {
    margin-left:30px;
}
```

This rule overrides the rule you set in step 9. Save the page and preview it in your browser. The paragraphs in the sidebar now have a left margin of 30 pixels, and in contrast to the other elements, are now indented.

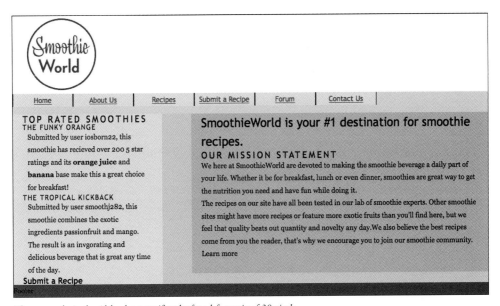

The paragraphs in the sidebar have specific rules for a left margin of 30 pixels.

With the exceptions of the changes you made in this exercise, all the margins and padding for the elements on your page are set to zero based on the reset style sheet. Add new values to the top and bottom margin values for most of your elements as indicated in the next step.

11 Locate the empty p, h1, h2, and h3 rules in your style sheet. Add also the h4 selector to cover the elements on your page, and modify this rule set as follows (highlighted in red):

```
p, h1, h2, h3,h4 {
    margin-bottom:20px;
}
```

Save the page and preview it in your browser. Most of your elements now have some added space from these margins. To add a top margin to the heading 2 in your sidebar you could add another rule as shown in the next step.

12 In your text editor, add the following rule set:

```
#sidebar h2 {
    margin-top:15px;
}
```

Save the page and preview it in your browser. Your heading 2 in the sidebar has been pushed down by the top margin.

TOP RATED SMOOTHIES

THE FUNKY ORANGE

Submitted by user iosborn22, this smoothie has recieved over 200 5 star ratings and its **orange juice** and **banana** base make this a great choice for breakfast!

THE TROPICAL KICKBACK

Submitted by user smoothj282, this smoothie combines the exotic ingredients passionfruit and mango. The result is an invgorating and delicious beverage that is great any time of the day.

Submit a Recipe

Your sidebar with a top margin of 15 pixels applied.

A review of using margins and padding for layout

In this lesson, you have learned two methods for adding space between the elements in a page. The first method is to add padding to a `div` element. The advantage with this method is that all the elements inside the div are affected simultaneously, making it quick and efficient. A disadvantage to using padding for a div container is that increasing padding changes the width; to compensate, you must take into account the extra width.

The second method is to add margins to the elements inside the divs. The disadvantage to this method is that it requires more code and attention to detail because you must notice how individual elements are positioned. The advantage is that column behavior is more predictable, since there is only one width property to consider.

There is another, less obvious advantage to the second method that has not been discussed. For reasons that will be covered in more depth in Lesson 9, this method is more reliable for achieving similar layouts across browsers and it solves a bug found in Internet Explorer 6.

Finally, you should note that a combination of methods (using margins and padding) might be necessary for some situations. Consequently, you should understand the cause and effect of each method you use.

Styling your footer with a background image

So far, the structure of your page has been defined by the background colors of your `div` elements. In this section, you will learn to add images. To do this, you will add a CSS background image to your footer.

1   Locate the `#footer` div and replace the placeholder content inside the div with the following code (highlighted in red):

```
<div id="footer">
    <p>Copyright SmoothieWorld 2011 </p>
    <p>Registration on or use of this site constitutes acceptance of
    our <a href="useragreement.html"> user agreement </a> and
    <a href="privacy.html">Privacy Policy.</a></p>
</div>
```

2   Save the page and preview it in your browser. Each paragraph is styled based on the current rules for paragraphs. You will adjust the rules for the footer, but you must know the size of the footer, which will be based on the dimensions of the background images you will add.

3 In your internal style sheet, locate the current rule for the footer. Add a new rule (highlighted in red) to apply a background image from your images folder:

```
#footer {
    clear:both;
    background-color:#BA2B22;
    background-image:url(images/footer_background.jpg);
    background-repeat:no-repeat;
}
```

Save the page and preview it in your browser.

Your footer now has a background image applied.

Your background image is now applied to the footer. This allows the footer text to be visible above it. Notice the `background-repeat` property in the code above. CSS background images tile by default, so setting a value of `no-repeat` ensures that this image will *never* tile. This code might seem redundant when your background image is the same size as your footer; however, if the footer expands, the code will ensure the image does not tile.

Set the footer dimensions to match the background image as indicated in the next step.

4 Modify your footer rule as follows (highlighted in red):

```
#footer {
    clear:both;
    background-color:#BA2B22;
    background-image:url(images/footer_background.jpg);
    background-repeat:no-repeat;
    width:960px;
    height:128px;
}
```

Save the file and preview it in your browser. Your footer is sized correctly and you can adjust your paragraphs. Use another contextual selector as shown in the next step.

5 In your text editor, add a new rule for paragraphs inside the `footer` div:

```
#footer p {
    margin:10px 0 0 20px;
    width:280px;
    font-family:Verdana, Geneva, sans-serif;
    font-size:0.689em;
}
```

This rule adds 10 pixels to the top margin and 20 pixels to the left margin of each paragraph in your footer. By defining a width for the paragraphs, you can force a break approximately where you need it: inside the white space of the image. The font properties define a different font family and a smaller font-size.

6 Save the page and preview it in your browser.

Copyright SmoothieWorld 2011

Registration on or use of this site constitutes acceptance of our user agreement and Privacy Policy.

Your footer paragraphs with new styles.

In the previous section, you learned that applying padding and margins is a common technique. You could add more space between the first paragraph and the top of the footer, but increasing the top margin of the `#footer p` rule affects the second paragraph. In this case, add padding to the top of the footer as indicated in the next step.

7 Add the following declaration (highlighted in red) to your `#footer` rule:

```
#footer {
    clear:both;
    background-color:#BA2B22;
    background-image:url(images/footer_background.jpg);
    background-repeat:no-repeat;
    width:960px;
    height:128px;
    padding-top:10px;
}
```

Save the file and preview it in your browser. Notice that the additional padding increased the true height of the footer, but the red background color is extending out. You can solve this problem in several ways, but the simple solution is to subtract 10 pixels from the height of the footer.

8 Change the height of the footer div to 118 pixels (highlighted in red):

`height:118px;`

Save the file and preview it in your browser. Your footer is now positioned correctly.

The final appearance of the footer.

You have finished this lesson, and you have a good foundation to build your page. In the next lesson, you will continue working on this design, add more images, upgrade the style of your navigation bar, and add other elements to your page.

In this lesson, you learned the difference between table and CSS layouts. You also learned to use the float and clear properties to create columns on your page. Finally, you explored the advantages and disadvantages of using margins and padding to control your layout.

To compare your work with a complete version of the final page, open the file named "07_final.html" in your web07lessons folder.

Self study

1 To practice styling with margins and padding, add new content to your main section. For example, add a new heading 3 and an unordered list between your two paragraphs:

```
<h3>Recipe of the Day:Honeydew Melon</h3>
    <ul>
        <li>3 cups Honeydew Melon (seeded & chopped)</li>
        <li>2 tsp Lime Juice</li>
        <li>1 cup Vanilla Nonfat Yogurt</li>
        <li>1 cup Ice Cubes</li>
    </ul>
```

2 After adding this HTML, use what you learned in this lesson to experiment with positioning these elements on the page.

Review

Questions

1 What is a fixed-width layout and what is a flexible layout? What are some of the advantages and disadvantages of each?

2 What is the CSS `float` property and where would you use it?

3 Cheri added a paragraph to the `sidebar` div she created. However, the paragraph is flush against the side of the sidebar. Name two options Cheri could use to move the paragraph away from the edges of the sidebar.

Answers

1 A fixed-width layout has a defined width (usually in pixels or ems) for the primary container. One of the main advantages to this type of layout is that this primary container provides a reliable way to position the other page elements. One disadvantage to this type of layout is that it does not resize with the web browser and some features, such as text reflowing, are lost. Flexible layouts resize based on the browser or device; however, this creates a more challenging layout for the designer.

2 The CSS `float` property lets you remove an element from the default flow of HTML and move (or float) it to either the left or right of its containing element. You would use floats when you want to wrap text around images, create horizontal navigation menus, or use columns for page layout.

3 Cheri could add some padding to the sidebar (which would move any content inside away from the edges). She could also add a rule for paragraphs inside the sidebar; specifically, Cheri could add margin values that would move the paragraphs away from the edges. (Cheri could also use a combination of padding and margins.)

What you'll learn in this lesson:

- Using comments in your style sheets

- Using background images

- Creating navigation styles

- Working with absolute positioning

Advanced CSS Layout

In this lesson you'll learn how to refine the appearance of your page layout by adding graphics, color, and additional page sections.

Starting up

You will work with several files from the web08lessons folder in this lesson. Make sure you have loaded the weblessons folder onto your hard-drive from *www.digitalclassroombooks.com/webdesign.* See "Loading lesson files" in the Starting Up section of this book.

See Lesson 8 in action!

Use the accompanying video to gain a better understanding of how to use some of the features shown in this lesson. You can find the video tutorial for this lesson at www.digitalclassroombooks.com *using the URL provided when you registered your book.*

This lesson uses the TextWrangler text editor to create the markup, but you can use any of the text editors covered in Lesson 3.

Building your page layout

In this lesson, you will be working with the two-column fixed-width layout from Lesson 7. In Lesson 7, you added background colors to the various page elements. In this lesson, you will remove the background colors to unify the appearance of the page.

You will also create a more attractive and useful navigation bar, add more images, create a styled data table, and add form elements for a contact page. At the end of the lesson, you will look at a few alternative page layouts based on the one you create.

Removing the background color

Your first task is to remove the background colors from the page. You do not need to delete the CSS properties for these elements, just comment them out in the code.

1   In your text editor, choose File > Open. In the dialog box that appears, navigate to the web08lessons folder, choose the 08_start.html file, and click Open. Preview this page in your browser to see the current layout.

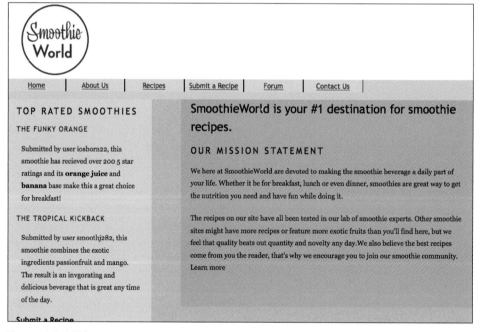

Your page in its initial state

2   Return to your text editor. Choose File > Save As, and in the dialog box that appears, go to the web08lessons folder. Name this file 08_layoutwork.html, and then click Save. This ensures you have a backup file.

3 Locate the `#wrap` rule in your CSS, and then add the following commenting code (highlighted in red) to the `background-color` property:

```
#wrap {
    /*background-color:#E0B3B9; */
    width:960px;
    border:thin solid black;
    margin:0 auto;
}
```

This code disables the style so the browser ignores it. You can remove these comments at any time to activate the style. Designers often keep either background-colors or borders in the code to help them identify layout elements in the future. Save the file and preview it in your browser. The purple background for the wrap is now gone.

4 Return to your text editor and repeat step 3, but this time add the commenting code for the `#sidebar` and `#maincontent` `background-color` properties. Save the file and preview it in your browser. Your page no longer uses color to define the two columns.

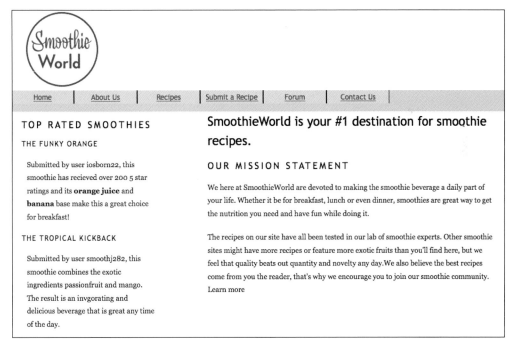

Your page with the background-colors for your columns removed.

Now that you have disabled the background colors of the columns, you'll add other colors, starting with the page itself. The CSS body selector allows you to do this; you need to open your external style sheet to modify it.

5 In your text editor, choose File > Open. Navigate to your web08lessons folder, select the base.css file, and then click Open.

Remember that your page is currently using three sources for the styles: the internal styles, which you have already modified; an external style sheet named reset.css, which applies margins and a padding of 0 to most of your HTML elements; and the base.css style sheet, which contains common styles, such as font family and font size.

Style sheet management

Learning to manage multiple style sheets is increasingly important in modern web design. Placing all your styles in a single style sheet can cause confusion and inefficiency, especially as the number of rules increases. Modern websites often use multiple external style sheets: one for the reset, one for layout, one for text, one for older browsers, one for mobile devices, and so on.

It is important to know when to use internal and external style sheets. On most completed websites, internal styles are used to style a unique page; the majority of the styles are in the external style sheets. However, during development, it is more convenient to experiment and refine the layout using internal styles; all the designer needs to do is scroll up the page and add or modify a rule. The point at which internal styles are moved over to an external style sheet is a matter of preference. However, designers often do this when the design is approved and they are beginning to build new pages.

6 In your base.css file, locate the body rule and add the following property (highlighted in red):

```
body {
    font-family:"Trebuchet MS", Tahoma, Arial, sans-serif;
    font-size:100%;
    background-color:#B3BBCA;
}
```

This adds a light-blue background color to the page. Save the file and preview it in your browser. You can see that with no background colors applied, your columns are transparent and the body background is visible. You'll fix that by applying a white background to the `wrap` div.

7   In your text editor, return to 08_layoutwork.html. Locate the rule for the #wrap div. Modify the color value (highlighted in red) and remove the commenting code:

```
#wrap {
    background-color:#ffffff;
    width:960px;
    border:thin solid black;
    margin:0 auto;
}
```

Save the file and preview it in your browser. With the wrap div using the white background, your page is beginning to take shape. Now you'll add some images.

Working with CSS background images

There are two ways to add images to a web page. The first way uses HTML to insert an inline image. You have already added an inline image when you inserted your site logo. Inline images rely on the HTML image tag, and the code is similar to this:

```
<img src="images/smoothieworld_logo.jpg" width="200" height="150"
alt="smoothieworld_logo" />
```

The second way to add images to a web page is by using CSS background images. You should generally use CSS background images as decorative elements and not primary content. In the following steps, you will add a CSS background image to the div container named #innerwrap that is nesting your two columns.

1   In your 08_layoutwork.html file, locate the div tag with the ID innerwrap. Here is a list of the containers currently on your page, from the top of your HTML code to the bottom: wrap div, masthead div, mainnav div, and innerwrap div. Currently, the innerwrap div is the parent container of the sidebar and maincontent div, which are the columns you created in Lesson 7.

The innerwrap is currently unstyled; however, its function right now is to provide a container for the two columns. Note the behavior of this container in the next few steps.

2   In your internal style sheet, locate the wrap rule and below it add a new rule for the innerwrap:

```
#innerwrap {
    background-image:url(images/inner-wrap_bg.png);
    height:450px;
}
```

The `background-image` property is pointing to a small gradient image located in your images folder. The `height` property gives the innerwrap some structure; this value of 450 pixels is arbitrary, and you will return to this shortly. For now, save the file and preview it in your browser.

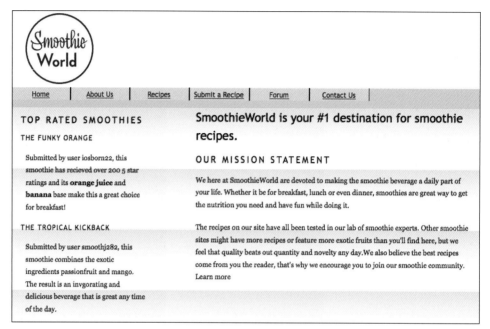

Background-images tile by default.

Your page looks strange because by default, background images tile both horizontally and vertically. In order to correct this, you need to tile the image horizontally (the direction of the x-axis).

3 In your text editor, add the following property and value (highlighted in red) to the `innerwrap` rule:

```
#innerwrap {
    background-image:url(images/inner-wrap_bg.png);
    background-repeat:repeat-x;
    height:450px;
}
```

Save the page and preview it in your browser. Your background image now tiles across the top of the `innerwrap` div, which creates the intended effect.

The many wonders of the background image

You can find CSS background images everywhere in web design, so you need to understand how they work. Following are some of the properties associated with background images.

To tile an image horizontally within the parent container, use the following value:

```
background-repeat:repeat-x;
```

To tile an image vertically only, use this value:

```
background-repeat:repeat-y;
```

To add a single instance of the graphic (in other words, with no tiling), use this value:

```
background-repeat:no-repeat;
```

Background-position

Another useful property is background-position. The default position for background images is the top-left corner of the containing element, as shown in the following figure:

A background image with the "no-repeat" value.

You can position this image in the bottom-right corner by adding this property:

```
background-position:right bottom;
```

You can use the keywords left, right, and center to position an image horizontally; by combining it with the keywords top, bottom, and center, you can also position the image vertically.

You can position background images even more precisely by using either unit or percentage values. The most common unit values are pixels, but you can also use other units, such as ems. When using unit values, the first value is the horizontal position and the second value is the vertical position, as the following example shows:

```
background-position:10px 40px;
```

The background image is positioned 10 pixels horizontally and 40 pixels vertically from the top-left corner of the box (the box itself is 100 pixels high by 300 pixels wide).

(continues)

The many wonders of the background image (continued)

You can use percentages for background images, particularly if the parent container has a flexible width. When using percentage values, the top-left corner is 0% 0% and the bottom-right corner is 100% 100%. The following example uses percentages:

The image above, as indicated by the following code, is positioned 20 percent away from the top and 40 percent away from the left:

```
background-position 20% 40%;
```

Using hacks to solve layout problems

CSS layouts that rely on floated boxes sometimes have unexpected results because various browsers render the same content differently. When an elegant solution does not exist, you need to resort to *hacks*. A hack is a solution where you use elements or properties within HTML or CSS for a purpose other than their intended application. You'll use a hack in the following exercise to properly apply the background image that spans across your two columns.

In the previous exercise, you applied a background image to the `innerwrap` div and you defined a height of 450 pixels. The problem with this method is that the two columns inside the `innerwrap` div are longer than 450 pixels and it's against best practices to have a containing element smaller than its content. To address this problem, you will remove the height value and then add new code to make the innerwrap work well in any situation.

1   In your 08_layoutwork.html page, locate the rule for the innerwrap and delete the entire `height:450px;` line.

Save the page and preview it in your browser. Your background image disappears because without a defined height, there is no content inside the `innerwrap` div.

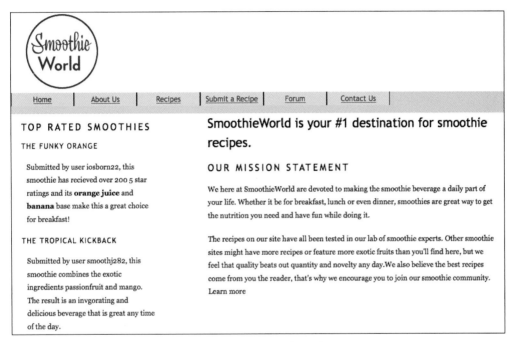

Your `innerwrap` *div has no defined height so it collapses and hides the background image.*

The `sidebar` and `maincontent` divs are contained within the `innerwrap` div; however, these elements are floated, and floated elements are removed from the flow of HTML. Also, the `sidebar` and `maincontent` div do not have height values, so the `innerwrap` cannot expand. You will now add code that solves this problem.

2   In the CSS below the `#innerwrap` rule, add a new empty rule (highlighted in red):

```
#innerwrap {
    background-image:url(images/inner-wrap_bg.png);
    background-repeat:repeat-x;
}
#innerwrap:after{

}
```

The `:after` is a special CSS property that allows extra content to be added at the end of an element using CSS. You will now add a series of rules that force the innerwrap to act as though there were content inside.

3 Add the following properties (highlighted in red) to this rule:

```
#innerwrap:after{
    content:".";
    display:block;
    clear:both;
    height:0;
    visibility:hidden;
}
```

Save the file and then preview it in your browser. Your innerwrap now displays properly. (If you are viewing this page in Internet Explorer 6 or 7, you might not be see the intended result; you will address this shortly.) It goes beyond the scope of this lesson to explain exactly what each one of these properties is doing, but essentially they are forcing the innerwrap to behave as a true container with content, not just a background image.

For more information about how this code works, go to www.positioniseverything.net/easyclearing.html.

The solution from the previous step will not work reliably in Internet Explorer 6 or 7, so you have to add a special set of rules for these browsers.

4 In your 08_layoutwork.html document, scroll to locate the links to your external style sheets. Type the following code (highlighted in red) below the link to the base.css style sheet:

```
<link href="reset.css" rel="stylesheet" type="text/css" />
<link href="base.css" rel="stylesheet" type="text/css" />
<!--[if IE ]>
<link href="iefixes.css" rel="stylesheet" type="text/css">
<![endif]-->
```

This section of code is called a *conditional comment*; you will learn more about this type of code in Lesson 9. For now, think of this as a link to an external style sheet that will only be used if the browser is Internet Explorer. All other browsers will ignore this code. The next step explains the content of the iefixes.css style sheet.

5 In your Text Editor, choose File > Open. Navigate to your web08lessons folder, select the iefixes.css file, and then click Open. It contains the following rule:

```
#innerwrap {
    zoom:1;
}
```

This is a special rule that forces Internet Explorer 6 to render the page as you intend. (You will learn more about these details in the next lesson.) Close this file without making any changes.

Enhancing your CSS navigation bar

Now you'll make your navigation bar more aesthetically pleasing. Currently, it uses the positioning and colors you added in Lesson 7 to understand how floats work. You'll now use CSS to add styling and interactivity. To review how the menu works, modify some of the properties to create a navigation menu better suited for the style of your page, as indicated in the following steps.

1 In your 08_layoutwork.html internal style sheet, locate the `#mainnav` rule. This rule sets the height of the div to 40 pixels and gives it a pale-green background color. Below this rule is the `#mainnav li` rule, which is floating the list items to the left as well as setting styles such as width, height, background color, and more.

Preview the page in your browser to see how the navigation bar is currently styled. The list items (with a background color of grey) are not the same height as the `#mainnav` div, which is why there is a gap. You'll fix this now.

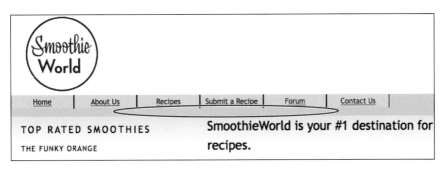

Your list items are not the same height as the surrounding navigation section; this accounts for the visual gap.

2 Return to your text editor. To make the list fit into the mainnav, both elements need to be the same height. Make the following changes to your rules (highlighted in red).

```
#mainnav {
    background-color:#60668B;
    height:35px;
}
#mainnav li {
    float:left;
    width:120px;
    height:35px;
    background-color:#7D83A4;
    text-align:center;
    border-left:1px black solid;
    border-right:1px black solid;
    line-height:35px;
}
```

Save the page and then preview it in your browser. By making the heights the same value, you now have a narrower navbar. By changing the background colors to shades of blue, you now have colors that are more compatible with the background color of the page. Unfortunately, the default hyperlink color is also blue, and the rule below the links is not very attractive. You'll now change the link color and remove the underline next.

3 Below your `#mainnav li` rule, add the following rule:

```
#mainnav ul li a {
    color:#ffffff;
    text-decoration:none;
}
```

This rule is necessary because you are targeting hyperlinks inside the `mainnav` div. The `color` and `text-decoration` properties set the style of these links to white and also remove the underline. Save the page and preview it in your browser.

Styling the appearance of the hyperlinks by removing the underline and setting the color to white.

This navbar is aesthetically pleasing. You can improve its usability by making the nav items change color when the user moves the mouse cursor over them and by providing a visual indicator of which page the user has navigated to. See the next step for instructions.

4 In your text editor, add the following rule below your `#mainnav ul li a` rule:

```
#mainnav ul li a:hover {
    background-color:#29336B;
    color:#F8F068;
}
```

The `a:hover` property is an example of a *pseudoclass*, which are special properties of elements (links, in this case) based on user interaction. The `a:link` property defines the default appearance of a hyperlink before it is first clicked by a user. The `a:hover` property defines the appearance of a link when a user hovers the mouse cursor over it (this action is sometimes known as a rollover). The `a:visited` property defines the appearance of a link on the page after it has been visited. (This helps the user identify the links she already clicked.) The last pseudo-class is `a:active`, which defines the appearance of a link when it is being clicked (when the user is pressing down but not releasing the mouse).

You do not have to create styles for all these properties, but you will often see them in groups of four. To see the `a:hover` property in action, save your page and preview it in your browser.

Move the mouse cursor over your links to see the effect. The behavior appears odd because the background color is defined by the size of the text. Fill the entire block with color, as instructed in the next step.

5   In your text editor, add the following property (highlighted in red) to your `#mainnav ul li a` rule:

```
#mainnav ul li a {
    color:#ffffff;
    text-decoration:none;
    display:block;
}
```

This property and value override the default inline value of links in the mainnav so the entire block expands. Save your file and check the menu in your browser.

Setting the hyperlink element to display as a block element forces it to fill the menu area.

Return to your text editor. You will now set a style that defines the appearance of the menu when a user is on a specific page; this will help him identify which page he is on.

6   In your HTML, locate the code for the mainnav list. Add the following class names (highlighted in red) to each list item:

```
<ul>
    <li><a class="nav-home" href="index.html">Home</a></li>
    <li><a class="nav-about" href="about.html">About Us</a></li>
    <li><a class="nav-recipe" href="recipes.html">Recipes</a></li>
    <li><a class="nav-submitrecipes" href="submitrecipe.html">Submit
        a Recipe</a></li>
    <li><a class="nav-forum" href="forum.html">Forum</a></li>
    <li><a class="nav-contact" href="contact.html">Contact Us</a>
        </li>
</ul>
```

The purpose of assigning a unique class to each list item is to target the list items with a style. You must also find a way to identify the page the user is on. You can do this by creating a unique ID style for each page.

7 In your HTML, scroll up to locate the `<body>` tag, and add the following code (highlighted in red):

```
<body id="home">
```

By adding an ID to the body tag, you can set a style that applies to this page only. In this case, the style is for the appearance of the Home link on this page.

8 In your style sheet, add the following rule:

```
body#home .nav-home {
    background-color:#29336B;
    color:#F8F068;
    display:block;
}
```

This rule targets the class `nav-home` on the page with the ID "home." Now save your page and preview it in your browser.

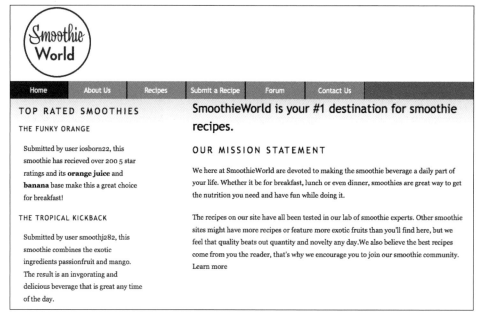

Setting a unique class name for the home page allows you to create distinct styles for it.

Notice that the Home link is permanently set to the same style as the hover effect. You can style it completely differently, for example, by choosing different values for the background color and color properties.

You will now add another page to your site and then style the navigation accordingly.

Moving your internal styles to the external style sheet

Currently, the majority of the layout styles for this page are internal. However, these styles will not automatically apply to new HTML pages that you might want to add. To avoid this problem, you will cut the styles from this page and paste them into your base.css external style sheet.

1 In your 08_layoutwork.html document, select all the rules between your opening `<style>` and closing `</style>` tags. Press Ctrl + X (Windows) or Command + X (Mac OS) to cut the style rules.

2 Choose File > Open, navigate to your web08lessons folder, and select the base.css style sheet. This style sheet currently contains the style rules for your text. At the bottom of the style sheet, after the last `<ol>` rule, press Return a few times to add some space, and then press Ctrl + V (Windows) or Command + V (Mac OS) to paste all your rules. Choose File > Save to save your changes.

3 Keep this file open because any future additions or modifications that you make to your pages will be made here. Switch to your 08_layoutwork.html page and choose File > Save. Preview it in your browser to ensure you followed the steps correctly. There should be no change in the page. Your styles are now contained in the base.css page, not the 08_layoutwork.html page.

Creating a style for the active page

Now that you have saved your styles in an external style sheet, you will create two new pages that will use these styles: the Contact page and the About Us page. You'll create additional pages at the end of this lesson.

1 In your 08_layoutwork.html page, choose File > Save As and rename this file **08_aboutus.html**. Scroll to locate the heading 1 content: *SmoothieWorld is your #1 destination for smoothie recipes.* You'll change this heading to help you identify this page, and later you'll add more content to this page. Type the following (highlighted in red):

`<h1>`**About Us**`</h1>`

2 Add an ID to identify this page as the About Us page as you did with the home page adding the following code (highlighted in red) to the body tag:

`<body id= `"**aboutus**"` >`

Choose File > Save. Now you'll add a rule to your style sheet to target the `nav-about` class attached to your About Us link, as instructed in the next step.

3 Choose File > Save to save the HTML file, and then toggle to you base.css file. Locate the rule you created for the home page and add to it as follows (highlighted in red):

```
body#home .nav-home, body#aboutus .nav-about {
    background-color:#29336B;
    color:#F8F068;
}
```

This appends the new rules for the About Us page (make sure you include the comma after the .nav-home class). Choose File > Save, and then preview 08_aboutus.html in your browser.

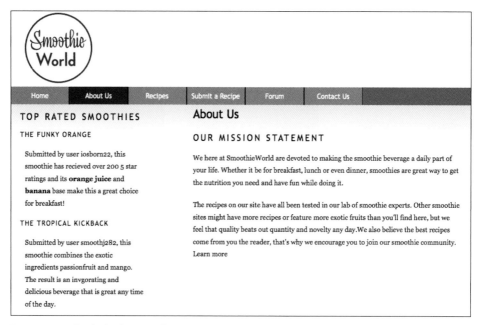

Setting a unique class for the about page allows you to create distinct styles for it.

Repeat the steps above for the Contact Us page, as instructed below.

4 In your 08_aboutus.html page, choose File > Save As and rename this file **08_contact.html**. Scroll to locate the heading 1 content: *About Us* and change it to **Contact Form**.

5 Add an ID to identify this page as the Contact pageby adding the following code to the body tag (highlighted in red):

```
<body id= "contact" >
```

Choose File > Save. Add the necessary rule in your base.css file to highlight the Contact link, as instructed in the next step.

6 Locate the rules you have been working with and modify them as follows (highlighted in red):

```
body#home .nav-home, body#aboutus .nav-about, body#contact
    .nav-contact {
    background-color:#29336B;
    color:#F8F068;
}
```

Choose File > Save and preview the page in your browser. The Contact link is now active. Click the About Us and Home links to activate them.

In the On Your Own section, you will repeat these steps for the Recipes, Submit a Recipe, and Forum pages.

Adding images to your sidebar

In the Home page, add two images to the sidebar and one to the main section, as instructed below.

1 Open your 08_layoutwork.html page. In your HTML, locate the `sidebar` div, and below the heading 3 code, add the following (highlighted in red):

```
<h3>The Funky Orange</h3>
<p><img src="images/FunkyOrange.png" width="235" height="130"
    alt="FunkyOrange Smoothie" /></p>
```

2 Add another image further down in the sidebar as follows (highlighted in red):

```
<h3>The Tropical KickBack</h3>
<p><img src="images/TropicalKickback.png" alt="" width="235"
    height="130" /></p>
```

Note that these images have been sized to the same dimensions of 235 pixels wide by 130 pixels high. These images are located in your images folder so they will be correctly linked, but ensure you type the file name correctly so the links to the images are not broken.

3 Save the file and then preview it in your browser. The two images you added are inside the sidebar. You'll now use a more advanced technique to add another image into the main area.

Working with absolute positioning

You now need to place a large splash image in the main column and place it below your heading 1 (currently labeled *SmoothieWorld is your #1 destination for smoothie recipes*"). You can create this layered effect of text on an image in several ways, but nothing you have learned up to this point would be ideal. The following paragraphs describe the methods you have learned, and explain why they would not work.

Method 1

Open Photoshop, add a text layer to your splash image, and save it as an optimized web graphic. The problems with this method are:

- Text in a graphic becomes invisible to search engines.

- You lose accessibility for other devices, such as screen readers.

- The method is inefficient when updating text, since it requires access to the original Photoshop file.

Method 2

Place the splash image as a background image within the maincolumn and position the heading 1 over it. The problems with this method are:

- CSS background images are to be used as decoration, not as replacement for content.

- You can only use one background image for any given div; multiple background images are not possible in CSS.

The method you will learn in this subsection takes advantage of relative and absolute positioning in CSS. Following this method, you will first insert your splash image as a standard inline image in HTML and add a new div container for the text. You will then position this new container as needed.

Start by adding the inline image into the maincontent div, as explained below.

1 Type the following code (highlighted in red) between the heading 1 and heading 2 in the maincontent div:

```
<h1>SmoothieWorld is your #1 destination for smoothie recipes.</h1>
<img src="images/frontpage_splash.png" width="551" height="270"
   alt="frontpage_splash" />
<h2>Our mission statement </h2>
```

Save the page and preview it in your browser. The image is located between the two headings.

Superimpose the <h1> text on the image (similar to a layer in Photoshop) by wrapping a new div container around it with the name splash, as indicated below.

2   Add the following code (highlighted in red) around the heading 1:

```
<div id="splash">
<h1>SmoothieWorld is your #1 destination for smoothie recipes.</h1>
</div>
```

Add a new style rule for this ID, as shown below.

3   Open the base.css external style sheet, scroll to the bottom, and add the following:

```
#splash {
    position:absolute;
    width:290px;
    height:230px;
    top:0px;
    left:0px;


}
```

Absolute positioning allows you to define the width and height of the div (as you did earlier), and then it allows you to move this box along a set of coordinates (in this case, a top value of 0 pixels and a left value of 0 pixels). Note that the default coordinates of 0 top and 0 left are defined as the top-left corner of the page.

Save the file and preview it in your browser.

Your heading is absolutely positioned, but it is incorrectly using the entire page as a reference.

Recall that you nested the `splash` div inside the `maincontent` div, but this box appears in the top-left corner of the entire page. This is because absolutely positioned items are positioned independently of their containers by default, but you can change the position so it appears relative to the container.

4 Locate the `maincontent` rule in your base.css style sheet. Add the following property and value (highlighted in red) at the top of your list of rules:

```
#maincontent {
    position:relative;
    width:600px;
    float:right;
    /*background-color:#ADA446; */
}
```

Save the file and then preview it in your browser. Although not positioned exactly where you need it, the `splash` div is now positioned in the top-left corner of the `maincontent` div.

By setting a `position:relative` *property on the* `maincontent` *div, your heading is using this div as a reference.*

Setting this div to `position:relative` instructs the absolutely positioned `splash` div to use the top-left corner of the `maincontent` div, not the top-left corner of the page. To position the box exactly where you want it, you can change the top and left coordinates.

5 Modify the `top` and `left` values as follows (highlighted in red):

```
#splash {
    position:absolute;
    width:290px;
    height:230px;
    top:35px;
    left:35px;


}
```

Save the file and preview it in your browser. Your `splash` div and the enclosed heading have now been pushed down 35 pixels from the top-left corner of the `maincontent` div.

The advantage of this technique is that your text is not a graphic, so it will be readable by search engines and by users browsing with images turned off. Also, the image and the text are independent from each other, which makes them easy to modify. For example, the text may be resized a bit smaller to avoid the crowding effect.

Positioning models in CSS

In addition to absolute and relative positioning, there is a property called `fixed positioning`, that is used less frequently than the other two. Here is a brief description of each of the properties:

Absolute positioning: An element that is set to `absolute` strictly follows the positioning values given to it, relative only to its containing element. The containing element can be another div or the actual page. Absolutely positioned elements are pulled out of the normal flow of HTML content, and regardless of the elements that surround them (such as, text content or neighboring divs), they always appear at the exact coordinates assigned to them.

Relative positioning: A relatively positioned element accepts values for position properties such as top and left, but it also takes the normal flow of neighboring HTML content into account. For example, a value of `left:35` would add 35 pixels to the element's left position.

Fixed positioning: This property generates an absolutely positioned element that is positioned relative to the browser window. In other words, by fixed positioning an element, you are anchoring it to your browser window. This effect is used for elements such as footers or menus that you want to stay in the same position in the browser window (even when the user scrolls down).

Self study

1 In the *Creating a style for the active page* exercise, you learned how to add IDs to the body tag of your Home, About Us, and Contact pages. Create a fully functional navigation bar by following the directions in that exercise to add similar code for the Recipes, Submit a Recipe, and Forum pages.

2 Try experimenting with different background images and applying them to your sidebar and maincontent columns. Although this requires an image editor such as Adobe Photoshop for best results, you can use the background graphic supplied for you in your images folder. Add the following code to your `#sidebar` rule:

```
background-image:url(images/sidebar_bg.png);
background-repeat:repeat-x;
background-color:#EAB8C3;
```

Note that the `background-color` property seamlessly matches the color in the sidebar_bg.png graphic, thereby creating a transition between the image and the sidebar background color. This effect is often used to keep your graphic files small. In addition, this technique avoids the problem of predicting how tall a column needs to be.

Review

Questions

1 What is the difference between an HTML inline image and a CSS background image? Indicate the optimal conditions for use each?

2 What is the purpose of the `a:hover` property in CSS?

3 What is the default behavior of an element that is absolutely positioned?

Answers

1 An HTML inline image is an image on your page that originates from the HTML `<img>` tag. A CSS background image is an image that originates from the `background-image` property in CSS. Inline images are most suited for important content within a page (such as a product image). CSS background images are generally reserved for decorative elements (such as a pattern).

2 The `a:hover` property allows you to choose a style for a hyperlink that is triggered when a user rolls over, or "hovers" over a link.

3 If you add the `position:absolute` property to an element in CSS, you can specify positional values for it, (most often top and left). These values will always position the object based on the corners of the browser page.

What you'll learn in this lesson:

- Testing your browser
- Using different browser testing tools
- Using conditional comments with Internet Explorer
- Dealing with future browser compatibility problems

Browser Compatibility

Browser testing is necessary because different web browsers render HTML and CSS code differently. In this lesson, learn to determine how much testing is necessary for any given project, as well as techniques for fixing browser issues or incompatibilities.

Starting up

You will work with several files from the web09lessons folder in this lesson. Make sure you have loaded the weblessons folder onto your hard-drive from *www.digitalclassroombooks.com/webdesign*. See "Loading lesson files" in the Starting Up section of this book.

See Lesson 9 in action!

Use the accompanying video to gain a better understanding of how to use some of the features shown in this lesson. You can find the video tutorial for this lesson at www.digitalclassroombooks.com *using the URL provided when you registered your book.*

Why browser testing is important

A web browser is a program that renders HTML, CSS, and JavaScript files according to a set of rules built into the application. Although web browser manufacturers use the recommended guidelines of the Word Wide Web Consortium's specifications for HTML and CSS, they can interpet these rules as required for their own purposes. Browser manufacturers can also add their own rules to the specifications to add features to their browsers that are not available in others.

Are web pages required to look the same in all browsers?

You can divide the answer to this question into two categories: 1) Technical considerations and 2) Time/budget considerations.

In the case of technical considerations, you must determine whether you could achieve your goal of making a web page look the same. For example, the earliest browsers, such as Internet Explorer 3 or Netscape 3, don't support cascading style sheets.

For these browsers, you couldn't apply the CSS layout techniques you learned in the previous lesson. In the case of time/budget considerations, you might find technical solutions to make your pages look the same, but if it takes you more time than you have allotted to identify and fix the problem you should determine whether the solution is worth it.

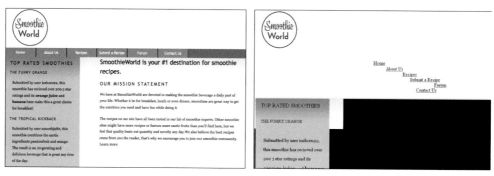

Your SmoothieWorld layout in a modern browser (left) versus Netscape Navigator 3 (right).

Attempting to make web pages look the same in multiple browsers is not as important as you might believe, due to several reasons:

- People browse the web in different ways.
- Monitor resolution. A website on a 17-inch monitor never looks the same as on a 27-inch monitor.
- Text resizing. Users can override the page layout by increasing or decreasing text size.
- Mobile devices, which represent a growing proportion of web browsers.

Who demands that pages look the same or is it something else when there are such inherent differences? Sometimes, it's designers with previous experience in the world of print design, because they are used to a single version of their work and might attempt to duplicate this experience with their site. Client expectations are often a factor as well, because clients are quite often less technically oriented than the web designer, so it becomes important for the designer to communicate exactly what will be delivered as well as the options.

Choose the level of browser support you want

The level of browser use partially accounts for your decision to support it. For example, you might find evidence that only 0.5 percent of all global browsers are Netscape Navigator 3, so you would decide not to spend much time designing for it.

The choice of which browsers to support becomes more difficult with more recent browsers. A good example is Internet Explorer 6. This browser was released in 2001, making it approximately 10 years old upon the publication of this book, yet it still remains a relatively popular browser. There are a number of reasons for this: Internet Explorer 6 was at one point the most popular browser in the world; some estimates gave it a market share of 80-90%. Many websites were designed with IE6 as the standard; in some cases, features found in the browser were tied directly into the functionality of the site.

Examples of Microsoft-specific features include DHTML extensions, ActiveX controls, and proprietary JavaScript.

As a designer, this could have an impact on your work. Recent estimates put the worldwide market share of Internet Explorer 6 between 15 and 20%; however, this number is hard to verify, and the incidence of IE6 amongst your client's target audience could be significantly higher. This scenario is not unusual, many corporate environments still use a combination of Windows XP and Internet Explorer 6. If your job is to redesign or add to a company's intranet (an internal website not accessible to the public), you would be targeting an audience that mostly uses IE6.

The special case of IE6

As noted earlier, Internet Explorer 6 is a 10-year-old browser, Internet Explorer 7 and Internet Explorer 8 have been released, and by the time this book is published, Internet Explorer 9 will likely be on the market. For the reasons mentioned in the previous paragraph, you should be prepared to support IE6 if required. However, there is a trend in the world of web design to stop optimizing for Internet Explorer 6. Companies such as Google have publically stated they will no longer support IE6. For large companies, this means they can free up resources to improve their websites, rather than spend resources to solve the layout and other problems that can add time to the development of a site.

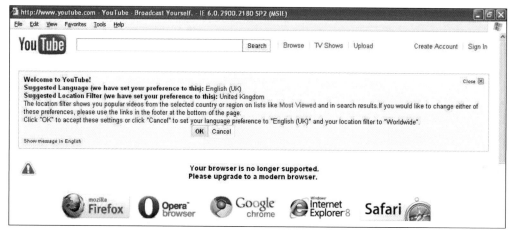

A visitor to Youtube (owned by Google) will find a targeted message stating that Internet Explorer is not supported.

Additionally, the capabilities of web browsers have improved since 2001, when Internet Explorer 6 was released. Modern browsers are faster and support new features that users of Internet Explorer 6 will not see. Still, for many website builders, it is often a business decision. If a client asks for a site that works well in Internet Explorer 6, you will need to deliver.

Even Microsoft itself has gotten into the business of phasing out their own browser. www.ie6countdown.com is a site launched by the company to help designers and developers track the decline of the browser.

Given an unlimited budget, many clients might choose to support the IE6 audience, but if budget and time is limited, you should clearly explain the available options and trade-offs to your client. For example, to support IE6 or to spend the same time and money to optimizing their site to take advantage of modern browsers and the growing mobile device market. As you will see in Lessons 11 and 12, we will help you frame that argument in our discussions of designing for mobile devices and using modern techniques, such as HTML5 and CSS3.

Browser Statistics

Locating an accurate number of the web browsers currently in use today is difficult. Individual websites can gather accurate information on their user's browser version (we discuss this Lesson 1 in the "Web Analytics" callout). However, websites don't necessarily release this data; therefore, the estimates that you might find online are guesses based on available data. Visit a some of the sites listed below for an accurate estimate; remember that the figures listed may not apply to your target audience.

Resources
www.statowl.com
This is a useful site because it also tells you the operating system and browser version you are currently using.

http://gs.statcounter.com/
Includes interactive graphs to help you understand browser trends over time.

http://w3counter.com/globalstats.php
W3counter offers simple to read and up-to-date browser statistics.

www.w3schools.com/browsers/browsers_stats.asp
The statistics from the w3schools.com site are not necessarily representative of the "average" web user, but they have been collecting data for years. Their site also offers additional information on how to interpret statistics.

Tools to identify browser problems

The first step in testing your page design is to view it in the desired browser; however, this isn't always easy, for various reasons. For example:

- You might not have access to the browser, which is a common problem when testing for cross-browser compatibility.

- Different Windows operating systems might not allow multiple versions of Internet Explorer to be installed on the same system.

Microsoft provides guidance on their website for users who need multiple browsers on a single machine.

A common solution is to have access to a separate computer. Many web designers invest in an inexpensive computer mainly used for testing. However, this option may not be practical for several reasons:

- Inefficiency. There might be a time lag involved in continuously changing computers.

- The debugging process involves making many small changes. It could become tedious to change computers after every change.

Virtualization solutions for the Mac OS

One way to avoid the time and investment of a separate computer for browser testing is to install software on your primary computer that allows you to switch operating systems. This ability is known as *software virtualization* and refers to the ability to add secondary operating systems to your computer. For example, recent Mac OS X versions have this capability built in with Apple Bootcamp.

Apple Bootcamp

Recent versions of Apple Bootcamp allow you to install a Windows operating system (XP, Vista, or Windows 7) on your computer, but you still need to purchase the Windows license independently. Although this option is useful, it still has drawbacks. To switch from one operating system to another, you must restart the computer. This introduces a time lag similar to moving to a second machine that is not necessarily efficient.

Learn more about Apple's Bootcamp at www.apple.com/support/bootcamp.

Parallels and VmWare Fusion

Parallels and VmWare are software virtualization programs for the Mac that allow you to run Windows operating systems without the need to restart your computer. The benefit is the ability to quickly switch operating systems, which is much more efficient in the browser testing process.

Virtualization solutions for Windows

As noted earlier, there is no equivalent on the Windows operating system to Apple Bootcamp or Parallels/VmWare Fusion, so if a Windows computer is your primary device and you need to test your designs on a Mac, you will need a separate computer, or explore some of the alternative options discussed later. However, there are Virtual Machine options that allow you to install separate versions of the Windows system on the same computer. For example, you could have Windows 7 with a modern browser as your primary system, and a virtual machine that runs Windows XP with Internet Explorer 6.

Windows Virtual PC

Windows Virtual PC is Microsoft's native virtualization tool that allows you to install one or more virtual machines on your system. The process is fairly straightforward; however, you need sufficient system resources, such as hard-drive space and memory, to make this a viable option.

Browser compatibility applications

Software virtualization programs have many benefits, but they are better utilized for more than just testing web browser. An alternative is to use a browser testing application or service whose only job is to test web pages. Although the details differ, the basic concept is the same: to provide "snapshots" of your web pages in different browsers.

Adobe BrowserLab

Adobe BrowserLab is an online service that you can use as a stand-alone product or in conjunction with Adobe applications, such as Dreamweaver CS5. BrowserLab lets you preview your page in a number of different browsers and platforms, so you are not limited to Mac or PC. The basic steps are to enter the URL of the page you would like to preview to generate a screenshot of the page. Once the screenshot is generated, you can compare the screenshots if you define multiple browsers.

Adobe BrowserLab with a split view of Internet Explorer 6 on Windows XP (left) and Safari 3.0 on OS X (right).

Microsoft SuperPreview

SuperPreview is a standalone software application connected to Expression Web, Microsoft's web editor. SuperPreview works much the same way as BrowserLab, but it can preview your web pages locally. SuperPreview can define different browsers for comparison. There are significant benefits if you want to test your pages for problems with Internet Explorer 6, since SuperPreview has the code for the IE6 browser built into the program. SuperPreview is a Windows application that only uses the browsers installed on a local system, but it also has a network feature similar to BrowserLab to let you view your page using Safari on OS X.

SuperPreview also features measuring tools and different modes that highlight suspected elements on the page that are likely to be the source of a problem. SuperPreview will not solve the layout issues, but it helps you to easily identify them.

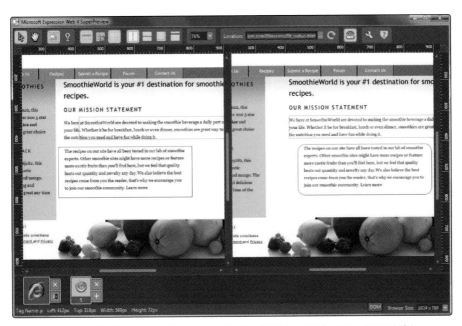

SuperPreview with a split view of Internet Explorer 6 on Windows XP (left) and Safari 3.0 on OS X (right).

Note that the full version of SuperPreview is not a free product, but Microsoft provides *Microsoft Expression Web SuperPreview for Windows Internet Explorer* for free. This is a stripped-down version of SuperPreview that you can use to test your pages with a version of Internet Explorer 6 (only IE6; there is no comparison feature).

Addressing browser incompatibilities with CSS fixes

The majority of the problems facing web designers and Internet Explorer 6 are the rendering problems this browser (and to a certain degree, Internet Explorer 7) introduces. The source of these inconsistencies stem from a few places: a different CSS box model than other applications, a problem with floated elements, and lack of support for transparent PNGs and some CSS properties.

In Lesson 8, you were introduced to conditional comments. Remember that a conditional comment is a unique style sheet that targets Internet Explorer browsers (the style sheet is called iefixes.css in the exercise from Lesson 8). Using this method, you would first develop your layout in a browser such as Internet Explorer 8 or 9 (PC), Mozilla Firefox (Mac/PC), Apple Safari (Mac/PC), or Google Chrome (Mac/PC). After you finish your layout, you could test it in Internet Explorer 6 and 7 using one of the methods listed in the subsections above.

After identifying any issues that appear in IE 6 (or 7), you would then find a solution and add a modified CSS rule to the iefixes.css style sheet. Although the majority of major issues are IE6 related, you might also find that IE7 also has rendering problems (to a lesser degree). You can also assign conditional comments to IE7. You will do a hands-on exercise with this later in this lesson, but first, you should review at the structure of conditional comments. The conditional comment you added in the last lesson was this:

```
<!--[if IE]>
<link href="iefixes.css" rel="stylesheet" type="text/css">
<![endif]-->
```

In this conditional comment, you instruct all versions of Internet Explorer to use the style sheet iefixes.css. However, this comment doesn't distinguish between the different versions of the browser, and a fix that resolves a problem in Internet Explorer 6 could create a problem in the newer version of the browser. In this case, you could use a more specific conditional comment:

```
<!--[if IE 6]>
<link href="iefixes.css" rel="stylesheet" type="text/css">
<![endif]-->
```

In this conditional comment you are targeting *only* Internet Explorer 6, but none of the other IE browsers. There are several conditional comment operators that let you be very specific regarding the browsers you target with your style sheet. For example, you could have CSS fixes that only apply to Internet Explorer 7 and below (6, 5.5, etc.). Such a conditional comment would appear as shown below:

```
<!--[if lte IE7]>
<link href="iefixes.css" rel="stylesheet" type="text/css">
<![endif]-->
```

This example uses the `lte` operator, which means *less than or equal to*. This is a style sheet that you would only use for browser versions 7 and below.

Conditional Comment Operators

Conditional Comment operators can be complicated, but you are only likely to use them when you have a high priority need to target specific versions of Internet Explorer.

Operator	Description
IE	represents Internet Explorer; if a number value is also specified, it represents the browser version
lt	less than
lte	less than or equal to
gt	greater than
gte	greater than or equal to
!	the NOT operator
()	subexpression operator
&	the AND operator
		the OR operator
true	evaluates to true
false	evaluates to false

Addressing Internet Explorer 6 issues with JavaScript

Addressing the numerous layout issues likely to appear in your page designs is impossible and it is beyond the scope of this lesson, but there are a few recurring issues that we can address in regards to Internet Explorer 6. Conditional comments are not the only solution. For example, there is a well-known bug in Internet Explorer 6 with transparency files in the PNG format.

This image was saved in the PNG file format and has transparent areas (the area to the left and right of the rounded corners and in the bottom half of the gradient). This effect allows you to change the background color of any page element the button is placed on to let the background color show.

Internet Explorer 6 does not support the transparency, so you would see a solid color in the transparent areas.

To avoid this issue, the first solution would be to replace this image with another file format. The GIF format also supports transparency to a degree, but not as well as PNG files.

PNG supports a form of transparency called alpha transparency. This means that areas that have less than 50% opacity remain transparent. The GIF format only renders anything that is less than 50% opacity as a solid color.

Modifying your images to address the PNG transparency issue is possible, but it can be inefficient. You would need to identify all graphics that currently use transparency and then change them, and it sacrifices the use of interesting visual effects in modern browsers not available in Internet Explorer 6. However, given that Internet Explorer 6 is approaching its 10-year anniversary, designers and developers have adopted solutions to this problem. A few different JavaScript solutions exist that forces Internet Explorer 6 to render transparent PNGs as if they were used in a newer browser. You can add a reference to this javascript file to force IE6 to show all images that use PNG transparency as intended.

The solution we recommend for the transparent PNG issue is named DD_belatedPNG. The explanation on how it works is beyond the scope of this book. For details and instructions on its use, go to http://www.dillerdesign.com/experiment/DD_belatedPNG/.

Browser incompatibilities in the future

Throughout this lesson, we have studied the issue of browser incompatibilities, particularly the issue of older browsers that do not render correctly compared to the current browser. However web browsers are constantly evolving, as are the languages of HTML and CSS. This means that there are new issues to resolve. In the race to include increasingly sophisticated features and to address the growing importance of mobile devices, designers now are able to use new CSS3 styles that add useful effects, such as rounded corners, transparent colors, and animation. However, some of these new features are supported in certain modern browsers, but not in others. In the next two lessons you will learn more about this situation, but here is an overview.

Future browser compatibility issues

HTML and CSS are continuously evolving languages. The original CSS code supported features that traditional HTML could not. For example, using CSS, you could add borders to any side of a box and then style the color, thickness, and pattern. However, the styling needs have changed, and they began to look for ways to do things such as create rounded corners for their CSS boxes. The original CSS specification had no way of doing this.

Now you can apply effects such as rounded corners using CSS; however the CSS code for this currently needs to be targeted at a specific browser and Internet Explorer 8 (currently the most popular browser) does not support this effect. The following steps show how the rounded corners effect works.

1 In your text editor, choose File > Open, navigate to your web09lessons folder, locate the 09_radius.html document, and open it.

This is a slightly modified version of the layout you built in Lesson 8. The box in the middle of the main column is a new div and currently has a thin blue border on all four sides; you will now change the radius of the corners.

> The recipes on our site have all been tested in our lab of smoothie experts. Other smoothie sites might have more recipes or feature more exotic fruits than you'll find here, but we feel that quality beats out quantity and novelty any day. We also believe the best recipes come from you the reader, that's why we encourage you to join our smoothie community. Learn more

A standard box with borders in CSS has four sharp corners.

2 In your base.css style sheet, locate the last selector and set of rules for the recipe box. Add the following property (highlighted in red):

```
#recipes {
    width:450px;
    float:right;
    border:1px solid #909;
    margin-right:100px;
    -moz-border-radius:24px;
}
```

The value -moz means this property is targeted for Mozilla browsers and is known as a *vendor-specific* property. Users with a version of Mozilla Firefox 3 and above will see this box rendered with curved corners on all four sides.

> The recipes on our site have all been tested in our lab of smoothie experts. Other smoothie sites might have more recipes or feature more exotic fruits than you'll find here, but we feel that quality beats out quantity and novelty any day. We also believe the best recipes come from you the reader, that's why we encourage you to join our smoothie community. Learn more

If you have a modern Mozilla-based web browser, you will see curved corners.

Other browsers will not understand this property and the box will remain in its default state. Another browser vendor is WebKit, and WebKit-based browsers, such as Apple Safari and Google Chrome, have their own property for radius.

3 Add the following property and value (highlighted in red):

```
#recipes {
    width:450px;
    float:right;
    border:1px solid #909;
    margin-right:100px;
    -moz-border-radius:24px;
    -webkit-border-radius:24px;
}
```

Save your page. If you have a recent version of a WebKit-based browser you would now be able to see the same curved corners as in Firefox. However, this still leaves out all versions of Internet Explorer from 8 and below. With the upcoming release of Internet Explorer 9, there is support for the "official" version of the border radius property which more closely resembles the CSS properties you have been used to working with.

4 Add the following property and value (highlighted in red):

```
#recipes {
    width:450px;
    float:right;
    border:1px solid #909;
    margin-right:100px;
    -moz-border-radius:24px;
    -webkit-border-radius:24px;
    border-radius:24px;
}
```

Save your file. With these three properties for radius added, you the `border-radius` property for most browsers. This might seem excessive for one rule, but consider the fact that all future browsers might eventually use the `border-radius` property. You can view these vendor-specific properties as testing ground for new and useful features. Browser developers might remove some of these features if they prove to be not useful, but other features such as `border-radius` a standard and form part of every web designer's toolbox.

What about browsers that don't support `radius` properties? Our suggestion is to evaluate the importance of the design elements to your page. For the example of the rounded corners, if a square box fits with your design, you can leave the box as is. If not, you will need to research other solutions, such as creating a conditional comment style sheet for Internet Explorer. This style sheet might target the boxes that use border-radius and add a background image with rounded corner graphic. A solution such as this requires an investment of time and effort, and you need to evaluate whether you or your client are willing to invest in it.

CSS3 features

The `radius` property covered in the last exercise is one of many new features available for use. Other CSS3 features that are available depending on the browser you are using are drop shadows (currently designated as `text-shadow`), multiple background images, the RGBA color standard (which allows you to set the opacity of colors), web fonts (the ability to embed custom fonts into a page), multi-column layout, animation, and much more.

CSS3 Resources

www.findmebyip.com/litmus/
A useful site that identifies the browser you are using and its support for CSS3 properties, and provides you with a chart listing more than a dozen current and old browsers and their support for CSS3 properties.

www.css3.info
This site has a CSS Preview section demonstrating CSS3 features available in browsers today as well as a weblog that tracks developments, books and articles related to CSS3.

www.alistapart.com/articles/understanding-css3-transitions/
An introductory tutorial to CSS3 transitions which provide the fundamental basis for animation using CSS instead of Flash or JavaScript.

With the number of current browsers in use today that do *not* support CSS3 features, you should consider the time you can spend adding these features to your site. You will also need to learn the vendor-specific properties (such as the `-moz border-radius` used in the previous exercise) so you can use them in your sites. Lesson 11 examines the use of CSS3 with mobile design and CSS3 media queries.

Self study

1 Evaluate the different browser-testing options outlined in the lesson. Depending on your platform (Mac/PC), begin testing sample websites or lesson files that you may have worked on.

2 For the CSS3 portion of this lesson, experiment with some of the more supported features, such as text-shadow and RGBA properties. Perform a research online for recently published articles on the web.

Review

Questions

1 What are three ways you can test how your web page will appear on browsers that are not on your platform?

2 What are conditional comments and when would you use one?

3 What are the strengths and weaknesses of using a feature such as border-radius that is currently part of the CSS3 specification and therefore not supported in older browsers?

Answers

1 Three ways you can test your web design on other browsers and platforms are: **a)** Using a separate computer with an alternative operating system installed. **b)** Using a "virtual machine" that allows you to install an operating system on your current computer and **c)** Using a web service or a standalone application such as Adobe BrowserLab or Expression SuperPreview to test pages.

2 Conditional comments are comments that target only specific versions of Internet Explorer web browsers. Conditional comment allows you to create separate external style sheets commonly used to create styles that fix problems with older browsers, such as Internet Explorer 6.

3 CSS3 properties allow designers to add interesting effects, such as `border-radius` or drop shadows. However, they often require special vendor-specific code that will only work in certain browsers. Additionally, web browsers that don't support the CSS3 features will not display them. This requires the designer to be careful when using these properties as central design elements.

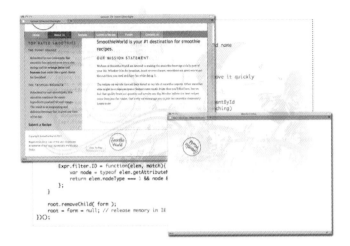

What you'll learn in this lesson:

- An overview of how to use JavaScript
- How to use the jQuery framework
- How to add Flash content to a page
- How to add Silverlight content to a page

Introduction to Interactivity

In this lesson, you'll learn the fundamentals of adding interactivity to your pages with JavaScript and adding rich media such as Flash and Silverlight to your web content.

Starting up

You will work with several files from the web10lessons folder in this lesson. Make sure you have loaded the weblessons folder onto your hard-drive from *www.digitalclassroombooks.com/webdesign*. See "Loading lesson files" in the Starting Up section of this book.

See Lesson 10 in action!

Use the accompanying video to gain a better understanding of how to use some of the features shown in this lesson. You can find the video tutorial for this lesson at www.digitalclassroombooks.com using the URL provided when you registered your book.

This lesson uses the TextWrangler text editor to create the markup, but you can use any of the text editors covered in Lesson 3.

Interactivity on the web

The web is an interactive medium by nature, and hyperlinks are good example of this. Even the most basic website requires user interaction, and the decisions made by the designer can affect the user's perception of the site as well as their experience. HTML offers very few possibilities for interaction, but by adding CSS, you have options such as CSS rollovers and the ability to style hyperlinks. CSS does have certain limitations, which you can overcome by using the JavaScript scripting language and interactive media such as Flash.

A form button with no JavaScript attached will do nothing when the user clicks on it.

JavaScript

JavaScript lets you extend the functionality and appearance of a website through a range of interactive tasks that vary from the simple, such as validating a form, to the complex, such as animated slide shows. JavaScript is a scripting language and that is more complicated to learn and use than HTML and CSS. However, the rise of JavaScript libraries has made it easier to add interactive elements, which has resulted in an increase in the number of developers using JavaScript. JavaScript libraries provide interactive functions largely hidden from view from the designer that can be added to a page with little effort. Later in this lesson, you will learn about jQuery, one of the JavaScript libraries.

Adobe Flash

Flash was designed in the early days of the web to perform interactive tasks. It began as a way to create and share animations on the web, and quickly grew to include sophisticated interactivity and the ability to display and control video. In recent years, alternative technologies, such as Microsoft Silverlight and the HTML5 family, have emerged as an alternative to Flash and share many of its benefits and disadvantages. The functionality and role of Flash and Silverlight often overlap with HTML, CSS, and JavaScript and sometimes even replace them.

The next part of this lesson provides an overview of working with JavaScript technology, and you will create an interactive photo gallery.

JavaScript basics

JavaScript is a scripting language that has its own syntax and structure. A full description of JavaScript and how to use it is beyond the scope of this book. This lesson provides a brief introduction, but there several books and training courses where you can learn about JavaScript. Some references are listed below.

JavaScript References

These are a few resources we recommend for learning JavaScript.

Eloquent JavaScript: An Modern Introduction to Programming
Eloquent JavaScript provides an introduction to the JavaScript programming language and programming basics that you can apply to other languages. This HTML version includes interactive examples and a way to use interactive code.

http://eloquentjavascript.net/

JavaScript Bible
This book is a JavaScript reference guide written for designers who want to improve their programming skill-set.

DOM Scripting: Web Design with JavaScript and the Document Object Model
This book by Jeremy Keith was written with a designer audience in mind and focuses on how to add enhancements to your web pages.

In this lesson, you will gain a basic understanding of how JavaScript interacts with HTML, which will serve as a foundation you can apply to more advanced scripting languages, such as PHP. In the following steps, you will work with a simple form to understand some of the basic concepts of JavaScript.

1   In your text editor, choose File > Open and navigate to your web10lessons folder. Choose the subscribe.html file, and then click Open. To ensure you have a backup copy of this file, you'll save the document with a new name.

2   Choose File > Save As and name this file **subscribe_work.html**. Be sure to save this file in the web10lessons folder.

Take a moment to examine the HTML code; note that it is completely created with HTML and as such, lacks functional interactivity.

3 Preview the page, and then click the Submit button. Nothing happens, except for the default behavior of the button, which is a non-functional element on your web page.

HTML cannot validate whether a form field was filled out; you need JavaScript for this functionality.

You need JavaScript to make this button interactive, since HTML lets you perform activities such as control the text that appears on the button, but offers no interactivity control. You will add JavaScript code to trigger a window to appear in your browser and prompt you to type your name. When you type your name and click OK, your JavaScript code will write your name on the page.

4 Below the `<title>` tag in your page, type the following code:

```
<script type="text/javascript">

</script>
```

You need to indicate in your HTML that you want to use JavaScript, just as you do with CSS. You can place these instructions anywhere in the HTML code, but best practice is to add them to the `<head>` section of your page.

5 Add the following code (highlighted in red):

```
<script type="text/javascript">
function show_prompt()
</script>
```

A function in JavaScript is code that will be executed by an event on the page. In this case, the code is called `show_prompt()`, and it is unique code that tells your web browser to open a small pop-up window. The event that triggers this function is the user clicking the Submit button.

The `show_prompt()` function needs more information to work.

6 Add the following code (highlighted in red) below the function:

```
<script type="text/javascript">
function show_prompt()

{
  var name=prompt();
}

</script>
```

In this line of code, you have declared a variable and its value. This variable, called `name`, obtains its value from the `prompt` function. One line of code is the minimum amount of information you need to make something happen in your JavaScript.

To trigger the JavaScript code, you need to add an instruction to your HTML button that describes how to trigger the code and what function to use.

7 Add this code to the HTML for your button (highlighted in red):

```
<input type="button" onclick="show_prompt()" value="Submit" />
```

The `onclick` code is known as a JavaScript event and the value "`show_prompt()`" is the JavaScript function that you declared in step 5 in your `<script>` tag. Now you have completed a logical chain that essentially says "When a user clicks on this Submit button, call the `show_prompt` function. When the `show_prompt` function runs, it will call another function named `prompt`.

8 Save your file and preview the page in your browser. Click the button and you see a pop-up window appear in your browser.

Clicking the Submit button triggers the pop-up window.

Now that you have created the pop-up window, you will add more code to populate your prompt window with information, as instructed in the next step.

9 Close your browser and add the following code (highlighted in red) to your JavaScript variable declaration (added in step 6):

```
var name=prompt("Please enter your name","Chris P. Bacon");
```

Save your file and preview it in your browser. The prompt window had space available for these values. You will now add code to your JavaScript to take the value of the text box and write it out onto a new HTML page.

10 Close your browser and add the following code (highlighted in red) to your JavaScript code:

```
<script type="text/javascript">
function show_prompt()
{
  var name=prompt("Please enter your name","Chris P. Bacon");
  if (name!=null && name!="")
    {
    document.write("Hello " + name + "! How are you today?");
    }
}
</script>
```

This code is composed of two parts: an *if* statement and a *then* statement. The *if* statement looks for a value in the text field; if there is a value, the document.write line is run, and the name value is displayed.

The characters != *and* && *contained in the code (*name!=null && name!=""*) are known as operators in JavaScript and they help build the logic of any given function.*

The document.write code is a statement that instructs your web browser to write data on a web page. In this case, the statement writes the text "Hello" plus the content of the prompt window text field, followed by "How are you today?"

11 Save your page, and then preview it in your browser. Leave the default name value in for now and click OK. A new page is built based on the code you added in the previous step. Click the Back button in your web browser, click the Submit button again, and then type your name. Click OK; a new page with the new value is created.

The value from the text field is written on the page.

This is a relatively simple JavaScript function, but it should give you a basic understanding of how JavaScript communicates with the HTML elements on a page, as well as the basic logic of a JavaScript function. In the next exercise, you'll learna about JavaScript events.

JavaScript events

The JavaScript event you worked with in the previous exercise was an `onclick` event that triggered the code when you clicked the Submit button. There are other events available you can use, and to better understand how these events work, you will modify the example.

1 In your HTML code, change your `onclick` event to the `onmouseover` event (highlighted in red):

```
<input type="button" onmouseover="show_prompt()" value="Submit" />
```

2 Save your file and preview it in your browser. Now place your cursor over the button without clicking; the prompt window appears. The `onmouseover` event triggers the JavaScript as soon as the cursor enters the area of the button.

Events are often based on user interaction, such as moving the mouse cursor over an object.

The onmouseout *event is closely related to* onmouseover *and triggers the JavaScript when the cursor leaves the area of the button.*

Currently, this event is tied to your button, but you can move the event from the button to the actual page.

3 Select the onmouseover event and its value, and then press Ctrl + X (PC) or Command + X (Mac OS) to cut the code. Locate the opening body tag and press Ctrl + V (PC) or Command + V (Mac OS) to paste the code as shown here:

```
<body onmouseover="show_prompt()">
```

A mouseover event on the actual page will work, but but best practices is to use the onload event, which triggers your JavaScript as soon as the page is opened:

```
<body onload="show_prompt()">
```

4 After changing the event to onload, save your page and preview it in your browser. As soon as your page opens, you trigger the prompt window. You could enter the text here, but as the event is currently structured, it would write the text to the page, so click Cancel.

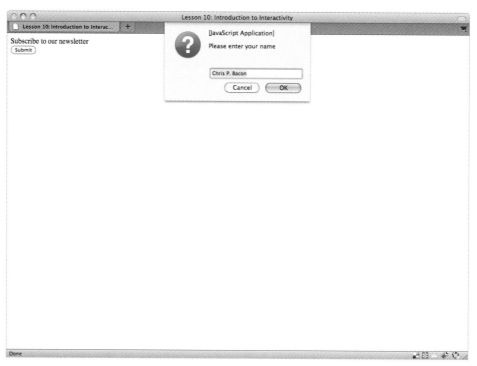

The onload event can be useful, but for this example, it would be distracting for the user.

With this exercise, you have learned that JavaScript lets you choose where and how you call it. In both cases, user interaction triggers the code, but the onload event gives the user little choice as to when to trigger the code, whereas the onclick event (attached to the button), gives the user more choice.

Placing your JavaScript into an external document

You can save JavaScript in an external file that is linked from your HTML pages in much the same way you do with external style sheets. The benefits are the same: to easily update code that's located in a single file.

1 In your text editor, choose File > New and then choose File > Save. In the dialog box that appears, save this file in your web10lessons folder as **promptwindow.js**. The extension .js is for external JavaScript files.

2 Return to your original document and select the code within the two `<script>` tags. Do not select the script tags themselves.

3 Press Ctrl + X (PC) or Command + X (Mac OS) to cut this code out of your document. Switch to the promptwindow.js document and press Ctrl + V (PC) or Command + V (Mac OS). Save this file.

4 Switch back to your HTML page, and add the following code (highlighted in red) to your opening `<script>` tag:

```
<script type="text/javascript" src="promptwindow.js">

</script>
```

5 Save your page and then preview it in your browser. The script works as it did before.

6 Close your browser and then close your HTML and JavaScript documents since you will be working with new files in the next exercise.

If your script is not working, check to make sure you spelled the name of the JavaScript file correctly. Also check to make sure that the JavaScript file is on the same level as your HTML file within your root folder.

There are multiple benefits to saving your JavaScript in an external file. Some of these benefits are:

- The ability to place multiple functions within a single document (although inline JavaScript has this benefit as well).
- Having a single reference for your JavaScript makes it easier for debugging purposes.
- The external JavaScript file can be cached by the web browser, thus preventing the need to reload the script on new pages.

The Document Object Model

JavaScript has access to objects within a browser; this is how the pop-up window from your previous exercise appeared on screen. This access takes advantage of the Document Object Model (DOM), which is a convention for accessing data within HTML pages. This model describes how all elements in an HTML page, such as forms and images, are related to the topmost structure, known as the *document*.

JavaScript has access to the document and the related elements on your page in a way that HTML does not. This access allows JavaScript to:

- Validate form fields
- Detect the browser a user has
- Respond to user events
- Store and retrieve information on a user's computer

Recall the first exercise and the section of code you added that was labeled `document.write` (the seventh line from the top).

```
<script type="text/javascript">
function show_prompt()
{
  var name=prompt("Please enter your name","Chris P. Bacon");
  if (name!=null && name!="")
    {
    document.write("Hello " + name + "! How are you today?");
    }
}
</script>
```

This section of code is referred to as a function and the behavior demonstrated on your page is one of the simplest examples in JavaScript because there are very few objects in the document. Most HTML documents have multiple objects, and it is possible to pass a text value to another part of the page, or to submit it via a form.

JavaScript frameworks

Imagine the following scenario: A designer is starting a new project and her client is interested in adding an interactive photo gallery to the site. The designer also needs to create a form that requires JavaScript validation. Since the designer is new to JavaScript, she finds code she can use for the photo gallery and the form validation, and adds it to her page. The designer later gets another job similar to the first, and she decides to reuse the code from her first project, so the designer saves the JavaScript code into an external file.

The designer now has a reusable library of code she can add to future projects. However, there are a few problems with this approach:

- The designer needs to organize, maintain, and update her library.
- The code the designer found could be poorly written.
- Poorly written JavaScript might contain twice as much code as necessary, might be difficult to modify, or might become slow and cause other problems if it was designed for simple projects and it's used for larger projects.

JavaScript frameworks are a better solution. There are several professionally written libraries available for use by designers. These libraries are large collections of functions built and tested by other designers and developers to form a common library. These collections of functions are available for immediate use, so if a designer needs to add an accordion menu (a menu that collapses and expands based on user events), he might readily find the code he needs.

You will now use jQuery, one of the most popular and accessible JavaScript frameworks for designers. jQuery is useful for designers because it uses CSS syntax to search and access the page, thereby decreasing the amount scripting language you need to learn.

Hiding an element with jQuery

In this exercise, you'll create an expandable container the user can toggle open and closed. The figures below show jQuery's animation features. The first image contains a box in its initial view; readers interested in the calorie content of the smoothie can click the *See calories* link to expand this section. The second image shows you the expanded box after the user has clicked the button.

An example of the collapsible box you will create.

As you will see, jQuery lets you experiment with different methods of expanding the box and with the timing. The collapsible box will take two exercises to complete; in this first exercise, you will hide the section.

1 (Optional) Perform this step to see the code of the jQuery framework. Choose File > Open. In the dialog box that appears, navigate to your web10lessons and open the jquery.js file. Scroll to see the functions contained within the file. This file is well commented, so you can get a sense of what the functions do. When you are finished, close the file without saving it.

```
// Check to see if the browser returns elements by name when
// querying by getElementById (and provide a workaround)
(function(){
    // We're going to inject a fake input element with a specified name
    var form = document.createElement("div"),
        id = "script" + (new Date).getTime();
    form.innerHTML = "<a name='" + id + "'/>";

    // Inject it into the root element, check its status, and remove it quickly
    var root = document.documentElement;
    root.insertBefore( form, root.firstChild );

    // The workaround has to do additional checks after a getElementById
    // Which slows things down for other browsers (hence the branching)
    if ( document.getElementById( id ) ) {
        Expr.find.ID = function(match, context, isXML){
            if ( typeof context.getElementById !== "undefined" && !isXML ) {
                var m = context.getElementById(match[1]);
                return m ? m.id === match[1] || typeof m.getAttributeNode !== "undefined" && m.getAt
            }
        };

        Expr.filter.ID = function(elem, match){
            var node = typeof elem.getAttributeNode !== "undefined" && elem.getAttributeNode("id");
            return elem.nodeType === 1 && node && node.nodeValue === match;
        };
    }

    root.removeChild( form );
    root = form = null; // release memory in IE
})();
```

You can reference the functions in the jQuery document in your web page, but you rarely need to modify them.

2 Open the document jquerytoggle.html located in your web10lessons folder. Preview this page in your browser. The section of the page you will hide is the list below the heading *Calories per serving*. Close your browser and return to your document. Scroll to locate the HTML for this section; the list is wrapped in a `div` tag with the ID `calories`. This is the div you will hide.

3 Add the link to the jQuery JavaScript file, which is located in your web10lessons folder: In your head section immediately below the closing `</style>` tag, add the following code:

```
<script type="text/javascript" src="jquery.js"></script>
```

Choose File > Save. Your document can now access the functionality within the library. Note that this link to the jQuery library should go on every page that might reference code within it. Now you will add another script tag to add code that hides your Calories box.

4 Immediately below the `<script>` tag you just added, type the following code (highlighted in red) to add an empty `<script>` element:

```
<script type="text/javascript" src="jquery.js"></script>
<script>

</script>
```

You will now add a line of code that is included in almost every project that uses jQuery.

5 Add the following code (highlighted in red) into your empty `<script>` element:

```
<script>
  $(document).ready(function() {

  });
</script>
```

In this code, the `$` symbol is a reference to the jQuery object and `ready` is the event to respond to (in this case, the document being ready). In addition, you are defining a new function with `function`. This section of code is referred to as a ready function and prevents your code from searching the DOM until the document is fully loaded.

For example, in the following code, you will hide text on your page, so you want this code to be hidden when the page first loads.

6 Scroll to locate the HTML code close to the bottom of the page that begins with the line `<div id="CalorieBox">`. This is the element on the page that you will hide; it contains a definition list that has the calorie values. jQuery allows objects in the DOM to be selected by several criteria. Since you want to select one specific element, you will search for that specific ID.

7 Add the following code (highlighted in red) immediately below your `document.ready` function:

```
$(document).ready(function() {
  $('#CalorieBox').hide();
});
```

The hash tag (#) tells jQuery to search for an element with the ID `'CalorieBox'` (using the CSS selector syntax). Once found, jQuery will run the selected element's hide function, which is also a jQuery function.

8 Save your page and then preview it in your browser. Your Calories section has disappeared from the page. Note that all the functionality for this effect is condensed in the line you added in the last step. This line works because the jQuery library is referenced in your HTML page.

The `CalorieBox` *before hiding it with jQuery*   The `CalorieBox` *after hiding it with jQuery*

This page lacks a trigger to cause the box to appear. You will now add this trigger by adding a link to the *Calories per serving* heading, as well as more jQuery code.

Adding an event to trigger the show effect

The effect you want to create is to expand the list currently hidden when the user clicks the *Calories per serving* heading. To do this, you will make the heading a link and give it an ID.

1 Locate the `Calories per serving` heading and add the following attributes (highlighted in red):

```
<h4><a id="triggerCalorieBox" href="#">Calories per serving</a></h4>
```

You are giving this heading an ID so you can target it with another line of jQuery. The href attribute is a dummy link that makes the heading a hyperlink, but is there only to serve as a trigger.

2 Scroll to your JavaScript code and add these four lines (highlighted in red):

```
$(document).ready(function() {
  $('#CalorieBox').hide();
  $('a#triggerCalorieBox').click(function() {
    $('#CalorieBox').show();
    e.preventDefault()
  });
});
```

The first line identifies the hyperlinked ID you created in step 1 and attaches it to a click event. The second line is the instruction to show the CalorieBox ID. The third line is needed to override the default behavior of the hyperlink. (As previously noted, before, this hyperlink doesn't go to another page, so this line is necessary.) The fourth line is the closing bracket for the new function. (The opening bracket for this function is on the `.click(function()` line.)

3 Save your page and then preview it in your browser. Click the *Calories per serving* link; the box expands. The style for this box has been defined as 450 pixels wide with a black border on all sides.

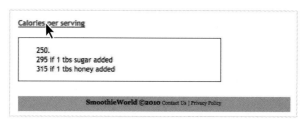

Clicking the link triggers the box to expand.

4 To enable the box to close again upon clicking, you need to add a line of code to hide the box after it has been expanded. The effect you want is for the user to toggle the box open and close by clicking the link. jQuery has a toggle effect you can use. You simply need to replace the show effect you have with the toggle. Replace the show effect with the following code (highlighted in red):

```
$('a#triggerCalorieBox').click(function() {
  $('#CalorieBox').toggle();
  e.preventDefault();
```

5   Save your page and preview it in your browser. The CalorieBox is still hidden when the page loads. When you click it, it expands, and when you click again, it collapses. Close your browser and return to your text editor.

Using the toggle effect, the user can now open and close the box.

To make the show-and-hide effect more interesting, you will use the animation capabilities of jQuery.

6   In the lines of code you have already written, you can add control for the speed of the show-and-hide effect. Add the following code (highlighted in red):

```
$('#CalorieBox').toggle('slow');
```

Save your page and then preview it in your browser. Clicking the link now results in a slow expansion of the box. If you want more precise control of the speed of the effect, jQuery allows you to control the speed using millisecond number values.

7   Return to your text editor and replace the `'slow'` value with a millisecond value (be sure to remove the single quotation marks, which are used for keywords such as `'slow'` or `'fast'`):

```
$('#CalorieBox').toggle(1200);
```

The 1200 milliseconds value is equivalent to 1.2 seconds. Save your page and then preview it in your browser. Clicking the link now results in a much slower expansion of the box. You'll now increase the speed of this effect.

8   Return to your text editor and replace the 1200 value with **500**, the equivalent of one-half second:

```
$('#CalorieBox').toggle(500);
```

You also have options to change the behavior of the box: in addition to `.show`, `.hide`, and `.toggle`, there are effects such as `.slideDown`, `.fadeIn`, and `.fadeOut`. You'll change your toggle effect to the slideToggle effect.

9   Add the following code (highlighted in red):

```
$('#CalorieBox').slideToggle(500);
```

Save your page and preview it in your browser. When satisfied, close your browser and your file since you will be working with a new document in the next exercise.

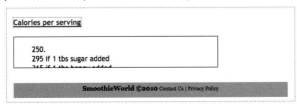

The slideToggle effect changes the behavior of the animation.

As you can see, jQuery allows different options for your designs. The ability to show and hide animated elements is just one thing you can do with this library. The best way to learn more about jQuery is to go online to the source at *jQuery.com* or to explore other online resources.

Taking jQuery further

jQuery and other similar JavaScript libraries are now used with increasing frequency on modern websites. User interface elements such as drop-down or accordion menus are two examples of these effects. However, you will also find jQuery used in slide shows, forms, multimedia, and much more.

As you explore jQuery, you will see that it supports plug-ins, which are sets of additional code that rely on some functionality in jQuery and then build upon it. For example, in the previous exercise, the ability to control the speed of the box was limited. You could choose to start expanding the box slowly and then speed up the expansion as it reached the end. In animation, this is referred to as easing, and several jQuery plugins have been created that give designers access to these effects.

Adding plug-ins involves adding another external JavaScript file to your site and then linking to it. This adds new functions that you can then refer to in your HTML. For more information on plugins as well as documentation and examples, go to *http://plugins.jquery.com*.

Adobe Flash overview

Adobe Flash was developed in the 1990s as a web technology that could perform tasks that HTML and JavaScript could not, especially animated movies. Design elements such as layout, text, animation, and sound were relatively easy to add to Flash projects. In addition, the interactive aspects of Flash gave designers another way to engage web users, and Flash was used for online presentations, games, and advertisements. Flash is still used for these purposes, but it has become a true platform with the addition of more complex features. Today, Flash delivers video, connects to databases for web-based applications, and is making an entry into the mobile device world.

Considerations when using Flash

Creating Flash content is not covered in this book; however, you will learn to add Flash content to your page. Some details to keep in mind:

- The Flash files you will add have the extension .swf. The authoring files that create the .swf file are also called Flash files, but these authoring files have the extension .fla.

- Flash requires a browser plugin called the Adobe Flash Player to work. If a user does not have this plugin, she cannot see your Flash content. However, the majority of web browsers have some version of the Flash plugin installed. You do need to be sensitive to which version your Flash content is targeted to. As of this writing, the most recent version of the Flash Player is 10.1. If a user comes to your website and has version 9 of the Flash Player, any incompatible content designed for version 10 will not be displayed. (You can find statistics on versions of Flash Player installed worldwide at *www.adobe.com/products/player_census/flashplayer*.)

- Flash has made great progress over the years, but some concerns about accessibility remain. Before choosing to deliver content in Flash, remember that search engines do not index the text content in SWF files with the same reliability as standard HTML, so important information about your site might not appear on your web page. Also, Flash might not be supported or might have limited support on mobile devices; take this into consideration when deciding where to use Flash on your site.

Generating code to add Flash movies to a page

In this exercise, you will generate the code necessary to add Flash to a web page. Adding Flash to a web page is similar to adding an image. However, the supporting code for Flash files is more complex because: **1)** over the years, different web browsers have managed Flash in different ways and you need to account for these scenarios; **2)** a user who does not have the Flash plug-in could visit your site, in which case you need to provide alternative content; **3)** a user who has an older version of the Flash plugin might visit your site, in which case you need to provide an upgrade. The only way to do this is by using code.

For this exercise, you will use a JavaScript-based solution that lets you embed Flash files while resolving these issues.

1 In your text editor, choose File > Open and then navigate to the swfobject folder located in your web10lessons folder. Open the file SWFObject_generator.html. This file is a stand-alone web page that will generate the necessary object code for you. This generator is based on a project called SWFObject, which is an open source project that provides designers and developers with a reliable way to add Flash files to their pages.

SWFObject is an open source project free for anyone to use with minimal restrictions. As of this writing, the latest version of SWFObject is version 2.2. You can learn more about the SWFObject project and access more in-depth documentation by visiting http://code.google.com/p/swfobject.

2   Preview this page in your browser; it appears as a form-based page. This page will generate the necessary markup and JavaScript for your project, but you will need to add a few properties related to your project.

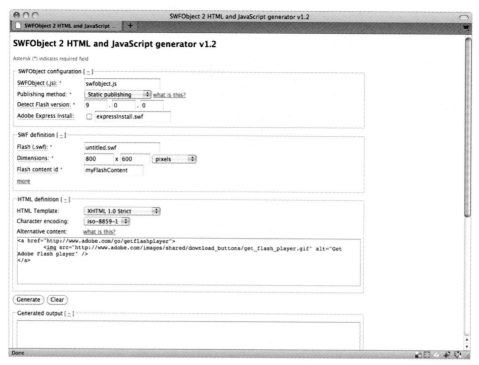

The SWFObject interface. This page will generate custom Flash code for your projects.

3   Locate the SWF definition section, and in the Flash (.swf) field, type the name of the Flash file you want to add to your page, in this case, **smoothie_ad.swf.** This file is located in the swfobject folder.

4   In the dimensions field, type **220** for width and **250** for height. Every time you insert an SWF file into a page using this method, you need to use exact values for width and height. To determine these values, you can access the original FLA authoring file and get the properties from there, or contact the creators of the Flash file and get the values from them.

Notice the Alternative content text field. This code will be generated and will provide users who do not have Flash with a link to the Adobe website where they can download the latest version of Flash Player.

5   Click the Generate button; all the code needed to use your Flash file is created.

6   Select the code in the Generated output field and choose Edit > Copy in your web browser. Return to your text editor.

7 Choose File > New and then choose Edit > Paste to paste this code into the new document. Choose File > Save. In the dialog box that appears, name your file **flashObjectCode.html**. Save this file into the swfobject folder. This is important because there is a generated `<script>` element that links to the external JavaScript file swfobject.js, so your HTML file needs to be in the same folder.

8 Preview the page in your browser to see your Flash file play.

The sample Flash animation running in your browser.

Close your browser when you are done, and return to your text editor. Keep this file open because you will use it in the next exercise.

You have successfully generated the code to play Flash content. If you want to add Flash content to an existing page, you don't need to use all the code from the Flash generator every time you want to add a Flash file to a page. You can copy and paste the code you need into a pre-existing page. You'll do that now to add a Flash file to a page from your Smoothie site.

Integrating Flash into a pre-existing design

In the previous exercise, you generated the code necessary to add a Flash file to a page. You will now add a different Flash file to one of the pages in your site by copying and pasting code that was originally generated by the swfobject generator.

1 Open the 10_insertFlash.html document located in your web10lessons folder. You need to copy the relevant code generated from flashObjectCode.html into this document. First, you will need the script tags.

2 Open the flashObjectCode.html document and select the following two script tags:

```
<script type="text/javascript" src="swfobject.js"></script>
<script type="text/javascript">swfobject.registerObject("myFlashContent",
    "9.0.0");</script>
```

Select Edit > Copy, or press Ctrl + C (Windows) or Command + C (Mac OS), to copy these two elements.

This first script tag is the link to the swfobject.js file. As with the jquery.js file, you do not need to open this document, but you need to ensure you are correctly linking to it. The second script tag defines the ID and the Flash Player version being targeted (in this case, Flash Player 9.0).

3 Open the 10_insertFlash.html file and locate the ending `</script>` tag from your jQuery show/hide code. We have added a commented line of instructions in the code to help you identify the correct location.

4 Now choose Edit > Paste, or press Ctrl + V (Windows) or Command + V (Mac OS) to paste this code. Remember that you are now in a different folder (web10lessons), so you need to update the link to reflect the script. Make the following change to your first script tag (highlighted in red):

```
<script type="text/javascript" src="swfobject/swfobject.js">
</script>
```

This updates the path to the external JavaScript folder named swfobject.

5 You also need to copy the supporting HTML code. Return to the flashObjectCode.html document and copy all the `<object>` code.

6   Return to your insertFlash.html file and scroll to locate the line `<h3>Recipe of the Day: Honeydew Melon</h3>`. Click once *above* this heading and paste the code you just copied.

```
<object classid="clsid:D27CDB6E-AE6D-11cf-96B8-444553540000" width="220" height="250" id="smoothie
        <param name="movie" value="ou_sidebar_ad.swf" />
        <!--[if !IE]>-->
        <object type="application/x-shockwave-flash" data="smoothie_ad.swf" width="450" he
        <!--<![endif]-->
            <a href="http://www.adobe.com/go/getflashplayer">
                <img src="http://www.adobe.com/images/shared/download_buttons/get_flash_pl
            </a>
        <!--[if !IE]>-->
        </object>
        <!--<![endif]-->
    </object>
<h3>Recipe of the Day:Honeydew Melon</h3>
```

Add the multiple lines of `<object>` code immediately before the `<h3>` heading.

Now you need to update the link to your new SWF file and a few other properties.

7   Locate the following line of code:

```
<param name="movie" value="smoothie_ad.swf" />
```

Change the value to point to a Flash file located in the FlashAssets folder in your web10lessons folder (highlighted in red):

```
<param name="movie" value="FlashAssets/smoothie_ad.swf" />
```

There is another object element nested within the first object element, so you need to update the link to the SWF file again. This second object element is needed for certain versions of Internet Explorer.

8   Locate the second object tag and modify this code (highlighted in red):

```
<!--[if !IE]>-->
<object type="application/x-shockwave-flash" data="FlashAssets/
smoothie_ad.swf" width="220" height="250">
<!--<![endif]-->
```

There are two remaining steps: you must update the ID name for this Flash object and update the reference to the ID in your JavaScript.

9   In the first `<object>` tag, update the name of the ID (highlighted in red):

```
<object classid="clsid:D27CDB6E-AE6D-11cf-96B8-444553540000"
width="220" height="250" id="smoothiead">
```

Scroll to your head section and make sure the reference to this ID is updated in your last `<script>` tag (highlighted in red):

```
<script type="text/javascript">swfobject.
registerObject("smoothiead", "9.0.0");
</script>
```

10 Save your file and preview it in your browser to see your Flash content. Close your browser and return to your text editor.

Adding an ID name as you did in step 9 is useful because you can create CSS styles that control the appearance of elements on your page. For example, you will move your Flash movie to the right side.

```
<object classid="clsid:D27CDB6E-AE6D-11cf-96b8-»
444553540000" width="220" height="250" title="smoothiead">
    <param name="movie" value="ou_sidebar_ad.swf" />
    <!--[if !IE]>-->
    <object type="application/x-shockwave-flash" »
data="ou_sidebar_ad.swf" width="220" height="250">

        <!--<![endif]-->

        <p>Alternative content</p>
        <!--[if !IE]>-->
    </object>
    <!--<![endif]-->

</object>
```

Assigning an ID to a Flash object allows you to use CSS.

11 In your CSS style section, add the following code:

```
#smoothiead {
   float:right;
}
```

Save your file and then preview the page in your browser. The Flash object is floated to the right.

Customizing the behavior and appearance of Flash objects

You can define several other features associated with Flash files called parameters. An example of a parameter is the ability to force a Flash movie to loop.

To access and modify the parameters of your Flash object in the SWFObject generator, locate the SWF definition section and click the *more* link to expand this section.

The recipes on our site have all been tested in our lab of smoothie experts. Other smoothie sites might have more recipes or feature more exotic fruits than you'll find here, but we feel that quality beats out quantity and novelty any day. We also believe the best recipes come from you the reader, that's why we encourage you to join the smoothie community. Read more

RECIPE OF THE DAY: HONEYDEW MELON

- 3 cups Honeydew Melon (seeded & chopped)
- 2 tsp Lime Juice
- 1 cup Vanilla Nonfat Yogurt
- 1 cup Ice Cubes

1. Take a blender, add honeydew melon and watermelon; blend until it smoothens.
2. Mix yogurt, ice and limejuice and blend it again.
3. Transfer it into tall glasses and drink it immediately

These parameters can help you customize the appearance and behavior of Flash objects.

Changing any of these values and then clicking Generate creates new code with any additional parameter code you might have added. For example, to loop an animation, you would click the loop menu and choose true.

Inserting Silverlight content into a web page

Silverlight is a browser plugin powered by the Microsoft .NET framework that has support for animation, advanced data integration, web video, and interactivity. As is the case with Flash, you need to know the width and height of the Silverlight content you want to insert. Just as Flash content has a unique file extension (.swf), Silverlight content has its own extension name (.xap). A sample .xap file is located within the web10lessons folder in the SilverlightAssets folder.

1 Open the 10_insertSilverlight.html file and scroll to locate the following code:

```
<div id="Sl_content"> </div>
```

This is where you will add the Silverlight content; in this case, it will be an animated footer at the bottom of the page. You will now add some CSS rules for this div.

2 Scroll to the head section of your page and locate the ID style rule we created for you called #Sl_content. Add the following code to define the width and height of this div:

```
#Sl_content
{
    position:absolute;
    left:296px;
    top:4px;
    width:657px;
    height:126px;
}
```

This code is absolutely positioning the Sl_content div inside the containing footer div. Also, the width and the height of the div are the exact same pixel dimensions as the Silverlight content (657 for width and 126 for height).

3 Choose File > Open and in the dialog box that appears, navigate to the 10_generatedSl.html document. This code was created by a Silverlight authoring program called Expression Blend. In Code view, locate the <object> tag.

4 Select the entire <object> element and press Ctrl + C (PC) or Command + C (Mac OS). Be sure to copy the entire 11 lines of code.

5 In your original HTML document, make sure your cursor is inside the Sl_content div and then press Ctrl +V (PC) or Command +V (Mac OS) to paste the <object> element. You now need to update the link to the XAP file to reflect your folder. Locate the following code:

```
<param name="source" value="ClientBin/test.xap"/>
```

Update the value to reflect the path to your Silverlight file:

```
<param name="source" value="SilverlightAssets/smoothiefooter.xap"/>
```

6 Choose File > Save, and then preview the page in your browser to see your Silverlight content. The code you added has a backup style rule that will prompt you to download the Silverlight browser plugin if it is not installed.

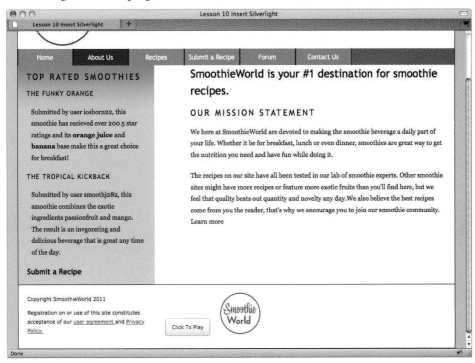

Your Silverlight file embedded within your page.

If you have the Silverlight browser installed, you can click the button to run the animation once. You can refresh the page to run it again.

Self study

1 Experiment with different effects for your jQuery calorie box. For example, replace the .slideToggle effect in the jquerytoggle.html page with the .fadeIn effect.

2 Experiment with the speed values in your code (currently set to 500 milliseconds) to see how they affect the behavior of the element.

3 Browse jquery.com, use the online interactive tutorials, and choose an example to integrate into your page.

Review

Questions

1 What is an event as it relates to JavaScript and HTML?

2 What is a JavaScript library, and what are the advantages of using one?

3 What are some of the advantages and disadvantages of using interactive media, such as Flash and Silverlight?

Answers

1 An event on an HTML page often originates from a user interaction, such as clicking a button or loading a page. These events can then trigger specific JavaScript code that runs in the user's browser.

2 A JavaScript library, such as jQuery, is a collection of JavaScript code that lives inside an external JavaScript file. You can easily reference a library to add functionality such as animated menus or user interface elements. Using a library is advantageous for designers because they can add relatively sophisticated behavior without writing complex JavaScript code.

3 Flash and Silverlight allow for the creation of content that goes beyond the capability of HTML, CSS, and JavaScript. This content might include animation and integration of video as well as a broader range of creative choices regarding layout and fonts. The disadvantages include the need for separate authoring programs and the need for users to have the appropriate plugin installed. In addition, due to technical limitations, important content within Flash and Silverlight files might not be indexed in search engines or be visible in mobile devices.

What you'll learn in this lesson:

- The challenges of designing for mobile devices

- Using CSS3 media queries

- Converting a fixed width layout to a single column layout

Mobile Design

For the web designer, the World Wide Web is no longer just accessible through a desktop web browser. In this lesson, you will learn how to design for the small screen sizes and limited bandwidth capabilities of mobile devices.

Starting up

You will work with several files from the web11lessons folder in this lesson. Make sure you have loaded the weblessons folder onto your hard-drive from *www.digitalclassroombooks.com/webdesign*. See "Loading lesson files" in the Starting Up section of this book.

See Lesson 11 in action!

Use the accompanying video to gain a better understanding of how to use some of the features shown in this lesson. You can find the video tutorial for this lesson at www.digitalclassroombooks.com *using the URL provided when you registered your book.*

This lesson uses the TextWrangler text editor to create the markup text, but you can use any of the text editors covered in Lesson 3.

The need for mobile-optimized websites

Until recently, the way a website displayed on a mobile phone's browser was only a peripheral concern for most web designers. Browsing on mobile devices still represents a small percentage of all browsing; however, mobile browsing is growing at an astonishing rate. Some estimates put the growth rate at 25 to 30 percent each year.

For estimates of web browsing statistics, see www.netmarketshare.com.

To illustrate the growing importance of optimizing a site for mobile devices, consider that 50 percent of mobile users start their activity with a search. If your site appears in a mobile user's search results, you have a unique opportunity to reach them.

How is the mobile experience of the web different than the desktop?

The most obvious answer to this question is screen size. The two most common screen resolutions in use today for desktop browsing are 1024×768 pixels and 1280×800 pixels. Mobile phone resolutions can range from 240×320 (for a non-smartphone) to 640×960 (for a smartphone). Screen resolution numbers change when you include mobile devices such as the first-generation iPad, which has a screen resolution of 1024×768. In most cases, however, a page of content that seems reasonable on the desktop may seem too long for a mobile device.

Comparing the screen resolution of a typical desktop screen (left) to a mobile screen (right). (This diagram is not to actual size.)

You also need to take into account screen orientation: for computer monitors, the default orientation is horizontal; for mobile phones, it's vertical. In addition, older mobile phones can *only* display web pages vertically, while newer smartphones can rotate the screen from portrait to landscape format. There are a number of other limitations for mobile users, particularly with older devices:

- Most websites are designed to be used with a mouse and keyboard. Modern smartphones address this with touch screens and QWERTY keyboards, but for many users, navigation on a cell phone is limited to arrow keys and numerical keypads.

- Older mobile web browsers have limited ability to render CSS. For example, they might ignore CSS layout such as floated divs, but maintain the text styles.

- Multimedia such as audio, video, and Flash have limited or no support on many mobile devices. JavaScript might also not be supported.

- The speed of the mobile phone's Internet connection is a major factor in the user's experience. In addition to multimedia files, large images can slow down the performance of a page.

- Many mobile devices have limited processing power and memory, which may result in incomplete or delayed page rendering. Features such as copy and paste may either be completely missing or limited.

Deciding which type of mobile device to target

Before deciding whether to spend time optimizing your website for mobile devices, you should determine the size of your target audience and address their needs based on your time and budget. For example, if only two percent of your visitors use legacy browsers and 15 percent use smartphones, you would optimize for the smartphone first.

The following figures show the SmoothieWorld site as displayed on a desktop computer, a legacy mobile browser, and the WebKit-based browser of the iPhone. The layout for this figure includes a fixed-width container of 960 pixels, which is centered horizontally within the page. This page structure will have some implications in all three formats.

The figure below shows the default layout view in a desktop web browser. Because of the decision to use a fixed-width CSS layout, the page will render predictably across different monitor resolutions. The designer accepts that in larger monitors, there will be more space on either side of the content, and in smaller monitors, the content may be cropped.

The fixed-width layout as shown in a monitor with 1024 × 768 screen resolution.

The figure below shows the same layout in a Nokia E60, a cell phone released in 2007. In this example, because the screen resolution is 240 pixels wide by 320 pixels high, the view is cropped to a small section of the top-left corner of the page. The user would have to use the arrow keys to scroll across and down the page.

The fixed-width layout as shown in a 240×320 cell phone screen.

The following figure shows the page in the Safari web browser included with the Apple iPhone. You can see that the entire page displays in the vertical orientation. The browser automatically scales the page to size, and it also uses the 960-pixel-wide container as the border of the screen. When rotated, the browser flips to the landscape mode and automatically scales again; in this mode, the largest text on the page is readable, but the main body text remains too small to read unless the user zooms in.

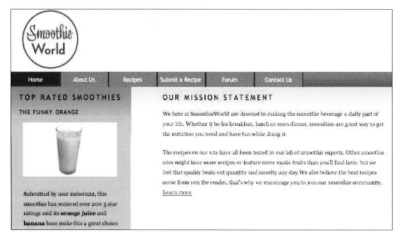

The fixed-width layout as shown in the iPhone 3GS 320×480—vertical layout (top) and horizontal layout (bottom).

Although the iPhone's rendering is better than that of the older Nokia's, it still presents problems. Largely as a result of the two-column layout, the body text of the page is unreadable without zooming. Also, the navigation bar presents a major problem in the default portrait mode: it is essentially unusable because the buttons are too small a target for the touchscreen (unless the user zooms in). In landscape mode, the navigation bar becomes more usable, but the target of the buttons is still small enough to frustrate the user who accidentally presses the wrong button.

How do websites know what browser you are using?

Whether you are browsing the web on your desktop or a mobile device, there are hidden communications taking place between your browser and the server where the website is hosted. All web browsers identify themselves with a user agent string. A *user agent string* identifies the visiting browser as Internet Explorer 6, Firefox 3.5, iPhone OS 3.0, and so on. In most cases, this information is never used by the website. However, you can add user agent detectors to your web pages. A detector can be a small piece of JavaScript code that identifies the user agent (in this case, a visiting browser), and then changes the default behavior of the website in some way. In some cases, the behavior could be as drastic as preventing the visiting browser from accessing the website. In other cases, this code might be used to send the visiting browser a different style sheet or to redirect the browser to a specific page.

The user agent string can be accessed in JavaScript with the Navigator Object. To learn more about using the Navigator Object and user agent strings, see *www.w3schools.com/jsref/obj_navigator.asp*.

The trouble with style sheets

A common problem in web design is the discrepancy between how something *should* work and how it *really* works. You saw this in Lesson 9 with issues of browser compatibility. Different browsers render the exact same page differently depending on various factors. This is especially the case with mobile web browsers. A solution to this problem was proposed in 1999 when the original specifications for CSS were developed. Using this solution, the browser defaults to the screen type when there is no other designation for the type of style sheet to use. In other words, this code:

```
<link rel="stylesheet" href="base.css" type="text/css" />
```

is the same as this code:

```
<link rel="stylesheet" media="all" href="base.css"
    type="text/css" />
```

Other media types are available for use: *screen*, which is the standard for desktop monitors; *projection*; *print*; *handheld*; etc. You can use the *handheld* media type by adding the following link to target handheld devices:

```
<link rel="stylesheet" media="handheld" href="smallscreen.css"
    type="text/css" />
```

In some cases, you can create a separate style sheet and attach it to your pages so that certain handheld devices will use this style sheet accordingly. However, mobile web browsers have not traditionally done a good job with these style sheets, and in some cases, will ignore or interpret them in different ways. An even greater issue today is that some of the most popular and high-profile mobile web browsers do not announce themselves as handheld devices at all, so a line of code such as the one indicated above would not work.

Using CSS3 media queries

When media types don't work, you can use media queries in CSS3 to recognize devices that are visiting your website. Instead of looking for a device that announces itself as handheld, a media query looks at the capability of the device, and then allows you to send it styles based on certain values. For example, the media query might look for the width and height of the browser window, the device width and height, the device orientation (landscape or portrait), and the resolution, among other things.

When the user has a mobile browser that supports media queries, you can write CSS specifically for certain situations, for example, to detect whether the user has a small device such as a smartphone. To understand how this works, you will create some styles for the mobile-optimized version of the SmoothieWorld site.

1 In your text editor, choose File > Open and navigate to the web11lessons folder. Locate the 11_home.html file and click OK. Preview this page in your browser. You will use the two-column design similar to the one at the end of Lesson 7.

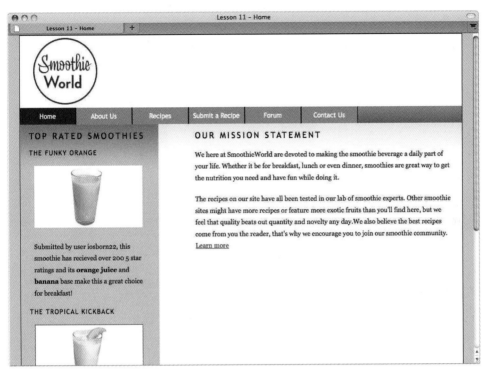

The two-column design you will be optimizing for a mobile device.

Close your browser and return to your text editor. You will now add a media query to your base.css style sheet.

2 In your text editor, choose File > Open, locate the base.css style sheet, and click OK. Scroll to the very bottom of the style sheet and add the following code:

```
@media only screen and (max-device-width:480px) {


}
```

A media query is a new category that has been added to the CSS3 specification. Most browsers use the CSS 2.1 specification and won't recognize the code, so you should be careful when adding CSS3 properties. However, in this case you are specifically targeting mobile browsers such as the Safari web browser on the iPhone, as well as all other mobile browsers that support CSS3, so you can use it.

3 Now you will add a new rule that sets a style for the width of the wrapper. Add the following code (highlighted in red):

```
@media only screen and (max-device-width:480px) {
    body {
            padding:5px;
            background-color:#FFF;
            background-image:url(images/smoothieworld_logo_mobile.jpg);
            background-repeat:no-repeat;
    }
    #wrap {
            width:auto;
            margin-top:80px;
    }
}
```

Note that throughout this lesson, you are adding new rule sets nested within *the media query section. The syntax here is slightly different than what you have created up to this point; study the code example carefully, and always add your new rules inside the* @media *section.*

This code accomplishes a few things: the 5 pixels of padding for the body will add a bit of space to any content you place inside your page, and the background image is a new image optimized for the mobile format. The rule for the `wrap` ID style redefines the main container of the page to an automatic width instead of the 960 pixels used for the current style sheet. Additionally, the top margin property adds 80 pixels of space between the `wrap` div and the top of the page, which allows your site logo to be visible.

4 Choose File > Save.

The most reliable way to test this page is to upload the entire site to a remote server and then point to the resulting link using your mobile phone's web browser. If you're not currently set up for this workflow, take time now to set up your remote server, or preview the page later.

Testing your designs on mobile devices

The best way to test your page designs is to have access to the mobile device in question. There is a category of software programs called *emulators* that allow you to test your designs in software versions of different mobile devices. The most reliable source for emulators is the manufacturer. For example, Apple provides an iPhone emulator with its iPhone development tools; Android and Windows Phone 7 also include emulators with their development tools. Using these emulators results in an accurate preview of your designs without placing your sample files online. However, emulators are often not cross-platform compatible. For example, the iPhone emulator (at the time of this writing) is only available for the Mac. Additionally, these emulators are installed with the assumption that you are using them for application design, not web page design; as such, the installation process might seem a bit overwhelming and unnecessary.

There are also a few online web services that claim to emulate your designs in the mobile format. However, these services are not always reliable and often require a hyperlink to your page online, rather than locally on your desktop. In this case, you could just use the actual phone.

5 Preview the page in your mobile web browser. Your page might appear somewhat broken, but the media query is working.

Your mobile design after adding rules for the body and the wrap container.

You currently have two logos; the second one (in the masthead) is redundant and you will remove it. Your page appears distorted because the mobile browser is attempting to fit all div elements that are floated and have fixed widths into a narrow space.

In general, mobile design works better with a single column for your content. In the following steps you will begin to override your existing styles using two methods: removing floats and changing pixel widths to a value of auto. First, however, you will remove the masthead, which contains the second SmoothieWorld logo.

6 Add the following code (highlighted in red):

```
#masthead {
    display:none;
}
```

The display:none property prevents the masthead element from appearing. This property is useful because it deactivates elements from the original style sheet. Now you'll configure your navigation.

7 Add the following code, which targets the list items in your mainnav div:

```
#mainnav {
    height:auto;
}

#mainnav li {
    float:none;
    width:auto;
    text-align:left;
}
```

Setting the height value for the mainnav to auto ensures that this container will expand and display the navigation items inside. Choose File > Save and then upload your HTML and CSS files to your server (if testing on your phone). Load or refresh your page in the web browser.

Your navigation section after removing the float *and setting the* width *to auto.*

Setting the `float` property to `none` and the `width` to `auto` turns your navigation into a vertical list. The `text-align:left` property places them on the left side of the menu. The auto width will work only after you have converted the rest of your page to a single column. You will continue to do that in the following steps.

Note that all the original properties for the appearance of the navigation list are still present, including the background color and the height. This is a benefit of the cascading nature of CSS. A single property, such as the 35-pixel height of the list items, can work in the desktop design and the mobile design, but you only need to specify it once.

Mobile Navigation Tips

Navigation that is easy to use is key to the success of your website. There are certain navigation guidelines you should remember for mobile devices, particularly touchscreen mobile devices.

- Navigation should be at or near the top of the screen so the user can easily access it. Consider repeating your navigation at the bottom of all your pages so the user does not have to scroll back up when she is done reading a page.

- For touchscreen devices, use a large target size for navigation links. This will prevent accidental clicking by your users.

- Touchscreen devices do not have a hover capability, which is triggered on the desktop by the cursor, so plan your styles accordingly.

- Refrain from using image-based navigation and use list-based navigation that is styled with CSS.

8 You will now add more styles in you media query for the sidebar and the main content. First, locate the rule for the `masthead` ID and then add the following selector (highlighted in red):

```
#masthead, #sidebar {
    display:none;
}
```

This removes the sidebar on the left side from the mobile page. Floats in a desktop layout can be useful, but not in a single-column layouts, so you will now remove the floated properties of your main content div. Remember that for mobile devices, simpler layouts work better.

9 To style the `maincontent` div, add the following code within your media query:

```
#maincontent {
    float:none;
    width:auto;
    background-color:white;
}
```

The key changes here are to set the `float` property to `none` and the `width` to `auto`.

Save the file and then upload your HTML and CSS files to your server (if you are testing on your phone). Load or refresh the page in your web browser.

Your maincontent section also fills a single column after removing the float *and setting the* width *to* auto.

Your content flows into a single column and you are getting closer to the intended layout, but your footer is still floated.

10 The last section of the page to style is the footer. Add the following rule set within your media query:

```
#footer, #footer p {
    clear:none;
    width:auto;
    height:auto;
    background-image:none;
    padding-top:20px;
    margin-top:0px;
}
```

In this code, you are setting the styles for the footer and the paragraph inside the footer. You need to use the `clear:none` rule to override the `clear:both` rule from the main style sheet. You set both `width` and `height` to `auto` in this case. Additionally, you set the `background-image` to `none` to simplify the page design. Finally, you add more padding and set the top margin to zero.

Save the file and then upload your HTML and CSS files to your server (if you are testing on your phone). Load or refresh the page in your web browser.

With all the floats removed and widths set to `auto`, you have a true one-column layout.

Test your page in both portrait and landscape modes. You are done with this lesson.

Diving deeper into CSS3 media queries

To learn more about CSS3 media queries to target and style content for mobile devices, see the resources listed below.

Safari Reference Library
Apple provides free and useful documentation on optimizing your site for WebKit-based browsers (used primarily for the iPhone, but also for other smartphone browsers). The organization of the website might have changed since this lesson was written, so you should perform a search for "Optimizing Web Content." This documentation explores the various ways to use media queries:

http://developer.apple.com/library/safari/navigation/

Responsive Design
This article by Ethan Marcotte explores techniques to build sites that are based on proportion and are better suited for creating desktop sites and mobile sites from start:

www.alistapart.com/articles/responsive-web-design/

Self study

1 Experiment with the design of your page. Add some left padding to the `#mainnav list` rules to give your navigation links a bit more space.

2 Improve the formatting of the second-level heading, "Our Mission Statement," by adding a new rule for `#maincontent h2` in your media query section.

3 Experiment with different font sizes and other text styling.

Review

Questions

1 Name three ways in which mobile websites provide a different experience for the user.

2 How are CSS3 media queries better than style sheets that use the handheld media type?

3 Rebecca wants to convert her pre-existing website to a mobile site and she begins to use a CSS3 media query to do so. She also wants to convert her multi-column layout to a single-column layout to maximize the screen space on the mobile browser. What are the two CSS properties relating to layout Rebecca should modify first?

Answers

1 First, desktop websites assume that you are using a mouse and keyboard, whereas mobile devices use arrow keys, numerical keypads, or a touchscreen. Second, desktop websites are often designed with the landscape format in mind, whereas most mobile devices use portrait format. Third, multimedia such as video, audio, and Flash are not always supported on mobile devices. A fourth difference is that mobile devices often have slower connections to the Internet than desktop computers.

2 The handheld media type was designed to allow mobile browsers use a special style sheet if the designer or developer added the correct code. This method works for many mobile devices, but it is inconsistent and newer devices, such as the iPhone, do not recognize the handheld value. These devices use CSS3 media queries, which are inside a style sheet and use a special syntax. The benefit of media queries is that they look for the capabilities of the mobile device (based on properties such as screen width and orientation) and allow the designer to create unique styles based on these capabilities.

3 To convert a multi-column layout to a single-column layout, Rebecca should first set a `float` property of `none` and a `width` property of `auto` to most or all elements using floats or that have fixed-width values.

What you'll learn in this lesson:

- Understanding key concepts of HTML5 markup

- Supporting technologies

- Evolving browser support

- Using HTML5

HTML5 Essentials

In this lesson, you will get an understanding of the different technologies related to HTML5. You'll discover the new elements that are available to help build HTML5 pages, and you will also learn about modern browser support.

Starting up

This lesson does not use any lesson files, so you do not need to load any files before starting this lesson.

See Lesson 12 in action!

Use the accompanying video to gain a better understanding of how to use some of the features shown in this lesson. You can find the video tutorial for this lesson at www.digitalclassroombooks.com using the URL provided when you registered your book.

Defining HTML5

HTML5 is a combination of new HTML markup tags, CSS3 properties, and JavaScript, as well as several supporting technologies that are connected to HTML5.

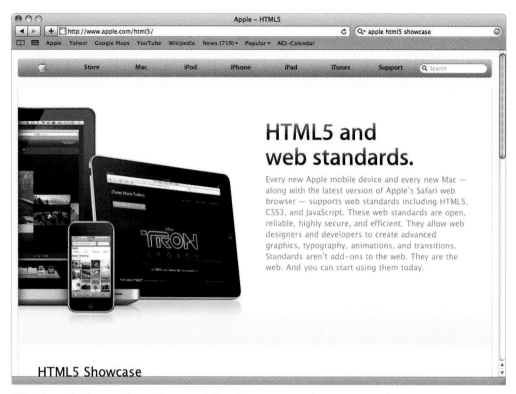

HTML5 is marketed as a significant evolution in web design; however, it is more than just a new set of HTML tags.

There is a difference between the HTML5 core and the HTML5 family. You can define the HTML5 core as new markup elements used to build web pages. Many of these elements include traditional HTML tags, such as `<p>`, `<ul>`, and `<div>`. The HTML5 family includes the HTML5 core and technologies such as CSS3, geolocation, Web Storage, Web Workers, and Web Sockets.

As web pages and web applications become increasingly sophisticated, there is a limit to what the current languages can do. HTML5 represents an evolution in the current capabilities of browsers.

The motivation behind HTML5

The version of HTML currently in use is HTML4.1. XHTML1.0 is largely the same as HTML4, but with stricter rules, such as requiring lowercase tags and for all opening tags to have a closing tag. The original specification for HTML5 was called Web Applications 1.0, and this name hints at some of what the new language is trying to accomplish: to provide a method of making HTML capable of doing more than its current format.

For example, HTML cannot currently play multimedia such as audio and video; it requires a browser plugin such as Flash or QuickTime. HTML also has no capability to store data. There is no native drawing format in HTML; graphics and animations are currently supplied as image files or through browser plugins such as Flash, Java, and Silverlight. Many of these limitations are addressed in the evolving HTML5 family. The next section describes the core changes in the HTML5 markup.

HTML5 markup

HTML5 markup introduces a number of new tags designed to make the structure of a web page more logical and functional. Recall the lessons on basic and advanced layout: you relied heavily on the `<div>` tag and often paired this tag with a CSS class or ID. For example, the code for your header was:

```
<div id="header"> This is my header </div>
```

The ID name "header" is arbitrary. Some designers might use the name `masthead`, `topsection`, or `rectangle_on_top`. To add logic and consistency, HTML5 uses a unique new tag named `<header>`, so you would use the following code:

```
<header> This is my header </header>
```

HTML5 has a few new tags based on this same concept, such as `<footer>`, `<nav>`, `<section>`, `<aside>`, and `<article>`. The goal is to reduce the current reliance on `<div>` tags and replace them with a more consistent and readable page structure. HTML5 doesn't replace anything you have learned in this book. The `<div>` tag has not disappeared, but it no longer has to support the whole load of a page layout. The new HTML5 element names come from the combination of HTML and CSS that most designers adopted: `<div id="nav">`, `<div id="footer">`, and so on.

The structure of your SmoothieWorld site with HTML5 elements
A. *Header.* **B.** *Nav.* **C.** *Section.* **D.** *Article.* **E.** *Aside.*

Section and Article

Most of the new HTML elements designed for layout use are logical, but some are not as intuitive as <nav>, for example, <section> and <article>. A section is a distinct and often self-contained block of related content. It is similar to the practice of defining a div as main or content:

```
<section id="smoothies">
    <h1>Banana Smoothie Recipes</h1>
    <p>The following list of banana smoothie recipes were collected from
        our readers </p>
    <h1>Facts about bananas</h1>
    <p>Bananas contain lots of potassium and their peels are often used
        for practical jokes </p>
</section>
```

An article is also a self-contained block of related content, but is used when the content could exist independently of the web site:

```
<article>
    <h1>Reviewing the Fruit-o-matic 10 speed blender</h1>
    <p> We put the Fruit-o-matic through its paces in various
        blending, ice-crushing, and puréeing tasks.</p>
</article>
```

The <article> element is useful because of its independent nature and the way people currently access content on the web. You can publish an article on your web site, but using technologies such as newsreaders and mobile devices, a user might have your latest articles delivered to their device without visiting your web site.

The <video>, <audio>, and <canvas> elements

One of the most publicized features of the HTML5 specification is the inclusion of native tags that allow you to add multimedia without the need for browser plugins. The <video> and <audio> tags allow you to embed video and audio into your pages the same way you would with the <img> tag. The <canvas> tag is designed to supply HTML with a native drawing and animation format. This tag could provide an alternative platform for displaying the type of graphics and animation most often found in Flash movies. As innovative as the development of these new tags might be, there are significant issues that must be addressed.

Embed media files using <video> and <audio> elements

The structure for embedding video and audio is simple. For example, the code for adding video to your web page is similar to this:

```
<video src="catz.mp4" width="400" height="300"></video>
```

Embedding an MP3 audio file in your page is very similar; you can also add built-in player controls and preloading capabilities with the *controls, preload*, and *autobuffer* attributes:

```
<audio src="high_seas_rip.mp3" controls preload="auto"
    autobuffer></audio>
```

An HTML5 video player with built-in support for volume, full-screen view, and other playback controls

There is an increasing demand to easily add video and audio; however, it can become complicated depending on the file formats of your video and audio and the browser support for them. In the above example for video, the `src` attribute is pointing to the file catz.mp4 (.mp4 is the extension for the MPEG4 video format). Currently, modern browsers that support this format include Apple Safari and Google Chrome, but not Mozilla Firefox or Internet Explorer. The upcoming version of Internet Explorer 9 will support the MP4 format, but the Firefox browser, which represents roughly 20 to 30 percent of the market share, will not. Firefox supports a video format called Ogg Theora (.ogg), which is not supported by Internet Explorer or Safari. There are similar discrepancies with audio: the MP3 format is not supported by default in Firefox.

The reasons for these incompatibilities are complex and are related to licensing issues for the video and audio codecs (the compression techniques used to reduce file size). To use these new tags, you should provide multiple versions of your video and audio, thereby allowing the browser to choose the first supported format it can find; so a more reliable method of providing video might look like this:

```
<video width="400" height="300" controls>
    <source src="catz.mp4" type='video/mp4; codecs="avc1.42E01E,
        mp4a.40.2"'>
    <source src="catz.ogv" type='video/ogg; codecs="theora, vorbis"'>
</video>
```

Note that older browsers that do not support the video and audio tags will need an alternative way of playing video; currently, the best way to provide this capability is to add the option to use Flash video, which is widely supported in current and older browsers.

The documentation for HTML5 is updated constantly; however, one of the best online resources is Mark Pilgrim's "Dive into HTML5" resource, located at http://diveintohtml5.org/video.html.

Provide drawing and animation features using the `<canvas>` element

The `<canvas>` element works as a drawing surface on your page. Within this drawing surface, you can create shapes, colors, gradients, and pattern fills.

This example might be visually unremarkable, but the addition of a native drawing format in HTML is notable.

You can interactively manipulate pixels onscreen, render text, and export these contents to a static image file, such as a PNG file. With the addition of JavaScript and the new CSS3 animation features, you can also make the objects you create move, fade, scale, and so on. Adding a canvas element is simple:

```
<canvas id="myCanvas"></canvas>
```

The work behind the scenes is performed by JavaScript, which provides a context for any objects you create:

```
<script>
    var canvas = document.getElementByI ("myCanvas"),
        context = canvas.getContext("2d");
    // x = 10, y = 20, width = 200, height = 100
    context.fillRect(10, 20, 200, 100);
</script>
```

This code creates a simple rectangle filled with the color black. This code might seem too complicated for such a simple result, but for the first time, HTML has its own drawing format. The current drawback is that you must draw your objects using code similar to the example above; there are no true equivalents to the drawing tools found in applications such as Flash. However, this might change quickly with the advent of third-party plug-ins such as Ai–>Canvas (available at *http://visitmix.com/labs/ai2canvas/*), which allow you to export vector graphics created in Adobe Illustrator to the canvas element.

HTML5 markup is still evolving

HTML5 markup will take a long time to become part of your standard toolbox. Many modern browsers currently support the new tags, but the final specification will not be delivered for years (current estimates aim around the year 2022). This means that tags such as <header> and <section> might change or be renamed. For the major elements, this is unlikely to happen because all modern browsers support them today; you can use a number of additional elements as long as you are careful.

Grouping headings and images

The <hgroup> element is designed to act as a container for one or more related heading elements. It can only contain a group of <h1> to <h6> element(s):

```
<hgroup>
    <h1>Today's News</h1>
    <h2>Recent Developments in Blending</h2>
    <h3>Dancer Chris Leavey explains his new style of smoothie
    making</h3>
</hgroup>
```

Identifying figures and captions

The `<figure>` element identifies diagrams, illustrations, and photos used within an article, and the `<figurecaption>` element identifies the captions that are often paired with these figures.

```
<figure><img src="blue_strawberry_smoothie.jpg" alt="Blueberry &
    Strawberry Smoothie">
<figcaption>A fresh blueberry and strawberry smoothie</figcaption>
</figure>
```

A fresh blueberry and strawberry smoothie

The figure element in HTML5 provides semantic tags to help identify images and their captions.

Web forms

The new form elements in HTML, when implemented, will make working with forms quite easily. For example, a common goal of many web designers is to create forms that require validation before the data is submitted. For example, a user must enter a value in the email field for a form submission to be successful. Currently, most solutions to this problem require JavaScript or another scripting language. HTML5 simply adds the *required* attribute to the list of form input types, as shown below:

```
<input type="email" required>
```

There are many new form input types, such as *email* (specifically designed for e-mail addresses), *search* (to designate form fields used with search terms), and *url* (to specify a form field that uses a web address). These new web form elements will take some time to become part of the official specification, but they are designed to fall back to generic input forms. In other words, you can use these new input types today, and if a browser doesn't support them, the new form element will use a generic (supported) element.

The rest of the HTML5 family

There are other developing web technologies that are not part of the HTML5 specification that deals with markup. However, these technologies are often grouped with HTML5, and they will let you perform tasks in web browsers and supported mobile devices that were not previously possible. The following is an overview of some of these features.

Geolocation

Geolocation is a feature that allows the web browser's geographic location to be pinpointed. This information is then used to send you relevant data based on your position. Version 3.5 of Firefox was one of the first browsers to use geolocation features. One example of how this could be useful is to connect web searches with map data; for example, in an unfamiliar city you might search for a restaurant within walking distance of your hotel. Rather than entering your address manually, a geolocation-enabled browser could deliver your results immediately based on your location.

With a browser such as Firefox 3.5, you can see can see geolocation working at www.flickr.com/map.

Web Workers

The Web Workers framework addresses the issue of browser performance. When you access advanced web applications, such as mapping or applications that generate charts and graphs instantly, there are a number of processor-intensive computations that can slow down the performance of your application. Much of the slowdown can be attributed to the competition between the user interaction (clicking, dragging, and so on) and the need for the application to access resources (graphics, data, and so on).

Web Workers are scripts that run in a separate thread. This separation means that processes such as pulling data from a database can take place independently of user behavior and create a more seamless environment for the user.

Web Storage

Web Storage is an upgrade to the current use of browser cookies. This is the process that allows a web site to store small pieces of data on your system so the site can save information for a later date. For example, sites that recognize your login information whenever you return are most likely using cookies.

Cookies are a limited technology and not particularly easy for designers to use; Web Storage aims to update the model to allow for greater storage space for modern web applications, as well as to make the addition of storage features more accessible.

HTML5 provides two ways to store data: `localStorage` and `sessionStorage`. Data saved as `localStorage` is available to the browser at any point, even if it closes or the user restarts her system. Data saved as `sessionStorage` is lost as soon as the user closes that window.

Web Storage is an HTML5 feature used in Apple iPhones. The iPhone has a default storage space of 5MB for data used in web applications, and as this space fills up, you receive a prompt asking you to expand your storage.

CSS3 integration with HTML5

Many of the examples that exist online as HTML5 are a combination of the HTML5 technologies described above, JavaScript, and CSS. Most of the the CSS techniques you have learned in this book are part of the CSS2.1 specification. These fundamentals will continue to be used, but the new and evolving specifications of CSS3 provide powerful new features that work very well with HTML5. It goes beyond the scope of this book to cover these features in depth but the following is a brief description of some of these elements.

- **CSS Animations**

  The ability to animate objects in the browser has traditionally been the role of technologies such as Flash; however, some of the same functionality can now be created using CSS rules and properties. The partnership of the HTML5 Canvas element and CSS3 transitions will potentially change the way designers create interactive and animated elements on the page.

- **CSS Transitions**

  CSS transitions are closely related to animation, but are fundamentally different. A transition allows property changes in CSS values to occur smoothly over a specified duration. For example, imagine a button that has a background color of green; when the user rolls over the button, it smoothly animates to a different background color. This is a very simple example, and you can currently do this transition with JavaScript or Flash, but transitions in CSS3 give designers a tool without having to become a scripting expert.

- **CSS 2D and 3D Transformations**

  The CSS `transform` property allows you to rotate, scale, or skew an element on your page. A simple transform might be the ability to rotate an image on the page slightly to one side for aesthetic effect. Transforms can also be animated, so animating the scale property might allow you to create an enlarging or minimizing effect on an image or other element. You can also use the `perspective` property to simulate an object being positioned or animated in 3D space.

Examples of CSS in 3D exist mainly as demos, but will likely become part of the visual language of the web.

- **CSS3 Backgrounds, Borders, RGBA Colors, Gradients, Drop Shadows, and Rounded Corners**

  There are several enhancements to the visual style of web pages that are now possible with CSS3. You examined the `border-radius` property briefly at the end of Lesson 9, but there are many new effects you can create, such as native gradients and drop shadows. Traditional effects, such as the `background-image` and `border` properties are upgraded in CSS3. For example, with the `border-image` property, you will be able to apply images to style a border and you will also be able to add multiple background images to a single container; this removes the current limitation of only being able to use a single background image.

- **@font-face Web Fonts**

  As explained in Lesson 6, the ability to use a wide range of fonts in your designs has been extremely limited for many years. There is increasing support for the ability to add custom fonts to your page designs using the @font-face property, which allows the designer to specify a particular font and provide a source link for the font; this, in turn, allows a user's browser to download the necessary font for use. This feature has the potential to dramatically transform the appearance of web pages worldwide, although it comes with many of the same browser support issues as the various HTML5 features.

These are just a few of the highlights of what is to come in CSS3. Remember that these HTML and CSS3 features are not supported by all browsers and it will still be some time before they become part of a web designer's standard toolbox. While it is exciting to contemplate what the future of web design will look like, it needs to be tempered by the reality of what you can use today.

How to begin using HTML5/CSS3

How and when to begin using HTML5 features has a lot to do with browser support. For example CSS animations are relatively well-supported in WebKit-based browsers, which include Apple Safari and Google Chrome. CSS animation is not supported in the versions of Firefox or Internet Explorer available at the time of publication of this book, but we expect it to be supported in the next major versions of these browsers.

Using web services to determine browser support

Given the shifting and evolving nature of the web browser and mobile landscape, a number of web sites have appeared to help designers and developers determine which HTML5 and CSS3 features are currently supported.

caniuse.com

This site provides a series of tables that illustrate the past, current, and future browser support for the various HTML5 and CSS3 properties. The site also has useful information such as the user statistics for any particular feature, which can help you decide whether to use that feature.

www.modernizr.com

This site automatically detects the browser you are using and displays the support for the various features of HTML5 and CSS3 on the home page. However, the site does not allow you to compare feature support of other browsers on the market.

www.html5test.com

This site is similar to the Modernizr site in that it automatically detects the browser you are using, but it then creates a score based on whether your browser supports different features.

Starting with an HTML5 foundation

When deciding whether to use HTML5, you are faced with the issue of whether you should use features that customers and users will want to use in the future, but may not work with many older browsers.

There are solutions currently available that bridge the gap in browser support. The best way to understand this is to consider the core HTML5 syntax you learned in the first half of this lesson. If you build a web page that uses the new tags, such as `<header>`, `<nav>`, or `<article>`, it displays well on many current web browsers, including Internet Explorer 9.

Older versions of Internet Explorer are not able to display most HTML5 content, and different versions of Internet Explorer are used by approximately 60 percent of users around the world. You can still use HTML5 and help users with older versions of Internet Explorer to view your site through the use of JavaScript.

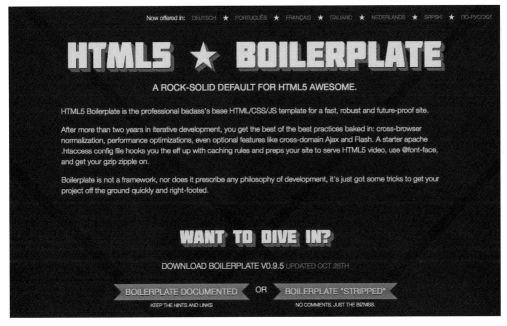

Sites such as HTML5boilerplate.com provide templates to help you start building HTML5 sites.

Supporting HTML5 in older browsers

The following solutions let HTML5 elements be styled by Internet Explorer 6 or other older browsers using some form of feature detection. In other words, when a browser that doesn't support HTML5 elements accesses your site, these JavaScript solutions allow you to use CSS that *will* work with the older browser.

www.modernizr.com

Modernizr.com provides a service that detects the support of any visiting browser and access to a downloadable JavaScript file that you can link to in your HTML5 pages. After linking to this JavaScript file, you can have better control over the styles used for different browsers.

www.html5boilerplate.com

This site offers an entire set of files, including HTML, CSS, and JavaScript, to provide designers a template for a generic HTML5 site that has been tested by professionals. This site is a great resource, but you should spend some time understanding the code.

html5shiv

This code is similar to the Modernizr code in that it allows Internet Explorer to recognize and style HTML5 elements. You can find it at *http://code.google.com/p/html5shiv/*.

Words of encouragement

When learning web design, remember that it is easier to learn something new than it is to replace a concept you already learned with new skills. This was the case for the first generation of web designers who created page layouts with tables. In many cases, when CSS layout became standard, it was not always easy to change habits and practices learned over the years.

The benefit of the rapidly evolving web technologies is that opportunities exist for entry-level designers. HTML5 and CSS3, for example, are still evolving languages and many working web professionals don't have the time to keep up with these developments. This book has focused mainly on the technical skills and best practices that are the foundation of a good twenty-first-century web designer. It has not focused as much on the aesthetics of web design, mainly because this is a function of experience, study, and a certain degree of subjectivity. Web design is a craft, and, as with most crafts, you will develop your own style through experience and feedback.

Self study

1 HTML5 is an evolving standard; however, you can read about the latest news and developments by visiting *html5doctor.com*.

2 Visit *html5boilerplate.com* and download the commented version of the template files. Modify these template files and reproduce your SmoothieWorld site using your existing assets. The WebKit browser engine used with Apple Safari and Google Chrome has the most support for advanced HTML5 and CSS3 features at the time of this writing. Download both of these browsers, perform a a search for HTML5 gallery or HTML5 canvas online, and explore the sites and experiments that designers and developers have created that take advantage of the new features.

Review

Questions

1 What is the difference between the HTML5 core and the HTML5 family?

2 What is the intent of the new HTML5 `<video>` and `<audio>` tags and what are the obstacles involved with using them today?

3 Name three advancements that are or will be possible in CSS3.

Answers

1 The HTML5 core represents the changes to HTML syntax, most noticeably the addition of new tags, such as `<header>`, `<nav>`, `<video>`, `<audio>`, and many more. The HTML5 family represents the new syntax and supporting technologies, such as CSS3, Geolocation, and Canvas, among others.

2 The new `<video>` and `<audio>` tags are designed to allow browsers that support them to embed multimedia within a web page without the need for a browser plug-in such as Flash. The issues involved with using these tags include the fact that older browsers will not recoginize the tags; therefore, you must provide a fallback. Additionally, even among browsers that support the tags, the video and audio formats are not standardized, so designers must still provide fallbacks if they want to ensure all users can view or listen to their content.

3 CSS3 is currently in various stages of support, but it will allow the following capabilities: CSS Animations, Transitions and Transforms, as well as rounded corner, gradient, dropshadow and other styles.

CSS Properties and Values

This table provides a reference to some of the most commonly used CSS properties in CSS 2.1. In addition to the name of the property, the allowed values have been listed. For a complete list of CSS properties visit *http://www.w3.org/TR/CSS21/propidx.html*. For a more in-depth discussion on how to add custom values, please review Lesson 4: Fundamentals of HTML, XHTML, and CSS.

Name	Possible Values	Default value
background-attachment	scroll | fixed | inherit	scroll
background-color	<color> | transparent | inherit	transparent
background-image	<uri> | none | inherit	none
background-position	[[<percentage> | <length> | left | center | right] [<percentage> | <length> | top | center | bottom]] | [[left | center | right] || [top | center | bottom]] | inherit	0% 0%
background-repeat	repeat | repeat-x | repeat-y | no-repeat | inherit	repeat
background	[background-color || background-image || background-repeat || background-attachment || background-position] | inherit	see individual properties
border-collapse	collapse | separate | inherit	separate
border-color	[<color> | transparent]{1,4} | inherit	see individual properties
border-spacing	<length> <length>? | inherit	0
border-style	<border-style>{1,4} | inherit	see individual properties

`border-top border-right border-bottom border-left`	`[ <border-width> || <border-style> || border-top-color ] | inherit`	see individual properties
`border-top-color border-right-color border-bottom-color border-left-color`	`<color> | transparent | inherit`	the value of the color property
`border-top-style border-right-style border-bottom-style border-left-style`	`<border-style> | inherit`	none
`border-top-width border-right-width border-bottom-width border-left-width`	`<border-width> | inherit`	medium
`border-width`	`<border-width>{1,4} | inherit`	see individual properties
`border`	`[ <border-width> || <border-style> || border-top-color ] | inherit`	see individual properties
`bottom`	`<length> | <percentage> | auto | inherit`	auto
`clear`	`none | left | right | both | inherit`	none
`clip`	`<shape> | auto | inherit`	auto
`color`	`<color> | inherit`	depends on user agent
`display`	`inline | block | list-item | run-in | inline-block | table | inline-table | table-row-group | table-header-group | table-footer-group | table-row | table-column-group | table-column | table-cell | table-caption | none | inherit`	inline
`float`	`left | right | none | inherit`	none

font-family	[[<family-name> | <generic-family>] [, <family-name>| <generic-family>]*] | inherit	depends on user agent
font-size	<absolute-size> | <relative-size> | <length> | <percentage> | inherit	medium
font-style	normal | italic | oblique | inherit	normal
font-variant	normal | small-caps | inherit	normal
font-weight	normal | bold | bolder | lighter | 100 | 200 | 300 | 400 | 500 | 600 | 700 | 800 | 900 | inherit	normal
font	[[font-style || font-variant || font-weight]? font-size [/ line-height]? font-family] | caption | icon | menu | message-box | small-caption | status-bar | inherit	see individual properties
height	<length> | <percentage> | auto | inherit	auto
left	<length> | <percentage> | auto | inherit	auto
letter-spacing	normal | <length> | inherit	normal
line-height	normal | <number> | <length> | <percentage> | inherit	normal
list-style-image	<uri> | none | inherit	none
list-style-position	inside | outside | inherit	outside

list-style-type	disc | circle | square | decimal | decimal-leading-zero | lower-roman | upper-roman | lower-greek | lower-latin | upper-latin | armenian | georgian | lower-alpha | upper-alpha | none | inherit	disc
list-style	[list-style-type || list-style-position || list-style-image] | inherit	see individual properties
margin-right margin-left	<margin-width> | inherit	0
margin-top margin-bottom	<margin-width> | inherit	0
margin	<margin-width>{1,4} | inherit	see individual properties
max-height	<length> | <percentage> | none | inherit	none
max-width	<length> | <percentage> | none | inherit	none
min-height	<length> | <percentage> | inherit	0
min-width	<length> | <percentage> | inherit	0
overflow	visible | hidden | scroll | auto | inherit	visible
padding-top padding-right padding-bottom padding-left	<padding-width> | inherit	0
padding	<padding-width>{1,4} | inherit	see individual properties
position	static | relative | absolute | fixed | inherit	static

quotes	[<string> <string>]+ | none | inherit	depends on user agent
right	<length> | <percentage> | auto | inherit	auto
table-layout	auto | fixed | inherit	auto
text-align	left | right | center | justify | inherit	a nameless value that acts as left if direction is ltr, right if direction is rtl
text-decoration	none | [underline || overline || line-through || blink] | inherit	none
text-indent	<length> | <percentage> | inherit	0
text-transform	capitalize | uppercase | lowercase | none | inherit	none
top	<length> | <percentage> | auto | inherit	auto
vertical-align	baseline | sub | super | top | text-top | middle | bottom | text-bottom | <percentage> | <length> | inherit	baseline
visibility	visible | hidden | collapse | inherit	visible
white-space	normal | pre | nowrap | pre-wrap | pre-line | inherit	normal
width	<length> | <percentage> | auto | inherit	auto
word-spacing	normal | <length> | inherit	normal
z-index	auto | <integer> | inherit	auto

Monitor resolutions, 32, 80, 119
`Mouseover` event, 219
Mozilla Firefox 3, 207–208
Mozilla Firefox Firebug, 51
.mp4, 259

N

Navigation
    Considerations for, 16–18
    List-based, 155–158
    Mobile devices, 251
    Usability testing, 18–19
Navigation bar, 183–186
Nesting tables, 142
New website
    in Dreamweaver, 46–48
    in Expression Web, 50

O

Omniture, 13–14
Operators
    Conditional comment, 204–205
    JavaScript, 217
Ordered lists, 130, 136

P

Padding, 135–137, 141, 160–167
Page layouts
    Building, 174–177
    CSS. *See* CSS, Layouts
    Fixed-width. *See* Fixed-width layouts
    Flexible, 145–146
    History of techniques, 142–145
    Mobile devices, 251–252
    Options, 145–146
    Table method, 142–144
Pantone Color Matching System, 97
Paragraph `line-height`, 127–128
Parallels, 201
Percent measurements, 119–122
PHP, 41, 44
Pixels
    Definition of, 119
    Ems conversion of, 123, 126
    Sizing text using, 118–119
Plain text editors, 37
Planning
    Creativity during, 23
    Defining goals and strategy, 12
    Information architecture, 15–19

Mockups, 20–21
    Overview, 11
    Prototypes, 21–22
    Research, 12–14
    Wireframes, 20
PNG image format, 86, 104–107, 205–206
Points, 118
Previewing
    GIF image, 97
    JPEG image, 89–90
Print design, 8–10
Prototypes, 21–22
Pseudoclass, 184

R

`Radius` property, 209
Relative positioning, 190, 193
Relative-size, 118
Research, 12–14
Reset file, 140–142
Resizing
    Images, 78–81
    Text, 118–119, 122
Resolution of monitors, 32, 80, 119
Resources, 5
RGBA colors, 265
Rounded corners, 265
Ruby on Rails, 41

S

Save for Web & Devices window, 87, 89–90, 100
Screen resolutions
    Desktops, 32, 80, 119
    Mobile devices, 240
    Web design considerations, 32–33
Scripting languages, 44
Search engine optimization, 61
`<section>` element, 258
Select Download Speed button, 88
Seminars, 5
Serifs, 115
Server log, 12–13
Server-side languages, 44
Sidebar
    Images added to, 189
    Padding added to, 160
Site management, 43
SketchFlow (Microsoft), 22
Slice Select tool, 108–109
Slices, 107–111

The on-line companion to your Digital Classroom book.

DigitalClassroomBooks.com

Visit DigitalClassroomBooks.com for...

 Updated lesson files

 Errata

 Contacting the authors

 Video Tutorial samples

 Book Samples

DIGITAL CLASSROOM

You have a personal tutor in the Digital Classroom

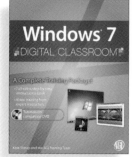

978-0-470-56802-6

978-0-470-60776-3

978-0-470-52568-5

978-0-470-60777-0

978-0-470-60781-7

978-0-470-59524-4

978-0-470-60774-9

978-0-470-57777-6

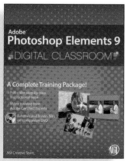

978-0-470-93230-8

978-0-470-60779-4

978-0-470-60783-1

DIGITAL CLASSROOM
A Complete Training Package

For more information about the Digital Classroom series, go to www.digitalclassroombooks.com.

Available wherever books are sold.

WILEY
Now you know.
wiley.com